Economics is regarded by many as a science, and it is generally reckoned to be 'for the public good' that the state should intervene decisively in the economy and control our lives. Alex Rubner, himself an economist, dissents from the typical 'economist's view'.

The Gross National Product, Forecasting and Central Planning are the sacramental instruments of the planning pundits. Mr Rubner debunks the GNP as a meaningful standard of measurement and rejects it as a significant gauge of human progress. He exposes the myth of forecasting, showing that even computers and governmental erudition cannot accurately foresee the main national economic indicators. He argues that in a mixed economy state planning must fail, and particularly castigates those who advocate free enterprise in the richer economies but favour the authoritarian directives of state planning (aided by international funds) for the poorer nations.

Mr Rubner suggests that in an affluent society a smaller GNP might actually bring more happiness than a bigger one. In this book he sets out to break the strong link that seems to be generally taken to exist between economics and soothsaying, and to strip economists of their spurious status as 'scientists'. He shows how economics, shorn of its magic frills, could be restored to the status of a discipline with sane and purposeful functions.

Three Sacred Cows of Economics

Alex Rubner

Three Sacred Cows of Economics

MACGIBBON & KEE

Granada Publishing Limited

First published 1970 by MacGibbon & Kee Limited
3 Upper James Street Golden Square London W1

Copyright © 1970 by Alex Rubner

ISBN 0 261 63230 2

Printed in Great Britain by Cox & Wyman Ltd
London, Fakenham and Reading

Contents

7

CONTENTS

Preface

The Three Sacred Cows are:

I   the GNP (gross national product) fetish;

II the myth of forecasting;

III the virtues of economic state planning.

These of course are not the only sacred cows of economics. The herd also includes the worship of investments, faith in the ability of trade unions to affect real wages under Full Employment, the notion that exporting is always good, the legendary preference of manual workers for fringe benefits, the putative merit of corporate retention of profits, the holiness of fixed (currency) exchange rates, and many others.

This book concentrates on the beatification of merely three sacred cows, which have close family links. They appear to be the most parasitical members of the bovine species. Politically-inspired planners envelop economic growth in sanctified garments, and glorify increases in material output. People who wish to establish their competence in implementing socialist policies have a vested interest to prove the meaningfulness of GNP calculations and the statistical significance of forecasts.

Most of my illustrations have been drawn from the current British scene but the conclusions, hopefully, have a wider application. Unashamedly, this is a partisan political essay. By exploring the nature of the GNP and its tributaries, I intend to shed some light on the intellectual arrogance which underlies much of the economic planning now executed in many countries of the world.

*

Readers will have to put up with a little shorthand. I differentiate between the GNP (or the conventional GNP) as it appears in the official national accounts, and the genuine GNP (also sometimes described as the 'social product').

In Appendix I, the various frameworks of the national product are described in some detail. National Income, Gross Domestic Product (GDP), and Gross National Product (GNP) are clearly not identical terms, but in the main body of the book they are employed interchangeably.

Unless the contrary is stated, time confrontations of national accounts are always arranged on the assumption of constant prices.

'Billion' denotes thousand million.

A.R.

Introduction

'The de-bunking of economic catchwords is a very useful exercise—and perhaps even one of the most urgent tasks of the present time.'

OSKAR MORGENSTERN

By pontificating on the television screens and other media, solemnly urging us to work harder in order to augment the national product, politicians implicitly affirm their belief that a growth of the GNP will lead to increased human satisfactions and magnified national welfare. What are the links, if any, between this vision of bigger doses of happiness and the conventional GNP?

Some theocratic theories deem human happiness on earth to be but a derivative of the happiness to be enjoyed after physical death. They underseal the Italian laws against divorce, the Israeli regulations concerning pork, the Irish legislation on the sale of contraceptives, the Indian prohibition on the slaughtering of parasitical cows—however much (direct) misery these secular laws may cause, they can nevertheless be rationally defended by those legislators, who consider that they enhance (indirectly) celestial happiness.* Consequently, no useful purpose would be served by a UN commission explaining to the Israeli government that its balance of payments would be improved through the breeding of pigs; it would be of no avail to prove statistically to the Indian government how the killing of surplus cows would help to feed millions of hungry mouths. Our discussion on the GNP will be limited to the enjoyment of human happiness on this earth without any

* There are tricky borderline cases, as the following two illustrations show: The Church of England castigated Harold Macmillan for introducing Premium Bonds (141). Some Rabbis contend that the Jewish objections to bacon-and-egg (imposed on the citizens of Israel irrespective of their religious beliefs) are founded on dietary grounds which make it unwise to eat pork in a hot climate. Once arguments are introduced to suggest that gambling is bad for a happy family life on this earth, or that the consumption of pigmeat is deleterious to health, the real theological strength of the underlying divine injunctions is seriously sapped.

reference to life in the next world. This is not to deride the importance of religious considerations; I specifically recognize that it is not illogical for people seeking maximum spiritual wealth in the next world to accept temporal vows of material poverty.

It does not follow, however, that because one seeks to restrict the discussion to the attainment of happiness on this earth, one must therefore put up with the servitude of the conventional GNP, that merely counts those things which can be given a monetary tag. The 'rat race', a hatred for tyranny, racial antagonism are but a few manifestations of human endeavours which are not represented in the conventional GNP. Their exclusion from the GNP is perhaps the strongest argument against its being a proper standard of measurement for human welfare.*

During those terrible days in the early fifties, when Senator McCarthy succeeded in terrorising the US establishment, the American economy rose to new heights of productive efficiency. British visitors to McCarthy's country had to endure scornful lectures on the teabreak mentality that was said to be the cause of the UK's backwardness; some even predicted that at the pace the British people were advancing economically, the majority of their television viewing would by the end of the sixties still be on black-and-white sets! These Jeremiahs, as we know, have been proved correct. But what does the dearth of colour television in Cardiff in 1969 signify? The conventional GNP measures the output of colour television sets but ignores the degradations brought about by McCarthy. If one drops the conventional GNP as the measuring rod for human welfare, one might even arrive at the conclusion that the genuine GNP (in which the pleasure derived from colour television is more than offset by the misery of the McCarthy hysteria) was and is bigger in Wales than in Wisconsin.

---

* 'The gross national product does not allow for the health of our youth, the quality of their education or the joy of their play. It does not include the beauty of our poetry or the strength of our marriages, the intelligence of our public debate or the integrity of our public officials. It measures neither our wit nor our courage, neither our wisdom nor our learning, neither our compassion nor our devotion to country. It measures everything, in short, except that which makes life worth while...' (114). Senator Robert F. Kennedy has fallen into the same pit of exaggeration as the protagonists of the conventional GNP. The latter imply that it measures practically everything of importance in human welfare; the Senator goes to the other extreme by saying that the GNP measures everything except that which makes life worth while. Surely the genuine GNP is to be found at some point between these two extremities.

But even if one does not seek to use the all-embracing concept of a genuine GNP, and merely aims at collating the items contained in the conventional GNP, sooner or later one must take a stand on whether the latter is really an accurate tool for any significant purpose. In the coming chapters I hope to demonstrate how highly misleading, or at best meaningless, are most *numerate*, international and time, GNP comparisons.

The material output of the UK economy went up faster in the five years of the first post-war Tory government than in the initial five years of the Wilson administration – but are the national accounts statisticians competent enough to determine the exact ratio? One is safe in assuming that the standard of living in Glasgow is superior to that of Calcutta, but it is either arrogance or stupidity to attempt to put this relationship into numerate language by drawing on the recorded GNP figures for the UK and India. This bandying about of the GNP is a particular hobby of several international agencies: it is used for fixing national membership fees,* the position of a country on the world's economic ladder, the relative weights of national tax burdens, the amount of aid an economy 'ought' to receive or dispense – and now that the creation of 'reserve money' is being propagated as a panacea for world liquidity, it is also suggested that the national contributions should be in accordance with the respective GNPs. One of the more ridiculous examples of this beatifying of the GNP cow by the UN was the proclamation of the sixties as the United Nations Development Decade; the developing countries were set the target of reaching by the end of the decade a minimum 5 per cent. annual rate of growth in their aggregate national income. The Organization for Economic Cooperation and Development (the Paris organization representing the developed countries) was not going to be beaten by the UN capturing all the headlines; it therefore set as its target the attainment of a 50 per cent. growth increase 'in the

---

* The voting procedure at the UN was always envisaged as 'one nation (however big or cultured or wealthy or wise) – one vote', but right from the days of the Preparatory Commission in 1945 it was considered expedient and socially progressive to lay down the membership fees in relation to the country's capacity to pay. A formula was consequently adopted, which depended mainly on comparative estimates of national income because these seemed the 'fairest guide' (117). This, however, was immediately modified to take into account per capita national income. But in the subsequent twenty years the UN, through resolutions at the General Assembly, has lost faith in the almighty justice of per capita GNP and has slowly whittled down this principle and now also employs other yardsticks.

combined national product' of member countries during this decade (i.e. 4·1 per cent. per annum). What fatuous number games! Did these targets change by an iota the course of economic events in either the developing or the developed nations? Quite apart from their loose use of the concepts of growth and national income, have the GNP acrobats helped, through these exercises, to feed a single hungry Pakistani child or aided in the manufacture of just one more Ceylonese steel rod? But the General Assembly of the UN lowered even further the intellectual tenor of its resolutions by resolving 'that the flow of international assistance and capital should be increased substantially so that it might reach as soon as possible approximately 1 per cent. of the combined national income of the economically advanced nations'.* One wonders what is meant by the 'combined national income'. Even more incongruous is the choice of 1 per cent.—why not 0·5 per cent. or 3 per cent.? Of course, it may be argued that these percentage figures of incomparable GNPs do little harm and the resolutions are merely words of exhortation. Such a defence may perhaps be applied to the cited OECD and UN sermons, but I doubt whether it can vindicate those many politicians and commentators who envelop GNP computations with a sacrosanct halo; to them it is as sacrilegious to doubt the scientific validity of past and projected GNP figures as to challenge conventional chemical formulas. One member of Parliament, Ian Lloyd, could not bear this balderdash any longer, but alas his protest failed to score the renown it deserved:

'Over and over again we have heard in the Chamber about whether the gross national product will increase by 2·4 per cent. or 2·6 per cent. ... With humble apologies to those on both sides of the House who may feel affronted, this is the most terrifying nonsense. It is terrifying because it is so plausible, so respectable, and apparently so important. But it remains nonsense, none the less.'

In theory it is possible to conceive that statistical craftsmen will succeed in arriving at GNP figures which mirror accurately the values of national output (according to the criteria of the conventional GNP). Would such arithmetically correct GNPs then—for comparative

* Even Balogh, who loves the GNP and all its tributaries, finds this approach illogical. He rejects the proportional concept and wants to introduce progression in the percentage of the per capita GNP devoted by the richer nations to international aid. (85).

16

purposes—be a significant guide to the economic purport, and social importance, of the national products? The single comprehensive GNP figure is made up of factors (capital goods, government services, military expenditure, etc.) which have widely differing meanings in diverse national contexts, and affect human welfare in uncertain ways according to individual tastes and desires. The conclusion is that even when two countries have the same GNP, say £100 Mn, this identical figure may hide varying material, and welfare, standards in the two economies. The UN, employing conventional GNP techniques, has judged the per capita GNP of Kuwait to be higher than that of the US (117). Arithmetically this is probably true, but what does it mean beyond being a mathematical ratio? Does the majority of the US population have a lower material standard of living than the majority of the Kuwaitis? Is life more worth-while living in Kuwait for the Kuwaitis than it is in the US for her citizens? By asking these questions, one is undermining the very purpose for which these single GNP figures are constructed. Similarly, personal consumption levels in countries with an identical conventional GNP differ widely, depending for example on the proportion of the GNP devoted to military expenditure, journeys to the moon, or investments. (And it also depends on the type of investment goods made: coalmining machinery, houses, or computers?)

Part I of this book, dealing with the gross national product, elucidates the non-theological postures of the GNP: its comprehensiveness, arithmetic accuracy, and socio-economic significance. I have addressed myself primarily to the intelligent laymen who have been doped with the slogan of GNP growth. The book may also strike a chord with those honest politicians, who (because of their own ignorance on the subject) unwittingly hoodwink the public with GNP platitudes. It is certainly not meant to enlighten professional economists. Those of my colleagues who specialize in national accounts know every single objection that I have raised to challenge the validity of the conventional GNP. Indeed, when they read papers at international conferences, publish academic treatises, hold forth in the privacy of the lecture room, or write esoterically in some obscure journal—then they bow their heads and shake their beards in order to emphasize how unsatisfactory are the national accounts; some will even go on record as to the degree of error in national accounts estimates. There are overall errors of up to ± 5 per

B

cent. in the presentation of the GNPs of advanced economies, and above ± 15 per cent. in the GNPs of some under-developed countries; many footnotes in national accounts allow for even larger errors in component parts of the GNP.

These footnotes, addenda and academic injections of *ceteris paribus*, testify to the intellectual honesty of the statisticians, but the wider public knows of course nothing about these reservations when they are sold some dose of government intervention on the basis of a single GNP figure. Two analogies come to mind: although the manufacturing chemists employed by detergent firms know the true performance potential of the competing products, their views are ignored to let merchandisers tell the public that article X washes whiter than article Y. The fuel analysts of the oil companies are experts on the chemical compositions of various types of petrol and discuss the implications in technical journals; they listen with a smile when advertising agencies spread the message that brand A drives faster than brand B.

Actually not all academic economists hide themselves in the ivory towers of their calling. Some write popular articles and speak in plain language on the BBC about economic matters; the nature of mass media permits them to mention GNP growth rates and numerate forecasts, but of course denies them the opportunity to introduce the qualifying reservations they would ordinarily make to academic audiences. Such behaviour constitutes misrepresentation. The task that I have set myself in this book is to lay bare the truth about the GNP which is known to the professional economists but generally withheld from the lay public.

The real culprits are those politicians who play around with figures prepared by national accounts experts. Many of the latter have cause to complain that the public is being duped, because the former cynically ignore the statistical limitations which they, the experts, have set out together with their GNP estimates. Actually many politicians think they can shrug off such protests based on academic scruples. Why? They know that the GNP—initials now familiar to dustmen and professors of chemistry alike—is popularly accepted as a reasonable standard by which the performance of a government can be judged; and they also know that most people are so ignorant of the real meaning of the GNP that few penalties await the politicians and journalists who employ the concept with distorted bases, averages and time spans.* As to forecasts—well what proportion of the electorate will check up three years later to ascertain whether they have come true?

There is, however, a more sinister aspect to the certitude with which GNP figures are often cited. Perhaps the most searching public examination of UK governmental statistical data is that made by a sub-committee of the House of Commons Estimate Committee (44). It is not surprising that many of the (temporary and permanent) civil servants and others, who gave evidence before it, believed in the ability and desirability of Whitehall to intervene actively in the economic life of the country. Reading between the lines of the Report, it is manifest that many of the witnesses considered their functions as statisticians and economists to be the suppliers of ammunition for socialist central planning. One of the most vocal was R. Stone who has spent much of his life constructing economic models with particular emphasis on forecasts; what he said in public only differed from the views of some of his colleagues in that it was openly spelt out: 'I assume that the main purpose of collecting economic statistics is to help in economic planning and control... None of these things can be done without quantitative data.' The conclusion is inescapable: GNP estimates must be made to look as if their constituent components were accurate and meaningful; without quantitatively significant national accounts it is useless to speak of quantitatively significant GNP forecasts—and without these the putative knack of governments to plan is soiled. Of course the collation of economic statistics may also serve other purposes, such as to enable private firms and individuals to plan intelligently their future activities or to enable historians to describe past events. However weighty these other purposes, their importance is swamped by the express wish of most governments to obtain enough quantitative economic and social data so as to establish credentials that proclaim them fit to make national forecasts and plan the economy accordingly.† If this is one of the main

---

* Apel (22) has delved into the misrepresentation of the GNP in American political demagogy; he has spiced his analytical research with examples from President Kennedy, Governor Rockefeller and other luminaries. A socio-economic study of the milking of the sacred GNP cow by British politicians has still to be written.

† With admirable candour Britain's Socialist Minister of Technology, Anthony Wedgwood Benn, once explained *why* 'the government should be allowed to know a great deal more than it does know about the community it was elected to

reasons why national accounts are prepared, it is the more urgent that one should investigate the soundness of the statistical basis of the GNP, and also to inquire how far the conventional GNP diverges from the genuine GNP. This is what much of my book is about.

---

serve'. He opined that 'you cannot manage an advanced society...unless the facts are available. That is one reason why we are now strengthening the statistical services... No economic policy can work unless its effects can be forecast accurately...'. (143).

Part I

The GNP Fetish

A Monetary Definition

'For so it is, oh Lord my God, I measure it; but what it is that I measure I do not know'.

ST. AUGUSTINE*

The concept of the conventional GNP is based on two working assumptions: One, that it is a tool enabling meaningful time and spatial comparisons to be made in numerate language. Two, that human welfare can be measured by it, with the corollary that the bigger the GNP the better for society.† In the following pages both these assumptions will be challenged.

Appendix I, which gives a more elaborate definition of the GNP, shows that the national product appears in three statistical guises (income, output and expenditure); in practice the statisticians come up with three arithmetically diverging numbers for each yearly GNP. Of course few of the television performers, journalists and politicians who so glibly use the 'national product' in their arguments, know that there are three sets of figures to play around with.

According to the expenditure approach, the GNP is defined as the sum of (the net foreign property income and) the values of all those goods and services domestically produced which can be given monetary prices. For goods and services to be represented in the GNP totals, they must have a money tag though this need not necessarily be a price freely obtained in a competitive market. (The attributed monetary values are sometimes notional, such as the measurement of doctors' output by

---

* W. Allen Wallis (45) has urged that this confession of St. Augustine, more than 1,500 years ago, about the concept of time, ought to be repeated daily by all who purport to measure economic growth.
† When Herman Khan, the famous strategic thinker, was interviewed on the prospects of Japan, he expressed the opinion that the Japanese were aiming at the highest GNP in the world, ahead of the United States. 'In America high school kids watch the baseball scores; in Japan they read the GNP.' (119). Khan implies that GNP growth is a good thing whilst the fostering of baseball is a less worth-while endeavour.

the amount of their emoluments.) As a rule, the national accounts technicians employ the artificial prices actually charged by governments or non-profit-making bodies for their output, as if these represented proper values based on true market prices.

A genuine effort is made to include in the GNP both material output *and services* although, as already noted, this may entail the incorporation of items at arbitrarily allocated values. This, however, still leaves excluded from the GNP the output of many human endeavours which, by the conventions underlying the construction of national accounts, is treated as valueless: feeding an ailing uncle, cooking at home, making a chair in the garden shed, playing with children, voluntarily driving an ambulance — these are but a few examples of human activities, generating material output and/or psychic pleasure, which find no expression in the GNP totals. The GNP statisticians exclude much of society's output — which is intrinsically valuable and quantitatively important — because they do not want, or feel unable, to give it a money price. I am re-emphasizing this, because it proves that the conventional GNP can only be comprehended within the framework of a rigid monetary definition. This in turn deflates the conventional GNP as a satisfactory yardstick in evaluating all human welfare-cum-happiness.

But even when the GNP includes items that have price tags which are derived from the free operation of the market, it is doubtful whether the recorded values always represent faithfully measures of output that are commensurate with the generated welfare. For the statistical purposes of the GNP it is convenient to ascribe to the croupier in a shady casino, who earns £5,100, the creation of a value which is said to be three times as big as the attributed output of a probation officer whose salary is £1,700.

To simplify matters, it will be assumed (in the following illustrations) that labour is the sole productive factor in society and that no other input contributes to the creation of GNP values; it is furthermore supposed that every working individual is paid £2,000 annually and consequently is deemed to be responsible for a £2,000 GNP output. Seven items of '£100,000 GNP value-output' then represent one year's work by seven groups of fifty people who have, in varying degrees, enriched society by supplying the following goods or services:

Teaching anthropology to 500 students; average *per capita* weekly tuition of fourteen hours to ten students.

Teaching 5,000 redundant miners enough knowhow to enter labour-hungry engineering factories; average *per capita* weekly tuition of twenty-eight hours to 100 miners.

Making X pop records (which are immediately 'consumed', i.e. thrown away after they have been played for a few months).

Building Y tanks in an ordnance factory.

Inspecting Z payroll sheets to collect Selective Employment Tax (i.e. participation in one of Britain's growth industries).

Constructing one computer which is anticipated, during its working life of eleven years, to replace the jobs of sixty people.

Manufacturing mining machinery, which once installed will necessitate taxing society in order to pay for part of the wages of its operators. (The latter will be producing with this new machinery coal that people only want if its cost-price is artificially lowered through substantial subsidies.)

This hotchpotch collection of seven hypothetical contributions to the GNP is meant to illustrate that in the narrow monetary framework of the national accounts, there are recorded items with equal values, which have a diverse impact on material and non-material welfare. The arbitrary nature of the conventional GNP forces on to a spurious common denominator the value-services contributed by philosophy lecturers, textile designers, croupiers and probation officers and the value-output by the makers of mining machinery, contraceptives, napalm bombs and television sets.

Many Western economists look disdainfully upon the national accounts practices in Communist countries (cf Appendix I). It is easy to poke fun at statisticians who are compelled by their Marxist heritage to work with infantile definitions of what is 'productive', and who must consequently define the national product in such a way as to exclude from it parasitical, non-productive endeavours, as selling and administration which are said not to create any values. Little erudition is needed to demonstrate that human welfare is enhanced just as much (or just as little) by teaching French and selling socks as it is by manufacturing blackboards and socks. But ought we, in the West, really to mock uninhibitedly the Communist statisticians? Both the Western and the Communist national accounts contain many arbitrary values, which are based on money prices that are partly (and in the case of the Soviet economies largely) artificial. One likes to think that the national income figures in the West are constructed on a somewhat more logical

25

foundation than that underlying the Soviet calculations, but as the distortions in the national accounts on either side of the Iron Curtain are very big, one may lump them all together as unsatisfactory indices for human welfare. People who live in glasshouses should not throw stones. We are not really *so* superior to the Soviets when it comes to the methodology of national accounts.

There are economists in the English-speaking world who beat their breasts to expiate for the shoddy and pretentious GNP data which they sell to the public; bemoaning their fate, they seek to elicit sympathy by asking how else can one construct national product figures than by using the admittedly unsatisfactory and arbitrary standard of monetary weights. Their dilemma is real but they weep crocodile tears. The genuine GNP is quantitatively indeterminate and therefore worthless for comparisons in time and space. Although the conventional GNP is an imperfect standard of measurement, it is hailed as useful because it allows for quantitatively determinant comparisons. If only its apologists would state plainly that the wish to forge a *determinate* tool has given birth to an implement with many imperfections, one could learn to appreciate and perhaps even to live with this creature. When, however, these imperfections are passed over as trivialities, and the conventional GNP becomes idolized as a gauge for national welfare, then the time has come to slaughter this sacred cow.

The GNP is not the 'Social Product'

'There are no economic ends.'
LIONEL ROBBINS

The thesis in Part I of this book is that the (conventional) GNP does not provide a meaningful index for human welfare. Before this is argued in more detail, I ought to disassociate myself from two types of criticism of the GNP, which — though sound in themselves — are irrelevant to my theme.

There are those who scorn the GNP on the grounds of faulty computational techniques and statistically inaccurate components. It follows that if economists were to succeed in sharpening their national accounts tools, the GNP could in time become a near-perfect instrument for the quantitative measurement of human progress. My strictures on the GNP, however, are of a more fundamental nature; they would not need to be much modified by an improvement in the collation of data.

Others are critical of the GNP criterion, because the nominal production costs of goods and services (as recorded in the national accounts) diverge from the social costs (i.e. the nominal costs plus or minus the unrecorded incidental benefits or sufferings society enjoys or endures as a result of their production). Thus, the GNP-registered values of chemical manufacture underscore the real costs of making chemicals borne by society, as they exclude the additional costs (or discomforts) imposed on people living in the vicinity of factories, whose clothes are sullied by obnoxious fumes. Another example is provided by the GNP-registered values of agricultural products, which leave out of account the fortuitous benefits enjoyed by those non-farming citizens, who are able to partake of rustic, aesthetic amenities without paying for them. Mishan (54) and others, who rightly stress these anomalies in the national accounts, perhaps do not emphasize enough that these divergences between nominal production costs and social costs can be, and increasingly are, whittled down by various statutory measures and

27

sophisticated taxes. Nevertheless, a differential element is bound to remain and this indeed lays the foundation for a sound objection to the GNP tool. I regard it, however, as a minor criticism as compared with the kernel of my attack on the GNP concept.

A short historical note may help to place the present GNP mania into its proper perspective. Once it used to be quite common to describe economics as a discipline dealing with the material aspects of human endeavours. Lionel Robbins is amongst those who have vehemently thundered against this notion; his onslaught, though launched forty years ago, remains valid today. He then showed convincingly (83), that the chief function of economists is the study of scarce means, and the analysis of relative valuations. This means dealing with the motives of egoists and altruists, of sensualists as well as ascetics and clearly includes non-material objects—even the sale of indulgences and the services of prostitutes. The GNP enthusiasts of today will of course gladly concede that non-material objects should be included—indeed many are—and lip-service is generally paid to the proposition that total human welfare is a wider concept than that covered by the GNP. But how sincere are these protestations?

In a frequently quoted passage, Pigou laid down that economic welfare is only *part* of total welfare, i.e. it is only that portion which can be brought directly or indirectly into a relationship with a money measure (23). Colm put it that 'as a statistical concept national income is defined...as the measurable part of social product' (52). It would seem as if there was no cause for complaint and that everyone concedes that not only the ham sandwiches and nylon stockings, counted by the GNP statisticians, but also such diverse factors as marital harmony, the aesthetics of arts, the enjoyment of friendship, religious freedom, etc., play a role in the creation of the totality of human welfare.

There is, however, reason to believe that most economists specializing in national accounts regard the welfare factors not represented in the conventional GNP as small, peripheral elements which ought not to interfere with their general conclusion that, on the whole, total human welfare can be correlated to the size of the GNP. As an erudite critic has pointed out (41), this implicit charge can even be laid against Pigou himself who seemingly was fully aware of the gap between the conventional and the genuine GNP (to employ the terminology of this book); Robertson suggests that if Pigou had been imbued with the spirit prevailing in the above quotation from his book, he would have called his masterwork *A Study of Economic Welfare*—in fact its title is *Economics of Welfare*. Many economists betray their real feelings by frequently describing the GNP (and its accounting satellites) as the 'social product'. When Britain's veteran in the preparation of national income and expenditure estimates, Richard Stone, describes his work, he too (apparently without any compunction) speaks of 'social accounts' (84). The United Nations, as the League of Nations before it, refers to the compilation of national accounts as the 'construction of social accounts'. The German nomenclature for the GNP is *Bruttosozialprodukt*.

Why do so many economists misappropriate the term 'social product', which (as Colm in the above quotation clearly implies) is different to, and often presumed to be bigger than, the conventional GNP? This is not a matter of linguistic hairsplitting or just a case of sloppy language; nor can it be explained by imputing ignorance to national accounts specialists as to the different attributes of the GNP and the 'social product' respectively. Why then these tendentious attempts to equate the arithmetic of the conventional GNP with that of the genuine national product? I suspect that a comprehensive welfare meaning is frequently attached to GNP exercises because of the crazy ambition of so many economists to raise their discipline to the level of an exact science.*

A.

The genuine GNP includes many human benefits which are not recorded in the conventional GNP (such as the 'free goods' of society, working on a hobby, voluntarily driving an ambulance from charitable motives, parental love, etc.).

* Galbraith (120) also refers to the dichotomy between what economists *think* about the essence of the GNP, and what they feel themselves obliged to *say* publicly. They regularly warn that economic judgements are not the total judgements on life. Having paid this lip service, they then proceed to treat the national accounts as the exclusive measure of social achievement, and the final test of public policy. 'St Peter is assumed to ask applicants only what they have done to increase the GNP. There are good reasons for this insistence on the totality of economic goals. It arrests what otherwise would be a disconcerting obsolescence in the profession of economics. For so long as social achievement is coterminous with economic performance, economists are the highest arbiters of social policy. Otherwise not. Theirs is an eminence not to be sacrificed casually.'

B.

The conventional GNP is necessarily computed on the working assumptions that the prices employed (a) always represent genuine price offers, and (b) that they quantify accurately the imputed benefits. The first assumption is clearly untenable when the state is able to buy and sell resources at artificial (i.e. non-market) prices. The second assumption is fallacious, because earnings of £1 have a variable meaning for different individuals. If the national accounts (presented from the income angle) record £500 Mn, the underlying assumption is that the cumulative earnings of individuals with a £1,000 income and those of individuals with a £10,000 income have the same welfare value *per* £1. This is nonsense, because – to use the technical language of economics – the marginal utility of £1 is a subjective criterion; it is not necessarily equal for people with identical earnings, and hardly ever equal for persons on heterogeneous income levels. The welfare significance of the conventional GNP can, however, also be undermined when one assumes, for the sake of the argument, that the marginal utility of £1 is in fact uniform, because it is absurd to divorce occupational earning standards from the incidental (positive or negative) benefits resulting from a particular job. The prestige of representing one's country abroad creates, per £1 earnings, a larger benefit than that obtained by a property tycoon who is bored with making money; indeed this is the reason why an ambassador is willing to work in his function at lower emoluments than he might obtain elsewhere where this incidental occupational benefit is lacking. When, on p. 24 a comparison was made between the £5,100 and the £1,700 salary of a croupier and a probation officer, it was urged that in most people's value judgement there was something incongruous about registering these gentlemen's respective contributions to the totality of human happiness in the ratio of 3:1. This was an evaluation of their offerings to the GNP, when it was dressed in its output uniform. Looking at it now, from the income angle of the genuine GNP, some might well arrive at the conclusion that the comprehensive occupational benefits enjoyed by the £1,700 probation officer are not one third of those of the casino employee – as the conventional GNP would have it – but actually larger than the latter's.

C.

The architects of the GNP pretend that the larger their edifice the better. The nature of the national product—its composition and distribution—may be vastly more significant, in terms of welfare, than its size as measured by conventional GNP standards. To some, a more egalitarian society is preferable to one with wide income disparities, even though the latter can boast of a relatively larger GNP. A pacifist prefers a smaller GNP to one swelled in size by the manufacture of arms. Elderly people wishing to enjoy pie on this earth will come out for a GNP which contains fewer investment goods and more consumption articles.

D.

Perhaps the most important criticism of the conventional GNP is that it measures, mechanically, the output of goods and services without taking into consideration the environmental and non-monetary costs of production. Pigou, Colm and all the others who make the obvious point that the GNP is merely *part* of the creation of human welfare are only telling half the story. Welfare is also vitally affected by the conditions under which the GNP output is produced, and by the quantities of physical and mental exertions that are expended in the process. Yet the conventional GNP merely dwells upon the end-product, and ignores entirely these cost elements. Countries A and B have the same population and an identical GNP—for the national accounts experts this clearly implies that they are 'equal'. For those who reflect on the more genuine aspects of life, this need not be a foregone conclusion, because the GNP equality may turn out to be a sham. In the national accounts of both A and B there is an identical item: '30 Mn socks, worth £3 Mn, produced by 1,000 workers'. The sock-makers of A are forced by the dictatorial régime of their country to engage in this activity although their inclination is to earn a livelihood by farming. B is a free country in which this output is achieved by the voluntary decision of people to make these quantities of socks. A is distinguished from B also by its inefficient working methods which bring it about that the makers of the socks must work daily twelve hours as against a six-hour working day needed in B to produce the identical physical output. The workers of B have enough leisure to engage in pursuits (unrecorded in the GNP) which bring them benefits additional to those obtained by manufacturing socks. The workers of A are prepared to work a shorter working week (with a consequently smaller output and fewer material rewards), because they seek to partake of some of the leisure benefits enjoyed by their colleagues in B, but the dictatorship—no doubt wishing to prove to the United Nations that the GNP is in A impressively large and that therefore A is a developed country—will not permit this.

Pigou, in his youth, could perhaps not conceive of a situation in which there was actually a contradiction between the size of the GNP and total welfare. His imagination clearly did not postulate the stage Western society has now reached, where a reduction in the size of the GNP may sometimes actually augment total welfare. The more capable a society becomes of producing material values in an ever increasing physical volume, the wider the potential gap between the conventional GNP and the 'social product'—and the more misleading it is to speak of them in one breath.

The GNP Wardrobe

'We delude ourselves into thinking that we live in a rather more
rational and scientific age than our forebears... We live in an age
of particular mysticism and the mystical religion today is
economics. The economists are the high priests and the statisticians are their acolytes.'

JOHN BIFFEN

The GNP can be dressed up in numerous guises, the choice of the
attire depending on the socio-economic occasion to which it is sum-
moned. Before dealing with four of its well-tailored suits, a few words
must be said about politicians who invite the GNP to appear, before the
gaping mass of their (economically untutored) electors, naked – without
even a fig-leaf. The crudest way of mentioning the national accounts
is to say: 'The GNP grew by x per cent....' It entails giving no explanation as to the *type* of (conventional) GNP, and is based on the tendentious assumption that there is only one form in which the national
accounts can be presented. A naked GNP hides many sins, and
politicians, batting on a sticky wicket, employ this vague term to compare one type of GNP in India with another type in France, one form of
the UK GNP today with another form of fifty years ago.

It is equally misleading to contrast the growth rates of different
countries or periods, when the GNP is given in *current* monetary
values, i.e. when no attention has been paid to the inherent changes in
money values induced by inflation. Clearly, the only proper way to
refer to GNP indices is to state *real* growth rates, based upon notionally
fixed prices. There are methodological obstacles in the way of calculating
real growth rates, but anyone not even trying to express GNP comparisons in real, as opposed to nominal, ratios is a charlatan.

The following two examples are meant to illustrate how an indiscrimi-
nate use of GNPs can deceive credulous audiences. In September
1967, the World Bank held its annual gathering in Rio de Janeiro and
the delegates were served up many GNP dishes, though few of the
cooks bothered to explain how they were prepared, and what criteria
and base periods determined their figures. The conference was divided:

33

there were those who thought that the rich West was not giving enough aid to the poor Afro-Asians, and to stress this they quoted GNPs with low growth rates in the backward nations. The others, who thought the West had been generous, selected GNP movements which bore out that view. Apparently G. D. Woods, the then president of the World Bank, belongs to the latter school for he told his distinguished listeners that 'over the last fifteen years, economic growth in less developed countries...has been proceeding as fast as in the industrialized countries'. According to Woods, the gross national product of the less developed countries 'has more than doubled' (94). Obviously, a marvellous achievement which was meant to imply that the Indians and Nigerians and Venezuelans were doing no less well than the Western nations. Unfortunately, Woods then went on to explain that the *per capita* income of the developing countries (a euphemism for what he had previously termed 'less developed countries') has increased in this period by only 40 per cent. It is clearly this last figure which tells us that the less developed countries, so far as their standard of living is concerned, have in fact been getting poorer in relation to their richer brethren, because—though Woods did not spell it out—the *per capita* GNP of the West has exceeded this miserable 40 per cent. average in the poorer parts of the world.

My second illustration revolves round an exercise by Beckerman (9), in which he worked out several alternative indicators of growth rates based on OECD statistics:

ANNUAL AVERAGE COMPOUND TREND RATES—PER CENT.
1950–62

Country	GNP	GNP per capita	GNP per head of employed labour force
Canada	3·5	0·9	1·9
United Kingdom	2·6	2·1	2·0

These three criteria, all written in the GNP language, are contradictory guidelines for an economic assessment of the two countries. According to the first, Britain's backwardness (compared with Canada) seems proven. The second criterion demonstrates that Canada's *per capita* growth lags behind that of the UK. The third criterion would have it that the UK's growth rate, mirrored in the productivity of labour, is more or less identical with that of Canada. It all depends on the costume of the GNP!

The four basic* uniforms of the GNP are:

A.

The most frequently employed, and one accepted by some international organizations for the object of determining national membership contributions, is the total current value of the GNP. (In some cases the values are calculated in accordance with the fixed prices of a base year, reading e.g. 'UK GNP revalued at 1958 prices'.) For purposes of international comparisons, these values are often translated into a neutral currency, mostly the US dollar, either at the official exchange rate or at one considered appropriate to the real purchasing power of the national currencies. This GNP score gives some idea of the relative material weight of national economies, but does not measure either labour productivity or the standard of living.

B.

A more helpful summation is provided by the GNP per capita of population, which is of particular importance for the merchandiser who wishes to know about the standard of living of the average citizen; it, however, tells us nothing about the relative economic performance of the active members of the labour force. In countries with a static population, the fluctuations in the national product, measured by criteria I or II, are identical. In economies with a population explosion or large waves of immigrants, this is not so and makes it highly tendentious to employ criterion I without any qualifications.

---

* The OECD, and the United Nations, regularly present the GNP on a market price basis, whilst most official UK sources tend to employ the factor price technique (cf Appendix I). With some little expert knowledge in national accounts the two divergent figures are easily reconciled. But how many non-experts have quoted the factor price UK GNP, and compared it with the market price GNPs of other countries? How many British politicians, citing glibly the size of the national product, say which of these two forms they are referring to?

The 54·3 per cent. growth of the Indian national income, at fixed prices, between 1948 and 1962, looks much more impressive than the corresponding *per capita* growth of 17·8 per cent. in the same period. Yet the latter dismal figure reflects more realistically the welfare significance of India's economic development. When Israel's Investment Authority boasts that 'in twenty years of statehood, Israel's Gross National Product has increased annually by an average of 9 per cent.' (121), thus beating the achievements of West Germany, Holland and the United States, the Statement itself is not to be censured; yet, it would have been wholesome to have added that the *per capita* GNP growth was in the order of half this recorded percentage.

C.

The first two GNP criteria are related to the standard of living. The third and fourth criteria deal with labour efficiency, adducing facts concerning technological advance and, by inference, the degree of capital-intensity in production. By computing the GNP per member of the labour force — criterion III — an index is moulded to allow for time and space comparisons of output per gainfully employed person. This criterion, however, is somewhat unsatisfactory as an accurate measurement of labour efficiency, because it compares output, per head of the labour force, in country A where a forty-hour week is the norm, with that in country B, where a sixty-hour week is still common.

D.

This is why I favour a hardly ever used criterion, that of the GNP per man-hour worked. Only when the GNP is dressed in this suit is it possible to ascertain the true economic efficiency of the national 'productive' apparatus.*

All the above mentioned criteria follow the traditional pattern of the GNP literature in measuring national accounts by one-yearly spans — a

---

* My ecstasy for criterion IV is sprinkled with a number of reservations, which relate to the — nationally variable — conditions and terms of labour under which the measured output of man-hour is attained.

dubious gauge. Droughts, for example, are rarely divine punishments, but are a (roughly) calculable factor that occurs in certain geographical regions once in, say, five years; it would consequently make much more sense to take the five-year average GNP of a drought-prone country and compare it with the GNP performance, over the same period, of a drought-free economy.

The need to view GNP achievements in the perspective of a longer period than one year is not conditioned merely by the impact of capricious nature, but also by the predominance of specific factors of production in undiversified economies. Keynes criticized the pioneers of national income statistics on the grounds that they overstated the value of certain national resources; in his view the real value of a factor of production ought not to be seen merely in the light of its contribution to the national product in year x, but should also be viewed by the case with which its specific character can be diverted in year y to other uses — at a small or big cost. In 1970 the *per capita* GNP of Kuwait is undoubtedly larger than that of the UK. Will this still be the case in 1985 when single-product oil countries may have been hit by the invention of a cheap electric car? I recall meeting a small furniture manufacturer, who had laid off part of his labour force rather than accept offered orders from a large buying organization, which would have resulted in more than half of his production being channelled into one outlet. He was a forceful character who swept aside my counter-arguments by declaiming strongly his ambition to remain independent for years to come, something which he hoped to ensure by never becoming dependent overwhelmingly upon a single supplier or buyer. It would probably be unrealistic to suggest that Kuwait should follow in 1970 in the footsteps of this proud Midland entrepreneur. I am merely proposing that one should treat with some detachment the present claim of Kuwait to head the GNP world league: what ultimately matters is how the Kuwait GNP shapes itself over the last thirty years of this century, as compared with the GNP performances of countries which in 1970 are 'inferior' to her. The nature of British industrial society is such that it is relatively easy to turn from the making of ploughshares to the manufacture of tractors and the building of computers. This agility may allow the average of Britain's long-term GNP performance to score over that of countries with very specific factors of production, which enables them to shine on the GNP sky for a short period only.

Growth of real UK GNP at Factor Cost

CRITERION	TYPE	1958	1967
I	TOTAL	1,000	1,325
II	PER CAPITA	1,000	1,243
III	PER GAINFULLY EMPLOYED	1,000	1,291
IV	PER MAN-HOUR WORKED	1,000	1,345

The above calculations of the GNP growth over a ten-year period, dressed up in the four uniforms, are based on official UK government statistics. They illustrate that there is no such animal as *the* GNP growth rate; for each occasion the appropriate dress must be selected from the statistical wardrobe. This exercise will, I hope, encourage heckling whenever some public figure glibly speaks about *the* GNP: it is as well to ask him which norm he means though such an impudent question may well embarrass the speaker.

The table elucidates that Britain's GNP growth, *per capita* according to criterion II, was considerably slower than the overall growth, measured by criterion I. The main reasons are that the British people chose to have more children, and that improved health conditions lengthened the average span of life. This, factually, does not confute the 'backwardness' of Britain's *per capita* GNP growth, though few would agree that the mentioned causes reflect adversely on British life.

The GNP, per head of the labour force, criterion III, rose less steeply than the overall GNP, criterion I. Why? The labour force increased by 2·6 per cent. in this period and consequently the 32·5 per cent. overall growth rate was only translated into a 29·1 per cent. rise in output per gainfully employed. I mentioned earlier in this chapter that many analysts use criterion III as a gauge for economic efficiency and accordingly this seems to indicate a certain retrogression in British labour efficiency. Such a conclusion, however, would be faulty and this is evident from criterion IV, the most sophisticated test: labour efficiency actually increased by 34·5 per cent., faster than the GNP growth measured by any of the other three norms. In 1967 the British working week was approximately four hours shorter than in 1958. The people in the United Kingdom had a relatively fast advance in output, as measured by man-hour, but chose to partake, in part, of the fruits of their additional endeavours through more leisure.

The expected raising of the school leaving age in 1973 will contribute to a reduction of the GNP, measured with criteria I and II, by about I per cent. Maybe some misguided gnomes in Zurich and the City of London will see this as a sad reflection on the UK's economic competitiveness, but I hope that the British people will learn to live with such a barren evaluation.*

In the previous chapter, I maintained that — whilst the genuine GNP is such a good thing that the more you have of it the better — the conventional GNP ought not to be judged only by its size, for it is conceivable that a relatively smaller volume may actually increase total welfare. This chapter, devoted to the measurement of the conventional GNP, will have driven home the same point. Relatively small growth rates do not necessarily designate regression in economic efficiency, but may be due to weighty and desirable welfare considerations.

* *One* of the reasons why West Germany's per capita GNP is higher than that of East Germany is that children in the latter stay on average one year longer at school than in the former.

A New GNP Dimension

'To many it will always seem better to have measurable progress toward the wrong goals than unmeasurable, and hence uncertain, progress toward the right ones.'

JOHN KENNETH GALBRAITH

A number of economists are suggesting that the growth rate of the national output is not as significant as that of the annual capacity output. Thus Beckerman (9) argues explicitly that 'the important comparison should be in terms of the growth of productive capacity, not output, of the different countries'. Particularly in the United States, many time growth series of national accounts are constructed with the percentage rates purporting to measure Potential GNP; the latter is defined as the notional output available 'through full utilization of the economy's existing resources' (45). I find it difficult to conceive of a more clumsy lever in the economists' tool-box than this new concept. Which purpose is served in estimating what the conventional GNP could be like? Surely welfare is measured by what is actually created and not by what could theoretically be produced. Those who think that it is useful to estimate the potential GNP, ordinarily admit that whilst it has no welfare significance it provides a measuring rod for the productive resources of an economy. I challenge the practical importance of such an exercise. What is meant by the assertion that country x has a potential capacity to produce y million tons of steel?* Is it based upon two-shift or four-shift working? When an economy is said to have a potential

---

* The nationalized British Steel Corporation (134) dropped the traditional publication of 'capacity utilization rates', because it found it misleading to lump together the potential output of all its production facilities for steel; there is no such thing as a customer demand for 'steel' – there is only demand for (and production of) steel product A, B, etc. When the autumn 1968 theoretical British steel capacity was recorded as 29 Mn tons, and actual production was only 25 Mn tons, the BSC nevertheless had to import certain slabs. Why? The demand for some steel products exceeded its production capacity, whilst there were idle production facilities for other steel products (like battleship armour plate) that the public were not eager to purchase. If it is therefore nonsensical to speak of steel capacity in the overall product sense, how much more incongruous is it to theorise about the total production capacity of an economy.

GNP of $z, are the statisticians basing their figures on everybody working sixty hours a week, the employment of all women and youths fit to work, and the closing down of most places of higher education? At the beginning of an unexpected war, it may make sense to calculate the amount of ammunition that could be produced on existing machinery when a four-shift working is introduced; in this example potential capacity is significant. But in an affluent society it is irrelevant to calculate how many stockings could be produced if a four-shift system prevailed, considering all the social inconveniences associated with night work and continuous employment at the week-end.

The total-capacity approach is, in my view, a barren concept except for one redeeming feature: it opens the door to a new dimension of the national product. Society's total capacity to generate welfare can be partially related to the measured output (registered in the conventional national accounts) by crossing two bridges. The first avenue reveals that certain reported GNP growth rates reflect fake phenomena, and the second suggests that gross welfare is enhanced by non-working (and therefore not contributing to the tight-drawn definition of the conventional GNP).

ILLUSORY GNP CHANGES

National accounts calculations are fundamentally based upon production which is measurable within the circumference of an exchange economy. When a country passes from a primitive stage, in which families satisfy most of their needs by self-production, to a sophisticated market economy, in which specialization prevails, statisticians record a rise in the GNP without this necessarily denoting an increase in the output of goods and services. The President of the World Bank found it expedient to boast (94) that the fastest rate of growth in the world is now being experienced by nations with an annual *per capita* income of less than $600, and he mentioned explicitly El Salvador, Nicaragua. Nigeria, Peru, Tanzania, Thailand. This attaches a socio-economic importance to a book-keeping exercise because these fast GNP growth rates hide, in part, the important fact that more and more citizens of these countries are becoming involved in a money economy.* No doubt

* The GNPs of under-developed countries include of course some imputations of untraded output, but when in the course of development this is transformed into traded output the total size of the recorded national product invariably grows *on that account*.

this is a worthy achievement, but such a metamorphosis distorts the actual accretion of additional welfare.

Woman's role in production statistics is similarly ambiguous. All first-year students of economics are taught that if a man marries his housekeeper the GNP is reduced, though clearly there is no change in output as a result of the wedding. (In fact the GNP ought to be re-written to record an increase, because the output of a loving wife is higher than that of a paid servant). It has been urged that as housewives' services are universally excluded from the GNP, this does not therefore distort inter-spatial and inter-temporal comparisons. This plea would be sound if the ratio of the GNP to the value of the (unrecorded) services by wives was constant, but in fact this is not so. Lindahl (110) has estimated that the Swedish pre-war GNP would have been swelled by 20–25 per cent. additional values, if this factor had been taken into account, whilst Kendrick (100) has calculated that the distortion of the US GNP through non-inclusion of housewives' output, was at that time 43·2 per cent., and is now 21·2 per cent. It follows that if all GNPs were re-written accordingly, there might be a significant change in the position of the various economies in the GNP league.

The GNP has grown in the Western world, in part, on account of married women working outside the home. (5 per cent. at the turn of the century, and more than 30 per cent. today in the United States.) To the extent that they continue to perform the same housewifely duties as before, their outside work represents a genuine contribution to the conventional GNP. In practice, however, the accretion to welfare is less because working wives more frequently send their families to eat in canteens and restaurants, make greater use of specially acquired consumer durables, and/or have more resort to outside service establishments such as laundries. In terms of welfare, the work-output of married women outside the home is therefore worth less than their actual output, because as a result of working they perform fewer household chores. To calculate this quantitatively it is of course necessary to work with a GNP model that does include the imputed value of domestic services by housewives.

Marshall (135) said that one ought not to count as part of the national income services 'which a person renders to himself', but he added in a footnote that 'it would be possible and for some theoretical purposes it would be best to include them'. I wonder whether this is just a matter of theory. 10 per cent. of male adults in the Western world are now said to have two jobs (one of which is part-time) as against 3 per cent. thirty years ago. If a moonlighting accountant opts to work as a waiter in the evening and at week-ends, and consequently cannot clean his own car but uses a car-cleaning service, this artificially increases the GNP. On the other hand persons who used to swell the GNP by giving employment to bus drivers, and now drive themselves, are responsible for a shrinkage of the national accounts. The same charge can be laid against various forms of self-service (cf also p. 70). There are powerful tax inducements for high-income earners to cut down their activities in the market economy in order to gain more leisure which in turn enables them to make valuable things for themselves that are not recorded in GNP statistics.

ALL POTENTIAL WORKERS

Product per man-year, corresponding to criterion III in the previous chapter, is nowadays calculated by dividing the national product by the number of people active in the labour force. Before the First World War, however, growth rates of the GNP, criterion III, were based on the demographic concept of 'working-age population'. Of course this present statistical refinement is helpful in portraying how those in employment apply themselves to the creation of wealth, but it clearly has the drawback of leaving out of account those citizens who are potential producers of wealth but either do not want, or are unable, to become active members of the labour force. A society in which 10 per cent. of the working-age population is involuntarily unemployed loses a great deal of wealth production (and consequently has a relatively lower GNP, measured by criterion I) even though it may hold the world record in GNP per gainfully employed. The proportion of gainfully employed, out of the total working-age population, is not constant but varies widely as between country and time. (Even within one country there are important time fluctuations: in the first half of the 1960's the level of unemployment dropped steeply in the US and was one of the factors for the growth in those years of the GNP, criterion I.) A good deal is therefore to be said for creating the notional concept of a working-age population, which embraces all physically fit persons in the age range of 10–80; this would of course include unemployed and housewives. It is important to give this potential labour force such a wide span, and this is particularly urgent if GNP exercises are made for international comparisons.

What advantage can be claimed for this approach? Above all, it lays bare the hollow proposition of the conventional GNP protagonists that there is a correlation between the creation of welfare and the size of the GNP. Let it be assumed that a dictator in an advanced industrial society forced everyone to go to work at the age of ten; the conventional GNP would be forced up in comparison with those nations in which a large number of persons do not enter the labour force until they have completed a university education. The worshippers of the sacred GNP cow would then be compelled to say that the welfare product of the dictator-country is larger than that of 'backward' countries where no one starts work before sixteen and many only do so after they have passed their twenty-second birthday. Those in whose thinking general welfare is not equated with the conventional GNP could profitably employ the total-capacity (ten to eighty) technique to counter this absurdity. How? The *voluntary* retirement of those in the sixty to eighty age group would be treated as the generation of positive wealth, i.e. the happiness of not-working; the college student, by not entering the labour force at the age of ten, would be seen to create a positive value;* an arthritic woman who is compelled to work in pain in India but is able to enjoy greater comfort by not-working in a Western country, would be regarded as responsible for producing a valuable object. If one accepts that these welfare-products are as valuable as manufactured mahogany tables and television sets, they may properly be added to swell the size of the national cake. The total welfare output of an economy in which no one is allowed to start work at ten and no one compelled to go on working until eighty, is likely to be considerably larger than the national product of a country in which everyone in the ten to eighty age range is actively employed.

---

* Most national income accounts incorporate, by imputation, certain unimportant products which do not enter the market economy, e.g. food produced and consumed on the farms. Kendrick (100) is working on a new extended dimension of the GNP which would include many hitherto unrecorded important products. One of these quantitatively significant elements, which he thinks should be notionally included in a comprehensive GNP, is compensation for school work by students 14 years of age and over. Kendrick's imputed values are 'the average earnings of persons in the same age-sex-colour groupings with the same attained educational levels'.

LEISURE

The above approach to the whole potential of the working population (including the sick, unemployed, married women, adolescents) aids in the construction of a more meaningful (enlarged) GNP. One can continue this line of thinking and apply the total-capacity technique also to the maximum working hours of all citizens of working-age, say a sixty-hour week. Walras and Barone are said to have been the first economists to refer to leisure as a positive element in the creation of wealth; they pleaded for its inclusion in estimates of the national income. Simon Kuznets was the pioneer who quantified leisure within the national accounts. In a path-breaking endeavour, published in 1952, he put a money tag on the increased leisure hours 'consumed' by the US population between 1869 and 1948 — and thereby of course radically augmented the size of the GNP. Kuznets maintained that this new-dimensional GNP was superior to the conventional GNP, because it took into account 'not only the material goods and services provided by the economy to its ultimate consumer, but also the amount of leisure' (55).*

His re-written GNP figures for the US ought to have made Kuznets a heroic figure amongst those searching for national accounts data that have some real bearing on the comparative measurement of welfare. Alas, applauding Kuznets for quantifying leisure would also have meant exposing the relative meaninglessness of the currently accepted GNP data.† A few only have acknowledged this revolutionary contribution; amongst them is Studenski who has denounced the conventional GNP as an 'ambiguous and misleading measure of welfare' (2). He arrived at this conclusion, *inter alia,* because he felt that GNP comparisons — by

* It is a matter of regret that Kuznets's pioneering work was seen by him to have 'only curiosity value'. I wrote to him to inquire how it is that he had opened a door but had not subsequently marched through it, dragging other GNP experts with him. In his reply, he said that he 'did not pursue the matter further because there were tasks that seemed to me of greater priority and interest' (127).

† The phenomenal growth of the per capita Japanese GNP is of course largely due to a true rise in productive efficiency. Nevertheless the superior growth rate of Japan — as compared with that of the Western world — owes much to a relatively long working week. During the sixties most Western countries operated a five-day week, whilst a five-and-a-half-day working week was still common in Japan; Holidays were also usually half the annual quota of most Western countries.

ignoring the welfare impact of leisure—do not ordinarily have sufficient regard for the differences that exist in the *amount of effort* required to produce a given output.

Georgescu-Roegen (57) supports the Kuznets approach, but has added an important qualification as to when it is meaningful to add leisure to other outputs in computing a comprehensive GNP. (Incidentally his brilliant exposition renders another proof of how silly are most of the comparisons between the national products of industrialized and under-developed economies.) Georgesco-Roegen accepts the premise that if national income is to be used as an index of economic progress, it must include leisure, but adds that this ought only to refer to *voluntary leisure*. In over-populated poor regions people may have greater leisure than in advanced countries, but this is imposed upon them by geopolitical conditions and not as the result of an opportunity choice between greater leisure and more material welfare. In an over-populated economy, therefore, leisure is not properly speaking an economic good, and its value is consequently zero; it is only in the more advanced countries that it is proper to include it, on the basis of Kuznets's approach, as a freely chosen welfare asset.

Environmental Conditions Affecting the National Product

'Not every kind of growth index would place Britain near the bottom of the list... If frequent teabreaks and other manifestations of disguised leisure are regarded as goods—and economics suggests they be so regarded—their inclusion in any index of output per capita might go some way to enhance Britain's comparative performance.'

E. J. MISHAN

Most of the preceding analysis has focused a searchlight on the numerate values of the GNP, and it has been suggested that even leisure and keeping children at school can be translated into values which ought to count in estimating the volume of the GNP. It is time to return to the basic difference between the conventional and genuine GNP, and to introduce additional arguments aimed at demonstrating that howsoever the conventional GNP is modified and improved, it will never approximate to the (numerately indeterminate) 'social product' which combines all the things that make for human happiness-cum-welfare.

As a result of a resolution by the General Assembly in 1952, the United Nations (aided by UNESCO and ILO) assembled a committee to explore the possibility of arriving at a definition, suitable for cross-national comparisons, which would enable the UN to publish annual reports on the 'differences and changes in the absolute levels of living of the different peoples of the world' (104). An impressive group of government officials and academic luminaries spent much time, and public money, to discharge this request in order hopefully to provide the statistical department of the UN with another set of figures to add to its annual output. Alas, with all the good will in the world to comply with the implied wish of the General Assembly, the experts finally arrived at a conclusion which less sophisticated people might have thought did not really warrant lengthy preliminary deliberations. The Committee of Experts 'was obliged to conclude'—a significant choice of words, denoting that they would dearly have loved to arrive at a positive judgement— 'that non-material elements are very often not manageable from

47

the point of view of measurement'. Drawing on profound wisdom they advised the members of the UN, who had initiated this feasibility inquiry, that 'the level of living is an organic unity embracing both material and non-material aspects of existence'. The Committee regretfully noted that a 'single unified index of the level of living was neither possible nor desirable for purposes of international comparison...' The result is that the UN statisticians do not publish Standards of Living, and have to make do with GNP figures, which they envelop with an aura that insinuates a correlation with standards of relative national welfare.

The theory that the conventional GNP is not just an enumeration of *certain* human activities, but bears directly on welfare comparisons, has many adherents. I have selected one such protagonist, Beckerman (99), who thankfully does not conceal his opinions: 'A society of ascetic monks who prefer to contemplate their navels rather than television sets may be much happier than a society of high income consumers caught up in the emulation process of an acquisitive society' — Beckerman thinks this is very funny though he means his inference to be taken seriously. 'This must not provide a pretext for failing to measure the relative amounts of goods that the two societies do produce and consume.' Of course, he then introduces the usual academic reservations about the existence of welfare factors which do not enter into the calculations of the national accounts, but these are not very important elements to him. In fact the amusing simile about the monks was deliberately used to proclaim that GNP measurements 'cannot indicate exactly' human happiness. My thesis challenges 'exactly'; I do not find that the GNP is slightly inaccurate as a measuring rod for welfare, but consider it a fundamentally distorted tool of social science. Elements of taste, culture and environmental living are, to my way of thinking, so crucial as to invalidate the social significance of the exercises Beckerman and his colleagues are engaged on.

A.

Let it be assumed that the *per capita* GNPs of both the UK and China are recorded as $5,000 by international agencies. This seeming equality hides a momentous inequality; the 'social product' of the UK is vastly bigger than that of China because British citizens enjoy political and religious freedom; in addition—a point detailed in the next chapter—the UK allows its people to spend their earnings on travelling abroad buying pop records, and viewing pornographic films.

The irrelevance of the Chinese GNP, as a welfare measurement, is but an extreme illustration. *Mutatis mutandis,* the same principle applies to a comparison of the GNPs of the US and the UK. Although I personally find much that is admirable in the dynamic American society and believe that all of us in the West owe indirectly much of our freedom to the deterrent effect of Washington's military might, I doubt whether on balance the 'social (*per capita*) product' of the US is really bigger than that of Britain. This is clearly a subjective value judgement, but I venture to think that even those who do not subscribe to it would at least concede that the gap between the genuine GNPs of the two major English-speaking countries is considerably narrower than the large disparity between their respective conventional *per capita* GNPs. Of course, the United States allocates more resources to space rockets, colour television sets and psychiatry than does poor Britain, but on the other hand the citizens of London were spared McCarthyism, can walk the streets in greater safety, and have usually been governed by a superior breed of politicians. Living in an affluent society, these non-material enjoyments may tip the balance in favour of Britain.

This environmental evaluation of the GNP is of course equally applicable to internal happenings in the British Isles. The Socialist government introduced, at various stages in the 1966–69 period, legislation controlling prices, wages and dividends and obtained reserve powers to punish culprits, in the last resort, with imprisonment. In theory this was supposed to push up the GNP. (I am not concerned here with the inimical effects upon the economy which in fact resulted from these controls.) It is arguable that even if the GNP was as a consequence increased by 1 per cent., the resultant moral damage (arising, for example, from the government edict that employers and employees shall be penalized if they do not break certain previously agreed contracts) and loss of liberty may well have diminished welfare by more than was gained by bigger material production.

B.

If the conventional GNP really mirrors a society's socio-economic strength, then surely everything ought to be subordinated to this.

c

Harold Wilson's favourite goods are machine tools; he has hinted more than once at the potential growth of the GNP which would ensue if such production were stepped up. In that case why not cut out from the school curricula such unproductive subjects as divinity, art, music and history? This would release resources that could be transferred to the making of his beloved capital goods. If this seems flippant and far-fetched, the attack should be directed not against my hypothetical proposal but against the belief that the fastest possible growth of the GNP is necessarily a desirable aim. Another example illustrates how alien is the optimisation of the GNP to our cultural ethos. In certain countries a young man can buy exemption from army service by donating a large sum to the military budget. The Western world has rejected such practices, even though in terms of maximum efficiency a £100,000 donation is probably preferable to the recruitment of a dis-gruntled rich youngster: the equitable bearing of sacrifice in wartime is usually treated with more deference than the maximizing of the material national product.

C.

Conventional GNPs are broken down into constituent groups, of which consumer expenditure is the largest. The enumeration of the produced physical goods disguises the important element of the psychic satisfac-tion obtained from so-called wasteful production, i.e. the manufacture of goods that are not actually consumed. The proportion of waste, out of total consumer expenditure, varies with the affluence of the society. There have been conclusive studies to demonstrate that in the rich English-speaking countries many people dropping accidentally one-cent or half-penny coins will not bother to pick them up. Naturally more stale bread is thrown away in Chicago than in Ceylon. Increased domestic electricity consumption contains a growing percentage of ex-penditure on fuel bills for keeping lights burning unnecessarily because lazy consumers seek the convenience of not having to switch on and off. The statistical data on tobacco sales do not give us an accurate picture of actual *per capita* national tobacco consumption. The wealthy American public leaves larger cigarette stubs in the ashtray than the poorer Indians and English. Long live waste! Yet, there are many, cf appendix VI, who look disdainfully on the happiness derived from not-actually-consuming produced goods; they want us to cut down on waste so that resources can be freed for what they think are more useful accretions to the GNP. I suppose if only the British public switched off the lights whenever they leave a room for a few minutes, many more machine tools could be manufactured!

D.

Just as there is waste in the utilization of consumer goods, so too it is possible to criticize certain environmental modes of production as being wasteful, in the sense that they discourage the achievement of the highest possible GNP. But if a nation is prepared to accept a lower conventional GNP, because wasteful production brings non-material happiness, I see no reason to discard the slogan: Long live inefficiency! The famous teabreak, which so many Americans remember from reading sneering and tendentious reportages on British industrial life, is a supreme example. (Of course, other economies also suffer from this alleged disease; the Italians call it '*prendiamo un caffe*'). Naturally long breaks in the working-day reduce output, but surely this is not a bad thing if workers are prepared to accept a commensurate lower remuneration. In a society where a living wage barely suffices to buy bread there will be an obvious incentive to work both intensively and extensively, but this inducement does not hold for members of an affluent society. They will be much more influenced by the atmosphere prevailing at their workplace: bullying foremen, prohibitions on talking, music-while-you-work. These conditions, underlying the creation of the GNP, are not counted by the national accounts experts though they form an important consideration in evaluating the genuine GNP.

E.

The exploitation of capital investments can be optimised, to produce with given resources a bigger conventional GNP, but at the expense of frightening social disutilities. Most societies could immediately augment their GNP if they re-arranged living conditions and switched over to a four-shift system. The Russians, after all, learned this from their Marxist textbooks and, after the 1917 revolution, abolished Sunday as the constant rest-day.* Brunner (98) has pointed out how wastefully Britain exploits her investments in electricity generation; if only weekly production were spread evenly over 168 hours, one would need much less equipment. And surely the same applies to theatres, restaurants, and swimming pools which are now underutilized because most of the population insist on working during the day and taking their weekly rest periods on Saturday and Sunday. Many machines are nowadays only exploited for 2,000 hours in the year, whilst a four-shift system could keep them busy 8,760 hours. Could we not learn a lesson in economics from some of the poor immigrant labourers in Birmingham, who pay for one bed-accommodation which they occupy in turn during the day and night depending on which shift they are engaged on? If only we followed their example, how many resources would be freed to swell Britain's GNP by more buttons, lipsticks and machine tools!

There are some service activities (telephones, nursing, water works) which, even in the richest society, necessitate a twenty-four-hour manning. Some industries are so capital-intensive that it pays managements to offer very large premiums to attract personnel for multi-shift working. But these are clearly marginal matters — affecting at the maximum 15 per cent. of the labour force. In countries, like India, where labour is plentiful and capital scarce, most persons are prepared, nay eager, to increase their income (and indirectly the GNP) by working in a manner which enables a full exploitation of equipment. Perhaps Britain's oracle on efficiency, the Right Honourable Aubrey Jones who heads the National Board for Prices and Incomes, deplores this, but the fact remains that the vast majority of British people prefer to waste capital equipment at the cost of a lower material standard of living. To GNP addicts this is of course a malaise from which Britain suffers. Its supposed victims do not think so. In July 1968, £25-a-week loom weavers at Kidderminster were offered a £40-a-week wage packet if they would regularly work through the night including a shift ending at 6 a.m. on Sunday. They turned it down because they said that they were not prepared to obtain these additional earnings at the expense of their regular Saturday night entertainment as well as missing out their midday pint of beer on Sunday (126). No doubt this sabotaged the growth rate of the conventional UK GNP, but did it diminish the genuine GNP which measures total human happiness?

* Christmas 1969 was officially postponed in Cuba till July 1970 to help harvest the country's sugar crop (203).

The Contribution of the State to the 'Social Product'

'In a society where statisticians thrive, liberty and individuality are likely to be emasculated.'

M. S. MORONEY

About half of the UK GNP is accounted for by activities under the control of the state. An order of magnitude of this kind underlines the importance of a meaningful recording of the state's output. The history of national accounting (long before the term GNP was coined) knows of an incessant debate on the virtues of including the state's contributions (110). Today the state is responsible for such a large segment of human endeavours that few would deny the desirability of registering most of its contributions to the GNP. The debate has moved to another plane: which of the state's output ought to be statistically grasped by the GNP experts? The output of, for example, the educational system or the railways is said to be readily ascertainable so that the only knotty problem is an evaluation of those state activities which 'do not yield marketable goods and services'. Looked at in this way, it would appear as if only a minute part of government expenditure needs to be excluded from the GNP. Usher (97) instances Parliament, the Ministry of Finance and the Home Office as state activities which, because they merely create the social conditions necessary for the functioning of the economy, ought not to be recorded in the national product.

This bickering on whether to include or exclude intermediate state products veils the existence of a much more weighty accountancy problem: do the prices or costs of the state output (which is agreed to be included) constitute accurate welfare gauges? Because of the ability of the government to manipulate the prices and costs of its products and services, are there not considerable distortions in comparisons between the measured output of the private and public sector?

John Hicks (17) has made it clear in his writings that he will have no truck with national accounts which are arrogantly presented as absolute

53

standards of welfare measurements, for he is well aware that 'there may be more than one money value of the social income, each corresponding to a different purpose of calculation'. He also has never had any illusions about the hazards of including the government's output within the GNP 'since the public services do not enter into the market mechanism'. At first, he therefore tended to exclude them from national income calculations, but finally succumbed because apparently — despite his intellectual doubts — he too thought it worth while to operate with comprehensive national accounts. Reluctantly, but nevertheless firmly, he concluded: 'I can see no alternative but to assume that the public services are worth to society in general *at least* what they cost' (my italics). What a surprising value judgement is implicit in the italicized words! It is challenging to find him explain his reasoning: 'One may feel considerable qualms about such an assumption — it is obvious that the government spends far too much on this, far too little on that; but if we accept the actual choices of the individual consumer as reflecting his preferences...then I do not see that we have any choice but to accept the actual choices of the government, even if they are expressed through a Nero or a Robespierre, as representing the actual wants of society...'* I have quoted Hicks at length, because he is one who is fully cognizant of all the pitfalls contained in his advocated methodology. Yet, so strong is his desire to work with the GNP tool that he is willing to put away his doubts. As the inclusion of government goods and services, at nominal and arbitrary prices derived from state budgets is the only objective and feasible manner of having a full GNP, Hicks is prepared to go along with an accountancy method which he himself has demonstrated to be faulty. His logic is convincing — once one accepts that the aim of presenting a comprehensive GNP satisfies an urgent need — but it does not remove a dark shadow from the validity of the end-result, the calculated GNP.

Here are a few categories which classify the distortions — in both directions — of the state contributions to the conventional GNP:

---

* Hicks published this in 1940. I wrote to him to inquire whether a quarter of a century later he still adheres to it. He has remained unrepentant. Whilst Hicks continues to point out the dangers arising from recording the state's contribution — for example, he repeats that a lot of government expenditure is 'very wasteful' — he still believes that if figures of the GNP are being put together 'the social accountant...must work upon some convention which is independent of his individual judgement' (128).

A.

Government goods and services are rarely bought or sold under the same conditions as exist in the private sector. Because the state has coercive powers, it can very often buy and sell at prices which do not correspond with those that would have prevailed if it had lacked this authority. (I am not suggesting that, in this context, coercion is necessarily something reprehensible; the government's predominance is introduced for the sole purpose of showing that artificial factor prices distort the measurements of the state's participation in the national product.) The real value of government-used inputs is either the value foregone by the sellers (of labour or materials) or the price which, *ceteris paribus*, would have had to be paid for their procurement by private buyers. When the state could command serfs to build roads for a given number of days each year, the nominal cost of the labour was zero although obviously a positive value-output was created. Israel used to have a statutory regulation whereby each owner of a lorry had to place it gratuitously at the disposal of the army for one month each year; this helped to keep the military budget down and minimized, statistically, the government's part in the GNP. There are many variations on the theme of forgiving direct and indirect taxes to individual and corporate suppliers of goods and services to the state. Credit from private banks is often obtainable by government agencies (or in the UK by nationalized corporations) at reduced rates; this is unconnected with the commercial risk element that might justify differential treatment but is based upon edicts or directions aimed at spuriously cheapening production under the control of the government. I know of a developing country which once issued an import licence for timber to one company — denying import rights to its competitors — on condition that it would sell half of the quantity to the government at cost price. In this case the size of the GNP was not affected because whilst the importer had anticipated selling the whole consignment with a 2·5 per cent. mark-up, he was now permitted by the price controllers to add 5 per cent. to the import price of the timber marketed to private buyers — all that had happened was that the proportion of government output out of the whole national product became understated.

B.

On the whole, the state buys more often than not at artificially low prices, whilst it is frequently guilty of selling goods and services at prices which over-rate their welfare-values.

The attitude of the UK tax authorities to some employer-financed fringe benefits proves a serviceable analogy. In December 1955 (129) a City firm arranged for its employees to receive a tax-free Christmas bonus by instructing Montague Burton, a multiple tailoring establishment, to supply each employee with a coat or suit; the price was not to exceed £15 and the invoices were to be sent directly to the employer. Mr Rogerson, the subject of a resultant famous test case, was one such employee. He had ordered a garment and the Inland Revenue treated its price, £14·75 (at which it was available to potential buyers), as emoluments on which he was to be taxed. The matter went through various judicial stages and ultimately the employee won a partial victory; it was held by the learned judges that the cost to the employer ought not to serve as the income-criterion. The real income, the welfare benefit of Mr Rogerson, was deemed to be the second-hand value of the garment (agreed by both sides as £5). As Lord Justice Harman put it: 'Income tax is a tax levied on income. The taxpayer has to pay on what he gets. Here he has got a suit. He can realize it only for £5. The advantage to him is therefore £5.' This judgement has established the following tax concept: a £100 money wage is the equivalent of £100 taxable income, but most gifts-in-kind* are taxable income only to the extent that they can be turned into money's worth. This makes good sense in elucidating that the welfare obtainable from £100 cash, which the recipient can spend according to his preferences, is usually larger than a £100-priced benefit-in-kind (that may be unwanted or can be turned into money's worth only at a discount on the original cost to the donor).

This principle is applicable to many of the public services furnished either free or at a subsidized price. When the state provides some or all of its citizens at no direct cost to them with coal, cough drops, the loan of

---

* This sound tax rule does not, however, apply to those culprits in society who receive benefits-in-kind when they are directors of the company concerned or are in receipt of annual emoluments of £2,000 or over. Both Tory and Labour governments have held that such people shall be penalized by having their fringe benefits assessed to tax in accordance with the cost to the employer of providing same.

Agatha Christie detective stories or lessons in anthropology, the formal size of the GNP is not distorted. These zero-priced goods and services appear in the national accounts as output, the price of which is determined by the outlay of the state (civil service salaries, purchase price of materials, etc.). The resulting falsification, in terms of human happiness, only becomes evident when one drops the formal accountancy conventions of the GNP. The state finances its gifts by imposing £x taxes on the population, which is thus deprived of spending the £x on goods and services of its free choice. Cash of £x ordinarily enables its owners to acquire products with a higher welfare content than is contained in the goods and services a benevolent government bestows on its citizens with the proceeds of £x taxes. (GNP experts know that this can be graphically verified with the aid of indifference curves, which are found in every economist's toolbox.)

C.

In terms of welfare, the value-output of the state sector is overstated in yet another manner. Some of the governmental administrative costs are clearly expenditure to provide services which are valuable *per se*. Salary payments to census officials, ambassadors, and fraud prevention inspectors yield a positive value to society and their output finds a place of honour in both the conventional and the genuine GNP. Other administrative costs, however, bloat the GNP proportion attributed to the state without commensurate benefits accruing to the population. Let it be assumed that the state does not impose taxes to provide free medicaments, and that people have to pay from their own resources for £100 Mn purchases of drugs and pills. Then a change of policy occurs—I am not concerned here whether this is a good thing or not—and the state offers to provide free £100 Mn of medical supplies. To accomplish this, the government spends £5 Mn to recruit staff for checking the accounts of the chemists and administering the scheme. The state imposes additional taxes for £105 Mn to finance free drugs; the state portion of the GNP is increased by that amount and the private sector's reduced accordingly, whilst the total size of the conventional GNP is unchanged It is arguable, however, that the true welfare content of the GNP has shrunk by £5 Mn because people now acquire the same volume of drugs by foregoing the welfare they had previously derived from their private expenditure of £5 Mn which is absorbed by the state for administrative purposes.

The two further examples, culled from Harold Wilson's public finance programme, both elucidate the same point that some state activities influence GNP growth in a perverse fashion. The Selective Employment Tax (SET) is a weekly poll-tax of £2·40 on each adult male employed (and proportionately smaller rates for women and youths), with an annual gross yield of more than £2 billion. From its proceeds the government refunds this tax, after a lapse of time, to the employers of certain categories of workers in the ordinary areas of the UK, and pays a weekly subsidy of £3·90 to employers in qualifying manufacturing activities in the development areas per each adult male employee. Only the residual amount, remaining after these two forms of expenditure, is net revenue for the Treasury. The avowed aim of SET is to tax parasitical service and distributive functions (like hotels, export houses and food stores) for the benefit of progressive manufacturing activities (including the making of bubble gum, cosmetics and one-armed bandits). The economists who inspired SET have drawn sustenance from dusty primers on Marxian economics which proclaim the superiority of 'making' material things. SET, apart from being an inequitable tax, involves the managers of many companies in the burdensome task of paying it and then (sometimes after wrangling with government offices) reclaiming some or all of it. Basically, SET does not affect the size of the national accounts because it represents transfer payments. In one sense, however, it produces a sham accretion to the GNP. The total government cost of administering SET is clouded in some uncertainty, and even fewer quantitative data are available to guestimate the additional number of staff which employers have had to employ to comply with its operation. Taking a low set of figures, it appears that about 1,250 men and women have had to be recruited within the private and public sectors to effect these transfer flows. They are playing a role —a dubious role—in contributing to Britain's GNP by virtue of the fact that their salaries are recorded as part of the national output.

In January 1966, investment allowances and accelerated depreciation were abolished as incentives and replaced by investment grants. According to government sources, investors were unlikely to be affected materially by this change-over, which replaced tax-credits with the cash payment of subsidies. Once again, it might be maintained that this was a technical financial arrangement that had no impact on the size of the

GNP. True in a way, except that the new method presented the Labour government with an opportunity to increase clerical employment. Under the simple replaced system investors had to file no special applications and the government in turn accorded the investment allowances through the existing tax machinery; Crawford (130) claims to know of an Internal Revenue estimate that it devoted only about fifty man-years of work to assessing the allowances. Investment grants, however, have necessitated the establishment of five regional offices, a central coordinating London office and the recruitment of about 1,150 extra civil servants. Companies claim that they have been saddled with an additional burden, involving an overall national recruitment of hundreds more employees for accountancy work. Does the execution of this new administrative function, created by the changed policy of providing investment aid and values to British welfare? The conventional GNP would have it that the answer is in the affirmative, though the 'social product' registers a drop as a result of the replacement of investment allowances by investment grants.

D.

This is an iconoclastic blast from Enoch Powell: 'It is no use producing, however efficiently, what people do not want. Much better to produce inefficiently what people are anxious to buy.' When the state employs its coercive economic powers to prevent certain goods from being manufactured, it intensifies the misrepresentation of the GNP as a mirror of the national welfare product. The nationalization of steel and footwear production makes state agencies the sole producers in these industries. As a result of these nationalizations, the physical output of rods and shoes may well be higher than that which, with the same productive resources, would have been reached under private ownership. Why? By cutting down on the number of products, and by limiting quality variations, unit output per man-hour may be raised. If this happens, the nationalized industries are then able to boast of contributing £105 to the GNP where previously, under competitive conditions, an output of only £100 was recorded. But when the style, taste, polish and shades of the products do not correspond to implicit consumer demand, the nationalized industries are selling 'second best' goods — in that respect there is a notional loss of welfare. £100 output, attained under conditions which satisfy the idiosyncrasies of free consumer choice, can be presumed to equal £100 welfare values. £105 of forcibly standardized goods are certainly worth less than £105 welfare values; they would be recorded in the genuine GNP at, say, £95.

The full force of Enoch Powell's epigram rarely applies. Nationalization does not lead to the manufacture of goods which people do not want, i.e. goods with no intrinsic welfare values. People buy standardized (nationalized) articles because they seek to derive some welfare utilities from consuming them. The intensity of their desire to buy them is conditioned by the non-availability of alternative articles, the consumption of which they would enjoy more. Polish ladies, visiting Western shops, look enviously at the choice of five hundred types of stockings that beckons buyers, whilst they—in the name of rationalization and efficiency of production—are limited at home to a selection of perhaps only five different styles and textures. Obviously they prefer to acquire stockings which are not exactly to their taste rather than go without stockings altogether and to that extent the output of the nationalized Polish stocking factories is creating welfare values. In contrast to the genuine GNP, the conventional Polish GNP is inflated by the exaggerated output-values of stockings. This is so, because the Polish ladies, purchasing the available stockings at their pre-determined prices, would probably not have bought these specific articles if a range of alternative stockings had been on offer.*

* South Africa has mammoth, *per capita*, sales of radios and, seemingly, this represents a true satisfaction of consumer demand. In fact, however, the extraordinary enthusiasm for radios is derived from a state prohibition on television. As in Poland, the South African consumers are driven to buy a product they would not have bought if they had been free to buy another.

A Bag of GNP Obscurities

'Most economists like to visualize themselves, in unguarded moments, as rising to the same sort of role as the astronomer who can predict a solar eclipse with dismaying accuracy and dependability.'

S. SCHOEFFLER

A fundamental appraisal of the conventional GNP must centre on its divergence from the 'social product' (the genuine GNP), i.e. the failure of the GNP tool to draw a comprehensive picture of the total human happiness generated by the efforts of a given society within a stated time span. The conventional GNP is, however, also open to the more prosaic criticism, that it fails to provide accurate welfare measurements for even those human endeavours the output of which it purports to record. The (money) values of which the gross national product is made up are not uniformly orientated links with the utilities people derive from them. The factors, listed in this chapter, are intended to sustain this two-pronged critique.

UNTRADED OUTPUT

Repeated references have already been made in the preceding text to a large volume of production that the GNP architects ignore, e.g. services given at no remuneration to the state or charitable causes; the work of women in their household chores; some bartered products. This untraded output clearly distorts the arithmetic value-output of each GNP. But worse than that; as these ignored services and goods constitute a variable proportion of the total output of each society, they undermine the feasibility of international confrontations, and can sometimes even knock out of shape a time comparison of growth rates within a single country.

ILLEGAL PRODUCTION

Most economists believe in a clean and simple life. Of course they have heard of graft, corruption, smuggling, illicit production, tax evasion and falsified returns to government questionnaires—but they shrug their shoulders and refuse to consider seriously such sordid interferences with official statistics, contending merely that these illegal acts represent marginal, and therefore quantitatively unimportant, phenomena. A German satirist, C. Morgenstern, once caricatured the bureaucrats of his country by accusing them of acting on the principle that what the law does not permit can *ipso facto* not have taken place.* Such an illusion guides many GNP experts.

In the developed countries illegal economic activities (some of which are caught in the GNP net) probably do not affect more than 3 per cent.† of the national product. But considering the fact that erudite discussions on growth rates often concern fractions of 1 per cent., even this relatively small element of illegality has some bearing on GNP forecasts. It is, however, in the less developed countries that illegal activities play an important role in distorting the national accounts. With the accuracy of their import/export data already impaired in many cases by multiple exchange rates, these countries frequently publish international trading figures that are perverted by crooked documentation and smuggling. (It is said that 30 per cent. of Lima's beef consumption is supplied by cattle smuggled into Ecuador from Peru.)

Where there is centralized government planning and controls abound, the black market and illicit production flourish. Despite the death penalty for 'economic crimes' in the USSR, Bulgaria, Hungary, Poland and Roumania, private enterprise has raised there its illegal head in supplying goods and services many of which are not recorded in official statistics. In one of the new Afro-Asian republics, independence was celebrated by introducing the rationing of price-controlled eggs for urban consumers. The system was supposed to work through government allocations of feedingstuff to farmers in exchange for eggs de-

---

* '*Weil nicht sein kann, was nicht sein darf.*'

† Perhaps I am underestimating this. In 1959 a survey (131) of the Licensed Beverage Industries Inc. guestimated that sales of $1,000 Mn of illegally made liquor were effected in the US. This moonshining racket is said to have involved a tax loss of $740 Mn, and accounted, in some areas, for one quarter of the total liquor consumed. There have been suggestions that in 1963 90 per cent. of Swiss cigarette exports were smuggled into neighbouring countries. The *Economist* (132) has calculated that whilst Switzerland officially exported in that year 361 million cigarettes, the unofficial exports exceeded 3.5 billion.

livered at (unrealistically low) official prices. Most farmers bought additional feedingstuff (including bread) on the open market, which enabled them to supply the black market. The GNP of this budding economy only took cognizance of the output of the official laying hens. When some years later rationing and price control were abolished, official statistics reported that egg production had almost doubled over-night. Agricultural experts from an international agency, who were sent to advise the government of this developing country, expressed surprise at this rapid growth rate. They were enlightened by the government statisticians, who explained that in fact production itself had not gone up, but that what had formerly been illicit production was now formally recorded in the national product. When it was pointed out to them that this cast a shadow on the accuracy of their previously published GNPs, they retorted that 'surely official statistics cannot take account of black market prices and output'.

'In the Philippines, traffic in contraband goods in both directions constitutes a very heavy element of foreign trade; but official Philippine figures cannot be expected to cover what is illegal without distinguishing it from what is not' (133). This description is undoubtedly factually correct, even if one does not accept the implied justification for the publication of a fake GNP, on the grounds that the Philippine government 'cannot be expected...' Vital, the author of this report, commits however a more heinous offence by first debunking the validity of the official Philippine figures, and then using them for his sophisti-cated comparisons of the Philippine GNP with the national products of the UK and other countries. It is, however, a not untypical in-congruity.

AUTARCHIC EVILS

The trouble about the conventional GNP is that it does not (and methodologically cannot) take into account the background aspects of production, such as tariff protectionism, intensity of work effort, the social environment, the number of hours worked per week, and other vital elements. The GNP records the product of the prices and quantities of output. When productive efficiency leads to a fall in unit prices, the consequence may be a fall in the volume of the current-price GNP. By translating current prices into notional constant prices, this particular distortion can be avoided through the constant-price GNP calculation. It is, however, noteworthy that the refinement of the constant-price GNP tool is not always feasible in confrontations of the national products of different countries.

This pitfall in international GNP comparisons is usefully examined after first considering the three sets of consequences which could flow from an improved mode of production of typewriters in country A; it is assumed that this leads to a 10 per cent reduction in labour time per unit manufactured.

(1) The price and the number of typewriters produced remain unchanged; the weekly wage also remains constant but the hourly wage rate is increased by 11 per cent., and the working week reduced from 40 to 36 hours.

(2) The hourly and weekly wage rates and the 40-hour week, remain unchanged, but the price of the typewriters is reduced so that a larger volume of goods produced can be marketed.

(3) The hourly and weekly wages and the 40-hour week remain constant; the price and the number of typewriters produced also remain unchanged; this will make 10 per cent. of the labour force redundant and it is assumed that they are transferred to the manufacture of electric tooth-brushes which have never before been made in country A.

How do the GNP alchemists treat these three possible consequences brought about by the more efficient manufacture of typewriters? In (3) both the current-price and constant-price GNPs record a growth of output which is equivalent to the value of the output of electric tooth-brushes. In (2) the current-price GNP records no growth (because the total sales revenue is presumed to be unchanged) but the constant-price GNP records an increment equal to the value-output of the additional typewriters. In (1) both the current-price and constant-price GNPs register no change. This last example shows up blatantly the absurdity of the GNP accountancy — as a measuring rod for welfare — because no provision is made to record the augmented human happiness that presumably ensues through the increased leisure of the typewriter workers.

The typewriter model shows that the sums in the national accounts ledgers do not reflect correctly and consistently welfare utilities. The same principle applies to international comparisons of GNPs, when these are built—as all are to some extent—on price tags that are artificial because of the restrictions on the free flow of economic factors across national boundaries. This is a world of arbitrary exchange rates, Buy America acts, South African government procurement regulations favouring products with a high local content, British protectionism for a high-cost coal industry, import controls and quotas, bilateral trade agreements, export subsidies, and other evils. All these influence the levels of welfare derived from purchasing, in country A, locally-made articles. In some cases their prices, and/or production costs, are determined by the artificial trade barriers which prevent consumers in A from freely buying substitutes made in country B. The arithmetic of national accounts is based on the actual market prices in country A although some are clearly higher under protectionist conditions than they would be under conditions of free trade.

A hypothetical example may assist to demonstrate how protectionism can pervert the welfare value of a GNP. Let it be assumed that North America is relatively inefficient in manufacturing generators, but highly efficient in making electronic devices. Furthermore it is presumed that, in response to official edicts and patriotic pressure, a given number of resources are employed in Detroit to construct a generator at a cost of $36 Mn, which sum swells the US GNP. What would happen if these same resources were switched to electronic work? The resultant output of $36 Mn could be marketed abroad and with the proceeds a Swiss generator purchased for $30 Mn, thus leaving $6 Mn for the import of bananas. In both cases the GNP contribution of the Detroit resources is the same, i.e. $36 Mn. But when one comes to measure the utilities derived from the output of these resources, there is, in the second case, an incremental benefit to the tune of $6 Mn. Simple people would clearly differentiate between these two cases, but the GNP arithmeticians imply that there is no welfare difference

There is not a single country in the world which does not somehow practise protectionism. If all did so to the same degree, the matter need not have been raised in this context, but of course nations vary widely in their autarchic habits. As a general rule, the more protectionist an economy, the lower is the welfare value per dollar of GNP. It follows therefore that, in seeking to arrive at meaningful comparisons between the national products of countries with respectively high and low degrees of protectionism, one ought certainly not to rely on GNP data.

THE QUALITY BUG

The government bureaucrats who think of themselves as competent guides of the economy are nowadays very proud of their computers with which they can count speedily the number of cars and cement bags produced. Multiplying these quantities by their retail prices they calculate the past GNP, forecast the future national product and thus, armed with a prescience denied to ordinary mortals, are equipped to plan our lives. They reject quality changes as nuisances which upset their orderly schemes, and in fact denigrate them as red herrings drawn across the track of the idyllic GNP concept. Paul Chambers's denunciation is succinct and biting:

'Certain economists who enjoy wallowing in masses of statistics for their macro-economic analysis regard this whole question of quality and reliability as just a marginal irritation of no importance because they cannot include these important factors in their calculations.' (95)

The theoreticians who equate human progress with GNP growth rates—cf, for example (124)—are of course well aware that their historical and inter-country comparisons are defective because not sufficient attention is paid to quality differentials. But does the wider public know? Let us assume that Britain's 1930 GNP included £100 Mn of goods which were sold as medical remedies though in fact they did not cure, and that this item is displaced in the 1970 GNP by £100 Mn of antibiotics which do cure. How can anyone claim that the welfare significance of this £100 Mn output item has remained unchanged? Yet, this is precisely what GNP accountancy implies. If only more people knew about the mystery of GNP growth rates which largely ignore such decisive quality changes, they would treat them with greater disdain as social criteria.*

Milton Gilbert has made a name for himself in comparing the GNPs

* Nicholson (96) has applied this same principle to demonstrate how quality changes distort the retail price index which serves in most countries as the standard of measurement for inflation. Although today the computation of the UK price index does take some account of quality changes (123), the index still overstates the actual increase in the cost of living because—with most items—the rise in prices is accompanied by a proportionally greater welfare benefit derived from the superior attributes of modern products and services. Just as the true

of different national economies. Naturally he has discovered that the price indexes are overstated and consequently the real rise of output is understated. Laymen may find it therefore extraordinary that Gilbert opposes rigidly the thesis that 'intangible quality improvements can be brought into the spheres of quantitative measurement' (178). The reasoning which he has set out in an academic journal ought to be more widely disseminated, because it tells us something about the mentality of people who have a vested interest in proving that international GNP comparisons are meaningful and necessary guides to welfare. Having denounced the prices indexes as inaccurate, because they fail to take sufficient account of quality changes, he then goes on to say that these quality-induced distortions must be ignored. If we do not heed this advice, 'in the end, they would make it impossible to construct measures of output and price changes that are useful in the study of economic growth'. It is the same story all over again. The GNP experts know the fallacies underlying their calculations, but want them ignored for otherwise GNP tables could not be constructed and that, to them, would be a major tragedy.

The more sophisticated the computer, and the more detailed the forms which the public must fill in for their bureaucratic masters, the greater the accuracy of the quantitative collation of production data. But fluctuations in quality, durability and taste can never be fully caught within the statistical net. They pose a problem which is insoluble. All one can assert with certainty is that in many fields these qualitative changes affect welfare more decisively than the measured changes in the price and quantity of recorded output.

Fluctuations in the quality of a £100 item, without a corresponding price change, can affect the accuracy of the GNP in two directions: If the quality has deteriorated the GNP ordinarily overstates, whilst if the quality has improved the GNP ordinarily understates, the satisfactions obtained from £100 current output as compared with the welfare utilities derived from £100 recorded in the previous GNP.*

growth rates of the national product (measured in terms of human satisfactions) are larger than those noted in the GNPs of the developing countries, so the real rise in the price index is lower than that given in official publications.

---

* Some quality deteriorations neither add to nor subtract from human welfare. Before the last war beds were manufactured to last for fifty years. Today they are made for a use of twenty-five years only. On the assumption that the real price of the beds has not changed, i.e. the price has not been reduced in accordance with the lowered durability, this seemingly constitutes a clear case of

The following illustrates a distortion of the GNP caused by a reduction in quality unaccompanied by a price change. It is assumed that labour charges are the only cost in providing postal services, and that consequently the wage bill of £3 Mn for 3,000 postal employees represents the output of the Post Office in the GNP. The staff are given a 50 per cent. wage increase but it is regarded as impolitic to put up the postal charges. Instead, one third of the postmen are declared redundant and retired prematurely. As a consequence, the public now has to fetch the letters from the post offices instead of having them delivered. The GNP will still register, unchanged, the output of the Post Office as £3 Mn, and thereby disguise the lowering of welfare which this reconstruction has brought about.

There are numerous instances of product groups where quality improvements outdistance price increases. (The GNP of course only embodies the latter). If £10 was the annual average family expenditure thirty years ago on cleansing materials for domestic washing-up purposes, and is still so today, this is recorded as 'no growth' in the national accounts, although handling greasy plates with detergents is clearly more pleasurable than performing this task with the aid of soap. Similarly, the enjoyment from textiles is growing yearly because of changes in textures, range of colours, weight and washability. Cars are safer and easier to handle. Which brings greater satisfaction from £100 fuel expenditure: open coal fires with the associated dirt and drudgery or labour-saving central heating which warms rooms evenly?

Quality improvements represent some of the invisible growth elements of our society. By their very nature they are numerately indeterminate, because quality means different things to different users. When a 12-page financial newspaper turns itself into a 24-page journal, by adding new sports and arts features, one might readily jump to the conclusion that, at an unchanged price, the new format represents 'better value for money'. For many readers this will be so. To the man, however, who only buys this paper to look up stock exchange quotations, the additional features will be worthless and he will not regard the new product as more valuable.

---

lower quality. In the formal sense this is wholly true; yet, for the majority of bed-purchasers in the last third of the twentieth century, the reduced durability is irrelevant because, unlike their grandparents, they are in the habit of buying beds more than once in their lives.

Finally, a hypothetical example in which an acknowledged quality enhancement actually induces—in the mind of the GNP experts—a shrinkage in the size of the national cake. Total medical expenditure on pneumonia contributed, say, £100 Mn to the 1939 UK GNP. In those days this was a serious illness that involved weeks of hospitalization and necessitated, on the average, eleven visits by the doctor. In 1969 the total medical expenditure on pneumonia is only £50 Mn because new drugs have cut down the hospitalization period and only three doctor visits are needed. There will be wide agreement for the proposition that the welfare value of the £50 Mn expenditure—in the form of safer, less painful and quicker treatment—is higher than that of the corresponding £100 Mn. Those, however, who pontificate on the GNP will note that Britain's medical output has been reduced, thus allegedly contributing to a lowering of the country's welfare!

The quality bug throws serious doubt on the accuracy of the cost-of-living indexes as criteria for the debasement of national currencies. The indexes make an inadequate allowance for quality changes because they are often based on the assumption that a price increase is due exclusively to a higher cost to the consumer in purchasing the identical product. In theory the index measures the price changes of an identical product, but in practice this is not feasible because all goods do not have sufficiently homogeneous, detailed and constant specifications. Housing is perhaps the most striking category in which the cost-of-living indexes overrate the steep slope of the upward trend. The housing expenditure of the average family, in current money terms, has of course risen tremendously in the last fifty years because of the debasement of the currency, higher land charges, and relatively more expensive construction costs. Another weighty change, however, is also causing the *per capita* housing expenditure to rise: more families lived in three-roomed hovels with outside sanitary facilities in 1920 than do in 1970: more families now reside in five-roomed double-glazed chalets with a twin garage than did half a century ago. The statisticians are doing their best to separate the pure price increases from these shifts in type of accommodation—they are also the first ones to admit that they are not fully successful. 'The housing expenditure of the average family' is a useful concept, but in comparing the respective 1920 and 1970 budgets more than price movements must be elucidated; unfortunately it is not practicable to highlight statistically how far a seemingly identical item of consumer expenditure has multifarious welfare functions over time and space.

If one therefore concludes that the cost-of-living indexes overstate the price increases of truly identical products, it then follows that they exaggerate the loss of purchasing power of the national currencies. This is of very practical significance in any examination of GNP growth rates. To make sense, the GNP is measured in real terms, i.e. the current-priced GNP values are adjusted for inflation, and in some cases the cost-of-living indexes are employed for this purpose.* If the UK GNP rises in one year by 10 per cent. at current prices, but the real growth rate is given as 3 per cent., because of the lowered purchasing power of the pound (measured *inter alia* by the cost-of-living index), this latter figure is bound to be wrong: the true growth rate is more likely to be 4 per cent. or above. Through ignorance, politicians miss the opportunity to tell the electorate that they are getting affluent at an even faster rate than is evident from the upward curve of the GNP.

SELF-SERVICE

Some forms of production for self-consumption are included with notional prices in the national product, for example farm produce which is consumed by the farmer and his family. The major part of the growing Do-It-Yourself activities are not represented in the GNP. John is a carpenter and Paul a decorator; if John makes furniture for Paul and the latter decorates John's house, then the output of both is reckoned as part of the national cake. If, however, John and Paul — perhaps in order to save paying income tax — do not work for one another, but each undertakes the carpentry and decorating jobs in his own home, the GNP will ordinarily not count their endeavours as part of the national output.

Work for self-consumption is methodologically allied to the conundrum of self-service establishments in the GNP orbit. The retail revolution of the post-war years has given birth to powerful supermarket chains where the prices are on the average 10 per cent. below those prevailing in the small family-owned shops. Methodologically, the

---

* To present the national accounts at constant prices, the statisticians employ various appropriate indexes, but the accuracy of most of these is impaired (like the cost-of-living index), because there are changes in quality and design which 'are not susceptible of measurement' — to quote Britain's official handbook on GNP data (105).

causes of this price reduction are dealt with under two headings in the conventional GNP.

Let us assume that in 1960 £100 Mn of blouses and pickles were sold in the UK, all of them in small establishments. In 1970 all of the same physical quantities are marketed through Woolworth, Marks & Spencer, Sainsbury and Tesco multiple stores for a combined revenue of £95 Mn. To the extent that the large stores were able to achieve this price-reduction by bulk buying, cheaper transport unit costs, lower overhead merchandising expenses, etc., they are in the same position as our efficient typewriter manufacturer mentioned on p. 64. Although the same quantities have been marketed in 1970 as in 1960, the current-price GNP has dropped by £5 Mn but the constant-price GNP has remained unchanged.

Let us now make the alternative assumption that the whole of the £5 Mn price reduction is due to the fact that the large stores have self-service facilities and consequently lower sales costs as compared with the counter-service small shops. This time the situation is truly different; Woolworth and Sainsbury and the others are seen to be enemies of both the current-price and constant-price GNP. If the national accounts statisticians do their job properly they will not compare the 1960 counter-service goods with the 1970 self-service goods because the latter are of lower quality in the sense that they lack the attribute of sales service.

In one sense, it is irrelevant whether I consume sweets served to me by a sales-lady or sweets which I have to put in bags myself, whether my tank is filled by a petrol attendant or whether I have to operate the pump myself. In both cases the consumer values obtained are identical. Yet most people would retort that the physical attributes of the sweets and petrol are not the only factors which create consumer values. If this is so then the purchases represent two kinds of sweets and two sorts of petrol, which is precisely what a strict interpretation of GNP accountancy would have us believe. I maintain, however, that in fact identical goods are consumed because in each case the consumer obtains the physical articles plus service. The real difference is that in one case the service is provided by persons who receive a monetary consideration — and therefore the GNP automatically classes their output as part of the national cake — whilst in the other case the service is production-for-self-consumption, i.e. the consumer creates a value without money changing hands, and his output is therefore not registered in the GNP.

So long as one accepts the premise that the GNP's job is merely to measure value-output (and that this in turn guides us to measure the relative welfare standard of the UK in 1970 in relation to the UK's welfare standard in 1960 and to that of Tanzania in 1970), it is incongruous to exclude production of goods and services for self-consumption just because they lack a monetary tag. It is only when the conventional GNP philosophy is set aside and one uses the tools of the genuine GNP that self-service and other forms of production-for-self-consumption fall into place. The genuine GNP not only seeks to measure total output but also takes into account the conditions under which it has been achieved. Looked at in this way it becomes highly relevant to inquire into the pains and inconveniences suffered by the buyer at a counter-service and a self-service shop respectively. The *net* welfare benefit at the former is on this basis relatively higher. So long, however, as national accounts are drawn up without any regard being paid to whether a given output is attained in a 40-hour or a 60-hour week, it is illogical to ascribe a lower value in the GNP to the lower-priced article in Tesco's self-service store and a higher value to the identical physical article sold at a higher price at a counter-service shop.

INVESTING IN HUMAN BEINGS

The asymmetry of the GNP and the 'social product' also manifests itself in the philosophical cloaks with which some economists attire investments (in the shape of food, health and education) seeking to improve human capital. During the last fifteen years the academic world has been inundated with a plethora of books and articles purporting to measure the relationship between this type of investment and the size of the national cake.* Schultz (111) believes that economists first began to be interested in the fruits of human investment capital when they were confronted by a puzzling rate of GNP growth which could not be wholly imputed to the recognized traditional inputs (labour, infrastructure, machinery, etc.). They were left with a 'residual growth', that

---

* I know of an unpublished thesis which argues that a person who acquires human capital by studying ought to be allowed, during his working life, to write off this investment through tax-deductions from his gross earnings. So far no country has recognized these investments as capital goods on which taxpayers may claim depreciation.

ostensibly could only be explained by an improvement in the quality of human resources.*

In the past any suggestion that this type of investment deserved special consideration in presenting the national accounts was taboo. In a Presidential Address to the American Economic Association (112) it was propounded that economists are loath to treat investment in human capital as ordinary investment, because they find it offensive to think of human beings as machines and naturally abhor slavery: 'To treat human beings as wealth that can be augmented by investment runs counter to deeply held values.'

These inhibitions now seem to have been dropped and the pendulum has swung to the other extreme. A special conference was organized by the International Economic Association which was devoted exclusively to this subject (21). Of course lip service was paid in most of the papers to the non-material impact of education, but the majority of the delegates presented findings that were easily accommodated within the circumference of the conventional GNP. Their thoughts were echoed in a policy statement by the Council of Economic Advisers (prepared for the President of the richest nation on earth):

'Failure to pursue vigorous educational and health policies and programmes leads to smaller increases in output in the long run... Failure to invest sufficiently in education means that we lose the additional output that would be possible with a better educated labour force...' (45).

Once one thinks along these lines, the temptation to quantify is too strong to resist. Becker (118) attempts the ludicrous task of estimating arithmetically the return on capital invested in providing a college education. One can only suppose that the National Bureau of Economic Research, which aided him, was pretty proud of his erudite output. We find percentage returns on this educational investment of 5 per cent., 7 per cent., 9 per cent., 10 per cent., 11 per cent., 12·5 per cent. and 15 per cent. − depending on whether the students were male or female,

---

* Estimates concerning the quantitative aspects of GNP growth attributable to human investment capital differ widely. Amongst the extreme calculations for education are those made by E. F. Denison − summarized in (9) − and in the 1962 Annual Report of the Council of Economic Advisers (45); these maintain that from 1930 to the middle fifties half of the growth of output (per employee) in the US is due to education. Estimates for the impact made by investment in health are even more vague. Mushkin (116) suggests that 'the decline in death rates between 1900 and 1960 in the US accounts for 10% of the...growth in the economy'.

white or coloured, studied in year x or y, attended faculty a or b, etc. Having calculated these percentages, Becker was still not satisfied; he called upon other economists to supply data on the various returns on capital invested in US businesses and then felt himself called upon to compare these with his own figures. His startling conclusion is that there is no significant discrepancy between the direct returns on college education and business capital; he therefore opines that direct economic returns do not justify increased college expenditures. This may or may not have been proved by his exercise. What is to my mind much more important is that it is a questionable proposition in the context of a comprehensive theory of human welfare. Becker and others, who defend the purposefulness of quantifying the direct returns on investment in education, are adamant that they are solely concerned with the impact of these investments on the supply of skilled personnel for the creation of wealth in the conventional GNP sense. They claim that though they are aware of the other effects, they do not seek to measure them because they have set themselves only one limited objective: the impact of educational capital on the size of the national product. To Merrett (115) this compartmentalization is artificial and impractical. At the conceptual level the economist is unable to deal with psychic income and changes in leisure activities which flow from education, because the human capital concept is not capable of evaluating them. As the economic and psychic benefit streams cannot be separated, Merrett rightly concludes 'that research into the rate of return on education should be discontinued'.

So far as the Western world is concerned, investments in human capital are not of great importance to GNP growth in the last quarter of the twentieth century, and have now as little relevance as the 'calorie theory'. Extensive research has established a correlation between calorie intake and labour output per hour: the more nourishing food manual workers consume, the greater is the productivity. This truism once had considerable practical significance in the Britain of the pre-1914 days just as it still has today in backward economies. But does anyone seriously maintain that output per man-hour today can be substantially augmented in the English-speaking world by more and better food? The law of diminishing returns applies equally forcefully to capital invested in education. In the first stages of the industrial revolution (practically all) funds spent on educational objectives produced many golden eggs – by giving youngsters a rudimentary knowledge of reading, writing and arithmetic the economies of those days were indeed helped to grow faster. But any additional educational expenditure today, aimed at raising the present level, will only marginally increase the national product.

Actually many of the learned papers, with their detailed statistics on education, implicitly ignore the fact that only a small part of educational capital is invested where it can have any but the slightest effect on the conventional GNP. Shakespeare and anthropology, divinity and history are taught in Japanese schools but these subjects certainly do not contribute to that country's advance in electronics. One third of all women college students in the US marry immediately after graduation and most of these do not put to commercial use their acquired knowledge: the investment in their education will neither have made them better housewives nor have earned them the accolade of becoming prolific contributors to the GNP. But even when one only considers the investment in the teaching of so-called productive trades, educational expenditure is not always helpful in augmenting the GNP, if the graduates cannot be absorbed into economic activities enabling them to employ their skills. India is today, in some fields, facing the problem of 'over-education', which in turn raises the social dilemma of unemployed graduates in a largely illiterate society.

Some investments in human capital may in fact be considered as an impediment to the growth of the conventional GNP. If investments in health did not prolong the life of many citizens to a ripe old age, the people looking after them in geriatric wards would be available for alternative activities with a potentially higher value-output, such as making television sets and cars. If resources now devoted to teaching archaeology and anthropology were freed, the redundant students and teachers could raise the national product by manufacturing computers and machine tools. Such considerations support Vaizey's assertion that 'a great deal of education which is cultural in content may be harmful to growth and certainly need not promote it' (113). Vaizey does not say explicitly what he means by 'growth', but he is presumably referring to the conventional GNP—and if so, he is certainly right.

The moment one abandons this restricted definition of growth and thinks in terms of the genuine GNP, investments in human capital, on the whole,* actively and positively accelerate the growth of total human

---

* I have written 'on the whole' because education can and does produce in some people feelings of frustration and unhappiness; this negative element must be deducted from the positive total of happiness generated by investments in human capital.

satisfactions. In my value judgement, our society—in which many have learned to derive pleasure from Bach or a book on Napoleon, are spared by modern drugs the pains of illnesses, and can look forward to care in their old age—has a greater 'social product' than preceding societies which lacked these non-economic goods. These intangible welfare benefits, however, are not all recorded in the GNP.

The Crux: GNP Comparisons*

'If bread is cheaper in the country than in the city, ordinary
national income accounting practice implies that a loaf consumed in the country constitutes less income than a loaf consumed in the city.'

DAN USHER

Sometimes the pleasure of cultivating roses is derived from beating one's
own past efforts or from surpassing the excellence of roses planted by an
envious neighbour. Such comparisons can indeed often determine the
intensity of enjoyment experienced by botanical enthusiasts. Yet it is
also not uncommon for some dedicated gardeners to glow with joy,
when—without any thought for the size and fragrance of other roses—
they lovingly behold the blooms of roses which they have grown from a
cutting, nurtured, watered and manured with dedication.

Unlike roses, GNP figures *per se* can never generate joy. To say that
the national cake has a value of $x or creates y utilities means nothing in
isolation. Such numbers only become significant once they are contrasted with the quantities of other GNPs. The *raison d'être* of calculating national accounts is to make possible comparisons over a period
and with other countries.

It is of course common ground that the path of GNP comparisons is
strewn with imponderable nails. The majority of economists affirm that
despite these nails, such comparisons do deliver a powerful message on

* I shall not repeat in this chapter my conceptual criticism of the conventional
GNP which seeks to invalidate the accuracy and purport of most national
accounts comparisons. In international juxtapositions there is also the additional
impediment of the uncertainties surrounding external exchange rates. Without
elaborating on it, reference must at least be made to the faulty character of
statistics in many parts of the world. As a distinguished UN expert on cross-
national research wrote: 'We are sometimes dismayed by the trusting manner in
which internationally issued statistics designed as unreliable or incomplete are
employed in scholarly publications, and by the elaborate structures and elegant
comparisons sometimes built up on the basis of very fragile data. It must be
kept in mind that under-developed countries tend to have under-developed
statistics' (137). To confront national accounts data of relatively high accuracy
with those of dubious accuracy, *as is frequently done*, is an intellectually dishonest activity.

77

relative standards of welfare. A minority claim that the resultant knowledge is flimsy. Some critics even argue that these GNP comparisons may actually do harm by producing distorted pictures which deflect from the study of national welfare by other, more substantive, indicators. Many national accounts experts have expressed themselves publicly on the accuracy and significance of GNP comparison. I have selected four such representatives (Clark, Beckerman, Kuznets and Usher), whose writings are readily available in English. In summarizing their views I have found it right to categorize the first two as belonging to the majority, and placed the last two in the ranks of the minority.

Colin Clark (43) is a fervent believer in 'objectively measurable economic welfare' and rather arrogantly denigrates those who disagree with him on this as intellectual anarchists. To Clark, any economist who denies the validity of economic comparisons between one country and another is guilty of engaging 'in the meaningless accumulation of facts'. He has no doubts or reservations: 'Economic welfare can be compared between times and places.'

Beckerman (99) is less haughty and does state reservations, but basically he subscribes to Clark's thesis. In an elegant way, Beckerman enumerates the many fallacies underlying inter-temporal and inter-spatial confrontations of national accounts. Having unburdened himself of these, he then pleads that they must not constitute a pretext for economists failing to carry out these measuring exercises. His philosophical approach is perhaps best summed up by recalling his protestation that, though the conventional national accounts are not perfect and 'cannot indicate exactly' variations in happiness, they still represent the best available technique for welfare comparisons. Beckerman's choice of the word 'exactly' is not likely to be regarded as fortuitous by any reader of his well-argued writings. I hope that I do him no injustice by interpreting his argument as follows: GNP comparisons are not 100 per cent. accurate and meaningful; they do not tell us the 'exact' truth but they come pretty near to it! According to the dialectics of Clark-Beckerman, the citizens of country A are better off than those of country B, if A has a higher *per capita* GNP than B. But what if the citizens of B live and work in a more pleasing environment than those of A? What if more non-material benefits, not included in the GNP, are enjoyed in B than in A? Beckerman tells us to ignore all this as a relevant argument against the validity of national GNP comparisons. First, he says, 'it is simply impossible to make quantitative allowance for such differences.'

Secondly, he observes sneeringly: 'The fact that "money can't buy happiness" has long been the consolation of everybody without much of it....'

Kuznets is the Grand Old Man of national accounts, and he would appear to have a personal vested interest in embellishing the significance of the GNP concept to the expositions of which he has devoted fifty years of his working life. Yet, from his earliest writings till today, he has always been very modest about claiming any comprehensive meaningfulness for his published national product data. Thus, in setting out his measured weights of 'national consumption', he emphasises that the latter is an accounting term which must not be confused with 'national income enjoyed' (138). This may be an obvious point, and one Clark-Beckerman do not dissent from; yet Kuznets's stress on the incomparability of 'enjoyment', as distinct from the limited comparability of the consumption item in the national accounts, is a wholesome reminder to those who tend to draw blind conclusions on welfare from conventional GNPs. Kuznets has pioneered the construction of *per capita* GNP tables, but he is careful to present them with the warning that though they may 'appear to measure the nation's economic welfare... further investigation reveals...that the clear and unequivocal character of such estimates is deceptive.' Kuznets divides the output of society into economic and non-economic products. The former are products which in the present state of statistics can, whilst non-economic products cannot, be translated into money terms for the purpose of arriving at a quantitative national income. Statistical exigencies therefore impel the choice of a narrow definition of national income, if one wishes to be reasonably accurate. If the ratios of economic and non-economic output were constant, comparisons of the GNPs (based on the former only) would not be invidious. But Kuznets is at great pains to point out that proportions of economic and non-economic output (out of the total output of society) vary as between countries and over time. Consequently, national income comparisons across wide time intervals (or between countries of greatly differing socio-economic structures) are 'highly misleading', unless one explicitly spells out that conventional GNP data are crude, non-comprehensive approximations of part of the total output. The part of the total output which has been selected for inclusion in the GNP is not necessarily the major or most important end-product of human endeavours — it merely happens to be output which is measurable with a relatively high degree of accuracy.

Usher (97) concedes that in order to conduct intelligent discussions about economic development and relative levels of poverty, one may be forced to attach numbers to degrees of prosperity.* He demands, however, that when this is done it is imperative to publicize the fact that any such quantifications of real income have in principle nothing in common with the measurement of, say, the density of a metal or the speed of light: they are inevitably subjective and lie on the borderlines between science and opinion. Usher may not himself be aware how much the economists and statisticians concerned resent it when international comparisons are stripped of their scientific cloaks.

It would not surprise me if there were statistics on national characteristics appertaining to runners of under-three-minute miles, the ownership of red-haired dogs, and the incidence of twin-births. If such indeed exist, they would provide the substance for *objective* international comparisons. I am not bursting with enthusiasm to study international comparisons of red-haired dogs, but undoubtedly these figures would be meaningful to people interested in such matters. The question that will now be posed is whether GNP comparisons are similarly meaningful in the sense that they tell an equally *objective* story that can be of professional interest to social scientists.

For the sake of simplifying the issues discussed in this section, it will be assumed that *per capita* GNP international comparisons can be constructed with arithmetically accurate data. To establish them, the statisticians would first have to agree on the denominator of a neutral currency, say the US dollar, into which all measured output would be translated at acceptable exchange rates. The volume of the national output would embrace, along the lines of the conventional GNP, such diverse products as steel, houses, air pollution controls, drinking water, poison gas, lessons in racial purity, and computers. Nobody can possibly object to the collation of such figures because it is obviously a harmless activity. Yet one may properly ask whether it will prove worth-while to have engaged on this mammoth task. Speaking only for myself, I do not profess to any intellectual curiosity to know the *per capita* output of different countries. If indeed such an exercise should reveal some worth-

* This does not make the choice of the GNP criterion inevitable. According to Usher, conventional *per capita* GNP analogies depend on 'theoretical imponderables and on the judgement and pure guesswork of the investigator' (33); he proposes that GNP confrontations should generally be avoided when superior criteria for income comparisons are available.

while message, one ought to be told about it by those who are engaged on this work. The onus of showing that *per capita* national output figures, calculated for the purpose of international comparisons, add significantly to knowledge falls on the GNP architects.

No one to my knowledge has ever been guilty of asserting that the measurement of national output is in itself a worthy endeavour. Clearly there is no intrinsic meaningfulness in a series of national output figures. Consequently all statisticians busy on this type of work tell us explicitly or implicitly of the purpose to which they seek to put the results. What is their rationale? The *per capita* GNPs are said to provide a measuring rod for national standards of welfare. As a corollary, they also reflect commensurate 'capacity to pay' in fixing national dues to international bodies, the countries' need to receive (or the countries' ability to give) foreign aid, etc.

Once one accepts that the collation of comparative GNPs is motivated by the purpose of comparing welfare, one has moved to another dimensional plane—away from the field of objectivity which characterizes the national measurements of twins, dogs and mile runners. I hope to demonstrate convincingly that the link between output and welfare is not definable in an objective fashion, because it depends on subjective criteria and national peculiarities. The GNP enthusiasts are caught between the devil and the deep sea. So far as their output tables are concerned, they may represent arithmetically correct and objective data but, on their own admission, these are by themselves meaningless. Once statisticians employ output figures to arrange international welfare comparisons, they are no longer measuring objective matters, because GNP output-values do not accurately mirror relative national standards of poverty or wealth. I have argued that international comparisons must be both *objective-accurate and meaningful*. The most damning stricture on GNP comparisons is that they cannot fulfil these two conditions simultaneously.

There are several weighty reasons why GNP output-values measure unsatisfactorily standards of living in time and space comparisons. A nation's welfare is not necessarily linked to its output, when either a substantial part of the latter is given away as an unrequited export, or when that society partakes of the fruits of another society's labour without paying any dues. (For details, cf Appendix I).

Even on the—blatantly untrue—assumption that the efficiency of labour, capital and management is the same in all countries, output-

values of the national GNPs (calculated in terms of a neutral currency) are not directly related to tangible output *in nationally identical ratios*. If the Dutch and Kenyan GNPs both record $100 Mn of road building, this could mean that the inhabitants of Holland have benefited from ten miles of new roads and the Kenyans only of five miles; this disparity would be due to the flat countryside of the former and the mountainous terrain of the latter. $100 Mn value-output of aluminium in Canada signifies 10 per cent. more tonnage than $100 Mn aluminium value-output in Wales, because of the relatively cheaper fuel costs in Canada. The costs of supplying one gallon of water and the price charged for it may be five times higher in Kuwait than in Eire. It is an untenable proposition to suggest that a mile of road, an ounce of aluminium, and a pint of water create welfare utilities in accordance with the varying national costs of producing them. Yet this is the logical conclusion from measuring welfare in terms of output-*value*.

It is not always understood by those who glibly compare national output-values that these are calculated by multiplying gallons of water, tons of steel, hours of tuition, etc., by their national prices. One way to resolve the incompatiblity of output-values is to construct one price-list, in terms of a neutral currency, of all the goods and services entering the orbit of the world's national accounts; the output-values of each country would then be reckoned by multiplying the physical quantities produced by the appropriate notional international price. It would obviate the present practice of calculating national output-values by the varying costs and prices prevailing in each country. This proposal would indeed make the comparisons more meaningful, but would raise other welfare incongruities that are set out on pp. 84–7.

The protagonists of international GNP comparisons try earnestly to prove that not only are their output-values objective criteria but that these also measure the corresponding welfare by an objective gauge. Consequently all output-values are treated alike as sources of identical welfare. Thus, when a dictator recruits one million persons to dig a canal and then employs another million to fill it in again, the output-values of these two million people is seen as augmenting the GNP of that country. When the Nazis devoted resources to a study of noses and Aryan physiognomy, the Burmese built pagodas, and the Texans hired students as paid cheer-leaders at football matches — all these activities were said to have increased the German, Burmese and US GNPs. One ought not to quarrel too deeply with the philosophy underlying this comparison of national welfare. If the citizens of Rangoon and Paris prefer to obtain happiness from pagodas and radios respectively, output-values may indeed (subject to the reservations above) constitute a guide to relative national welfare. Some types of output-value, however, are conditioned not by national welfare idiosyncracies but by genuine *sui generis* environmental, political and geographical *needs*. After a short digression, I intend to illustrate with concrete examples that if country A has greater needs than country B, the GNP of A must be commensurately higher than that of B before one can assert that both countries have the same standard of living.

The layman thinks that national accounts discussions are dry matters discussed dispassionately by academics who would certainly never dream of introducing personal matters and—Heaven forbid!—sex into GNP polemics. I am afraid that Beckerman does not live up to this popular image. In order to beat down his opponents, who plead for the 'needs approach', he is ready to reveal that he himself has a far greater need for caviare, fine wines and beautiful women than have most people. He makes these disclosures in order to stress that this may bring about a position where, at a given income level, he could be considered less happy than others who do not have these 'insatiable appetites'. Beckerman insists 'that it would be a very peculiar statistical procedure to consider my standard of living as being much lower than that of somebody else with the same income as me, but with much more pedestrian tastes, simply because my income may not go as far as does the other person's income towards satisfying my insatiable appetites' (99). Beckerman cites his own personal life to blast economists who concern themselves with different states of spiritual happiness. He has, however, a more penetrating objective: it is his intention to establish that just as individuals with the same income must be assumed to have the same standard of living, so nations with the same GNP output must be deemed to have the same standard of living.* His aim is to obliterate the 'needs approach' in comparing the GNPs of different countries.

---

* In a pungent paper, Frankel has warned of the dangerous tendency to draw welfare comparisons, particularly as between developed and under-developed countries, from the size of conventional GNPs (152). To Frankel, the process of measuring the national income is strictly an accounting procedure. His analysis was published almost twenty years ago, but I regretfully report that it is Beckerman's concept, and not Frankel's, which is today accepted by the political decision-makers who shape our lives.

Let me start by dissecting Beckerman's appetites. I deny that the emotions which he shows for caviare, fine wines and beautiful women are 'needs' — they are 'wants'. If he cannot satisfy these appetites he may indeed become unhappy and even frustrated but unless he can demonstrate that the full satisfaction of these appetites is a pre-condition for living and working, they are not necessities and are falsely described as 'needs'. Whilst I do not seek to follow Beckerman in laying bare my sexual and gastronomic appetites, I am prepared to disclose the personally intimate fact that I wear glasses which cost me on an average £3 per year. There are no hard and fast rules about what constitutes a 'want' and a 'need' respectively, and one must be guided by commonsense. It is in this conjectural vein that I suggest my appetite for glasses to be a 'need' whilst my desire to own a Jaguar (or Beckerman's craving for beautiful women) to be a 'want'. If Beckerman and I both have the same income but I *must* wear spectacles to earn my living, whilst he need not, my standard of living is lower than his.

Below are some concrete instances of — real or imagined — national 'needs' (Kuwaiti air-conditioners, Israeli arms production, the building of tall blocks of flats in an urban civilization, artificial rain-making, the construction of nuclear warheads). The 'needs approach' can of course be put aside as an irrelevancy if one merely compares *per capita* national output-values and assumes that these automatically mirror national levels of living. I maintain, however, that it is not only the size of the GNP which matters but also its composition. Hence, when countries A and B both have a *per capita* $500 GNP,* their respective level of living cannot be ascertained from this figure if, for example, country A has to spend $200 *per capita* on military preparations whilst country B does not feel this 'need'.

A.

The British 1970 GNP is in every way bigger than that of 1870. Part of today's national cake, however, includes output that does not bring about a superior standard of living; it satisfies needs that have been created by the urbanization of the economy which has raised living costs

* National accounts thinking relates to the mythical average citizen, who is assumed to produce and consume the *per capita* GNP. This begs the question posed by income differentials within countries which are almost always larger than *per capita* GNP country differentials.

without correspondingly enhancing welfare satisfactions.* Town life results in higher pro rata expenditure on lighting, roads, sewage disposal and infrastructure. Distribution costs go up because, instead of buying farm products in the village, food must now be specially packed, milk bottled and transported to a marketing centre. If high buildings are more expensive to construct, per square foot of dwelling, then part of the resultant increased rental costs are due to urbanization. If one assumes that people like spending some of their leisure time in rural surroundings, the additional expenses of travelling to the countryside must be counted as another cost element induced by the rural-urban transformation. The Indian farm worker regards with envy the Birmingham steel worker, who drives to work in his car. The former walks for five minutes to his workplace whilst the latter is compelled to drive bumper-to-bumper to the steel plant which is twenty miles from his home. That part of the GNP which is represented by car production devoted to urban transportation does not represent a supplementary welfare satisfaction enjoyed by the British and denied to the Indians. Usher (19) is amongst those who regard transport costs as one of the important segments of the national accounts which distort country comparisons by bolstering up the nominal standards of living of the richer countries of the world. Of course we are better off today than we were 100 years ago or than Tanzania is today, but the 1970 GNP of the urbanized UK overstates this welfare superiority when compared with the 1870 GNP of a less urbanized UK or the 1970 GNP of a rural Tanzania.

B.

The South African GNP contains a transport bias in its international trade because certain neighbouring African states impede the shipping and airfreighting of goods to and from a country practising racial discrimination. Some of the South African GNP is devoted to the operation of Apartheid which makes it necessary to provide duplicate social facilities (public lavatories, ambulances, swimming pools) for whites and non-whites, and to finance an administrative apparatus and special police forces to enforce segregation. Some would say that the white

* This problem is parallel to the one traced by Kuznets, in which a society moving from a primitive state to a highly developed money and credit civilization generates the need for banking, insurance, and similar services (55).

citizens thus forego the enjoyment of higher welfare benefits that might have accrued to them if the Apartheid resources had been available for other purposes. The whites argue, however, that without the GNP output, dedicated to making segregation work, they would be unable to enjoy their present high standard of living. There is strong substance in this argument when viewed from the angle of the South African whites. Thus to 'justify' Apartheid expenditure also implies that the *per capita* South African and UK GNPs are not congenial. In the British Isles there is no physical, social or economic threat to our way of life to give rise to the need to appropriate resources for similar racial segregation.* The white South Africans feel this need. The inevitable conclusion is that the South African GNP does not reflect the South African standard of living in the same ratio as the UK GNP mirrors the British standard of living.

C.

A similar evaluation applies to the Israeli standard of living which *compared to that of most other countries of the world*, is relatively lower than is indicated by the growth of Israel's buoyant conventional GNP. According to the Institute for Strategic Studies in London, Israel spends a larger portion of its GNP on defence than any other country except South Vietnam. Some reports suggest that it is 25 per cent. The military proportion of the Swiss GNP is perhaps only one-twentieth of Israel's. Rightly or wrongly, Israel believes that she would be wiped out by hostile neighbours if she did not have a strong military deterrent. Switzerland has no such fears and consequently sees no need to arm herself to the teeth. Under the circumstances UN comparisons about the *per capita* GNPs of Israel and Switzerland tell us little about their respective standards of living.

D.

Climatic conditions represent another factor preventing GNP confrontations from realistically measuring relative national welfare. Let it be

* This is not to be construed as a moral defence of racial segregation. I am merely noting that the white South Africans believe that they would be threatened if they did not practise Apartheid; they see it as a need.

assumed that Kuwait spends 6 per cent. of its national output on the need to desalinate water and manufacture air-conditioners, whilst Holland only expends 1 per cent. of its GNP on these two items. Let us further assume that Kuwait's *per capita* national income is 5 per cent. larger than that of Holland. Would it not be rash to surmise from these figures that Kuwait enjoys a standard of living which is 5 per cent. higher than that of the Dutch?

Countries which have not a consistently warm climate must expend a large part of their national product on efforts to combat cold. A few years ago an estate agent tried to induce me to emigrate to the Bahamas and, for that purpose, to buy a plot of land from him. I was given a brochure which explained that though the costs of many articles in the Bahamas were dearer than in Britain, this should not frighten one from living in this sunny paradise. 'Clothing is more expensive than in the United Kingdom but since the climate is tropical, shorts and beach-wear can be worn the whole year round, thus expenditure on clothing tends to be less than in the United Kingdom.' He did not succeed in selling many plots to the residents of foggy London—but the logic of his argument remains unassailable.

Usher (33) has estimated that the total cost of keeping warm in the UK, including heating, extra clothing and well-insulated buildings, comes to about £60 *per capita* out of an annual income of £406. This of course is a very substantial factor to be considered when comparing the UK standard of living with that of a tropical country which has no need to expend a similar proportion of its GNP on heating. (Even the countervailing need of tropical countries for more air-conditioners and refrigerators is not likely to wipe out the heating bias implicit in the UK GNP.)* If, therefore, a comparison between the Congo and UK GNPs implicitly overstates the British standard of living, a confrontation between the national accounts of Iceland and the UK implicitly understates the latter's standard of living because of the still greater need of Iceland to devote GNP resources to protecting its citizens from the cold.

---

* Morgenstern expresses the same thought by designating certain countries as having a negative income in that certain amenities are not required there. 'Even with a US *per capita* income, one would not heat a house in the tropics (though one may want to cool it) or wear fur coats. Therefore the financial inability to provide heat and furs is irrelevant in determining the meaning of tropical income levels' (16).

So far international GNP comparisons have been viewed through abstract lenses with the aid of mostly hypothetical examples. I shall conclude by citing two concrete case studies, relating to UK-Thailand and US-USSR GNP confrontations. There is no disagreement about Thailand having a lower standard of living (and *per capita* GNP) than the UK, and about the average Russian being less well off than the average American—the question is by how much? No social scientist would today maintain that when the world's per capita GNPs, denominated in national currencies, are translated into US dollars at the *official exchange rates*, they yield realistic quantitative indices. External exchange rates do not fully reflect internal purchasing power parities even of the currencies of countries which place no artificial restrictions on imports/exports and the movement of capital. Still wider is the disparity between the internal and external values of national currencies in those parts of the world, especially in the poorer countries, where the official external exchange rate is divorced from the internal purchasing power of the currency through distorting controls and manipulations, such as prohibitive levies on imports and export subsidies. The official exchange rate approach has therefore been found to be inappropriate for national accounts confrontations aimed at contrasting standards of living.

There has come into being a voluminous literature which seeks to establish alternative techniques for the measurement of relative national welfare. Some of the more persuasive proposals have come from people who reject the GNP altogether as a tool enabling the observer to say by how much one country is better off than another, and opt for non-monetary indicators. Others, still relying on published official GNP data, have adapted them—for two-country comparisons—in the following manner. Let it be assumed that the French and German GNPs consist exclusively of beer and bread, and that we are not prepared to use the official exchange rates for marks and francs to compare the respective volume of their national products. The two GNPs can both be placed on to a common denominator when the physical output-quantities of German beer and bread are multiplied by the franc prices of beer and bread prevailing in France, i.e. we thus obtain figures for the German and French GNPs which are both denominated in francs, and the ratio between the two is said to indicate the relative standard of living in the two countries. The same arithmetical calculation can also be repeated by multiplying the French beer and bread output-quantities by the mark prices prevailing for beer and bread in Germany. Though in theory the two resultant GNP relationships—in terms of marks and francs—could be identical, they are not likely to be so in practice. This means that one has calculated two ratios, one of which may suggest that the standard of living in Germany is 1·6 times higher than in France, whilst the other ratio might indicate that it is only 1·4 times higher.

Why not then average out the two ratios? This indeed is what is done in many GNP comparisons. The average of the two separately calculated ratios will probably be a very meaningful ratio provided the two countries are in the same class, i.e. are both very poor or very rich. (Being in the same class does of course not mean that they consume the same articles; in one country beer, and in the other wine, may be the staple alcoholic beverage.) But, as Usher has convincingly demonstrated, this averaging is highly misleading when a rich and a poor economy are compared, because in the latter the consumption of cheaper goods is predominant. In relation to a rich country, a poor country's GNP is slightly overvalued when both GNPs are computed with the prices of the rich country and it is highly undervalued when both GNPs are computed with the prices of the poor country. The ratio that reflects most accurately the relative standard of living of the two countries clearly lies somewhere between the two ratios—no one knows where, except that it is not necessarily nor ever likely to be the middle point.

Some idea of how indeterminate GNP comparisons are is provided by Usher's confrontations of the national income of Thailand with that of the UK. Drawing on three of his computations (19), (33) and (97), I have compressed the relevant data in the following table:

RATIOS OF PER CAPITA GNP, 1958, THAILAND AND UK

Criterion	Thailand	UK
UN INDEX*	100	1,930
OFFICIAL EXCHANGE RATE	100	1,430
THAI PRICE WEIGHTS	100	690
UK PRICE WEIGHTS	100	310

* Based on the rate of exchange used by the UN for cost-of-living allowances for its non-Thai employees on assignment in Thailand.

The average UK citizen is nineteen times better off than the average Thai citizen according to the UN index, fourteen times according to the official exchange rate, seven times when Thai prices, and three times when UK prices, are applied to the respective national products.

If the innocent laymen should think that, faced with a choice of several possible GNP criteria, the one chosen is always selected because it is the most reasonable measuring rod for relative standards of living, he ought to disabuse himself of this naïvety. GNP comparisons are often tendentious. Under-developed countries frequently wish to prove, with the support of their do-gooder friends in the international agencies, that they are poorer than they really are. Some seem to derive a perverse pride in having a low GNP. This puts to shame those wicked efficient developed countries and helps to squeeze out of them increased charitable aid.

Other rules apply to a parlour game played in the United States, that is concerned with the relative size of the national cakes of the US and the USSR. For most purposes American circles do not seek to inflate their official GNP balloon; they sometimes find it convenient to prove that the disparity between their GNP and that of Burma is not as big as the Burmese find it expedient to claim. In a comparison with Russia, however, national pride is said to be at stake and the superiority of life under free enterprise must, in some US politicians' views, be proved by suggesting that Russia's conventional GNP is even lower than it actually is.* Mechanical averaging of the two ratios, outlined above, helps to feed this ludicrous ambition.

Morris Bornstein, of the University of Michigan, reported to the Joint Economic Committee of the Congress — cited in (45) — that the 1955 Soviet GNP was 26·8 per cent. of the US GNP when both are measured in rouble prices, whilst it was as high as 53·4 per cent. when both are calculated in dollar prices. US politicians immediately pounced on these figures and, working out their geometrical average, concluded that the 1955 Russian GNP was less than 40 per cent. of theirs. After a phenomenal rise of the Russian GNP in the subsequent three years,

* The discussion on the size of the conventional GNP does not help to decide whether it is more pleasant to live in San Francisco or in Moscow. The real superiority of the American way of life over that of their Russian competitors is discernible in the size of the genuine GNP. Even if the Russians caught up with the Americans in the production of cars, life in America would still be so much richer because it lacks press censors and Siberian labour camps.

and only a small growth in that of the US, Bornstein's 1958 binary comparisons showed that the Soviet GNP was then about one-third or two-thirds, respectively, of the US GNP. Again official US circles drew political comfort from averaging these ratios to proclaim that the Russian GNP was still only 45 per cent. of theirs. This averaging is arithmetically sound, but it is almost certainly wrong to deduce from it that the resultant single ratios express correctly the relative magnitudes of the two conventional national accounts. It was noted above that whenever a poorer country's national product is valued at prices prevailing in a richer country, the results slightly overvalue the poorer country's GNP, whilst there is considerable undervaluation of the poorer country's GNP (relative to the GNP of the richer country) when both national accounts are expressed in the poorer country's currency. It is, therefore, reasonable to conclude that in order to arrive at a true ratio, one has to down-grade the rouble-calculated US GNP and the dollar-calculated Russian GNP. Russia undoubtedly remains poorer than the US but not by as much as is suggested by the geometrical average of the binary GNP measurements.

A dogmatic and definite conclusion can be drawn from our survey of GNP comparisons: the problems raised do not allow for a determinate solution. There are no objective, scientific GNP data. Comparisons of national income yield haphazard answers. Provided the subjective nature of all such exercises is clear to both the purveyors and buyers of the resultant figures, the game is harmless.

Divine infallibility is said to be a pre-condition of unquestioning faith. I like to think that I have at least raised enough doubts to have turned a few believers in the scientific validity of national accounts comparisons into atheists. There is nothing sacred about the GNP cow.

Part II

The Myth of Forecasting

Definitions Do Matter

'Dreams and Predictions ought to serve but for winter talk by the fireside.'

FRANCIS BACON

An attempt will be made in the following pages to evaluate economic forecasting by the two criteria that have been applied to the GNP: accuracy and meaningfulness. These, in turn, raise some disquieting questions. Are economists competent to make meaningful and accurate general forecasts? How far are some of the *published* forecasts deliberately contrived to give a false picture of future events, which the forecaster privately knows to be false? The answers to these disturbing inquiries point to the existence of a tripodal ideology of forecasting. Avid predictors of the future size of national economic indicators (total output, balance of payments, etc.) often subscribe to the political philosophy which inspires the measurement of human welfare by the dimensions of the GNP (discussed in Part I) and frequently embrace the faith that proclaims the wisdom of centralized state planning (to be discussed in Part III).*

GNP forecasters have been denounced as soothsayers, false prophets, latter-day astrologers, modern oracles, academic diviners, witchdoctors, econometric magicians, damned prognosticators, builders of toy models, crystal gazers, confidence tricksters, and economic alchemists.† These poisonous darts inflict pain, and those who throw them at economists clearly intend them to wound. The discipline of economics will continue to be suspect until GNP predictions are no longer described as scientific ventures, and until economists explain exactly what they mean by

---

* A senior civil servant in Britain's planning ministry has admitted with refreshing frankness that 'forecasting and planning...are closely related' (172). Jallow is even more explicit: 'Forecasting and planning are two sides of the coin... Forecasting is an integral part of the planning process... Not to forecast means simply not to plan...' (177).

† I have come across these pejorative designations during the last three years, but I feel certain that I have missed out many more.

95

viewing the future. 'Forecasting is a science of prediction; economic forecasting is the science of predicting economic change' – this is the type of arrogant rubbish that ought to be consigned to the dustbin. Of course there are a few forecasters whose purpose is to cheat for the exalted purposes outlined on pp. 136–55 and they have no compunction about persuading others that there is a scientific basis to their proclamations. Many more economists, however, honestly feel that they can contribute something useful by speculating on the future. If they truly seek to gain respect they must first come clean and admit to the limitations of their powers, even though this will topple them from the pedestals on which they now stand and that at present gurantee their oracular pronouncements headlines in the press. If they are willing to abandon pompous intellectual postures they will lose the enjoyment of mass-appeal, but their conjectures can then be placed in a proper perspective and they may thus make a valuable contribution to economic discussions. Kahn-Wiener's book on *The Year 2000* deserves to be treated as a serious work precisely because the authors abstained from representing it as a forecast, and remained content to have it judged as 'a framework for speculation' based on 'surprise-free economic projections' (125).

In this context a tight linguistic definition is something more than just adhering to pedantic rules. I am not alone in attaching here importance to the choice of words. Some years ago a research organization was founded in France, with the aid of the Ford Foundation, called *Futuribles*, that brought together people with a common conviction that the social sciences should orient themselves towards the future. One of its early distinguished leaders was Jouvenel, who in time became frightened of the term 'futurology' which some people wanted to attach to the society's work, with some actually describing it as 'The New Science'.* When he later wrote a book on the subject, he laid great stress on its title *The Art of Conjecture* (82). 'The reasons why the word "conjecture" appears in the title of this book is precisely that it is opposed to the term "knowledge".'

In our political and economic literature 'forecasting' is employed indiscriminately to denote many different things. I consider it vital to

---

* Jouvenel went out of his way to stress the non-scientific nature of his explorations of the future: 'In all ages men have gathered about fortune-tellers, and when these persons achieve a recognized position and are able to back their pronouncements with figures, they will attract a rash of customers who accept their words as "what science says".'

reserve the word 'forecasting' for the purport of a defined function. Consequently I have given it a specified meaning, which separates it from other functions also concerned with viewing the future. My purpose is not to serve terminological purism, but to emphasize the substantive nature of 'forecasting' and to set it apart from other activities that also speak of the shape of things to come. The sort of misunderstanding I want to avoid is contained, for example, in the following quotation from one of Ian Macleod's onslaughts on the Labour Government: 'We do not expect long-term forecasts to be accurate... We do not expect them to be more accurate than long-term meteorological forecasts.' I shall suggest below that if one divorces the concept of conjecturing from forecasting, one does so because one expects the latter to be accurate; this in fact is part of its declared purpose. It also follows from my definition that whilst observations on the economic future (which is what Macleod was talking about) cannot be accurate, meteorological prospects can become accurate with greater scientific knowledge; this is why I choose not to describe economic predictions as forecasting but find it right to describe as such the work of meteorological experts.

What distinguishes forecasting from prognostications or conjectures or predictions all of which also foretell the future? Forecasting depicts a future state or event in a definitive manner and has no room for ifs and buts, for hedging and conditions. It is just a play with words to say that 'a forecast is made on the basis of "unchanged policies"' (139). A forecast will ultimately turn out to have been right or wrong, but it cannot be optimistic or pessimistic—only accurate or inaccurate. If one regards a high GNP growth rate as an ideal, this is a value judgement which ought to be divorced from the forecasting exercise. A forecast of a 3 per cent. GNP growth rate is equally wrong whether the actual growth is 4 per cent. or 2 per cent. Forecasting is neither homiletics nor a pep-talk. There are several phrases in the English language to denote approximations—such as 'this figure is more likely than any other'—but 'forecasting' is not one of them.

A forecast must be definitive in nature and if a range is given it must be a very narrow one. When a writer, suffering from an incurable disease, consults his doctor about the likely date of his death—in order that he may so arrange his affairs as to complete an unfinished novel—an answer of 'within the next few years' is too vague to be useful, whilst a reply of 'in six to nine months' represents a forecast that can be put to practical use. In the autumn of 1967 the official British long-range weather predictions were attacked as 'little better than blind guesswork'. Those responsible for this censure did not maintain that the Meteorological Office's glimpses into the future were wrong; their complaint was that they were couched in vague or even contradictory language and thus useless for practical application. David Bowen (140) made a close study of the long-range forecasts and found them to be formulated in a general way, not mentioning specific dates or the expected lengths of rainy, wet, mild or cold spells, so that it was hardly surprising that the Meteorological Office could claim a 73 per cent. accuracy for its forecasts.*

There are three sets of circumstances in which definitive and unconditional predictions can be made with a high degree of accuracy:

A.

If one believes in strict divine predestination and the existence of persons who have been inspired to know of God's plans and are willing to divulge them one may properly classify their prophecies as forecasts.†

B.

In what situations do persons, who are not divinely inspired, have reasonable grounds for thinking that they *know* certain events will occur in the future? When they are expert enough to diagnose particular phenomena, which—on past evidence—suggest that they inevitably give rise to certain occurrences after a defined period of time. Examples to fit this category are to be found in the physical sciences only. I am advised that there are fewer instances than laymen might think in which the scientist can predict the future with certainty and thus qualify as a forecaster.

C.

A now largely obsolete meaning of forecasting, given by *The Shorter Oxford English Dictionary*, is 'to contrive or plan beforehand'. Though

---

* In one instance the weather forecast for June read as follows: 'Over the month as a whole some warm, sunny days are probable in all areas, but they are unlikely to be more frequent than usual for June.' Bowen comments that unless June was totally sunless or sunny every day—both unlikely—the forecast was bound to be correct.
† Most of the biblical prophecies are, however, not forecasts because the prophets usually foretell divinely inspired events on condition that their listeners act in a prescribed manner.

this definition is outdated, it points to circumstances in which fore-casting (in the modern sense of the word) is feasible. When I say that my daughter's pocket money will be raised next year from eight to ten shillings, I am forecasting something which is within my power to bring about. Ernest Breech, the former chairman of Ford Motor, is quoted (81) as saying: 'It is our business, and that of other large companies, to make trends, not to follow them.' Monopolists and some powerful cor-porations can indeed make certain successful forecasts because they are strong enough to have them come true in almost all cases, provided their resolve is sufficiently intense. This ability to make the future come true is, however, possible only in a limited target area. If Ford are really determined to sell 100,000 units in Canada, a sales forecast to that effect is almost a foregone conclusion. Ford, however, is not able to make such a certain appraisal of future sales in Canada if its objectives also include pre-determined prices, profit margins and labour emoluments. The reason Ford could make the sales forecast come true is that it has enough resources to vary its advertising expenditure, adjust prices if there is consumer resistance, raise wages sufficiently to stave off any strikes that might hold up production, and execute the sales (if necessary) at a loss. Corporate estimates of the future, relating to product sales, are there-fore rarely to be termed forecasts, except when the executives are single-minded enough to concentrate on isolated objectives—at the expense of other business objectives.

GNP predictions, of sufficient definiteness and accuracy to justify placing them into one of the three forecasting categories set out above, are inconceivable. It would be blasphemous to write that God had pre-ordained the 1970 British national output; consequently, one cannot impute to any Treasury official (however sincere his faith in planning) divine GNP inspiration. Unlike the physical scientists, national accounts experts cannot employ their expertise to prescribe future happenings on the basis of laws verified by the records of the past. Most governments are powerful enough to implement forecasts of particular social and economic objectives, but no state apparatus, however totalitarian, has ever succeeded in making a comprehensive GNP forecast come true. Unless they call Calvin to help, even illustrious Cambridge economists (aided by the most sophisticated IBM computer) have no right to announce their GNP predictions as forecasts.

Predictions that are not Forecasts

'A man, asked about the age of a river, states that it is 3,000,021 years old. Asked how he could give such accurate information, the answer was that twenty-one years ago the river's age was given as three million years. There is a fair amount of this in economic statistics.'

OSKAR MORGENSTERN

There are many ways of appraising discerningly the future. Some are the results of honest and productive toil; others are not. But all the nine predictions which I have enumerated below have this in common: they are not forecasts (according to the definition given in the preceding chapter) even though they are often misnamed as such.

I

Football pool promoters claim in their sanctimonious publicity that punters placing funds with them exercise putative skills in 'forecasting' results. I have shown elsewhere (141) that skill, i.e. knowledge as to the relative winning capacities of football teams, plays no role in winning the glittering high prizes. Applying football expertise is in fact less helpful than prayer or making a wild random selection, because the top prizes are not won primarily for predicting correctly eight drawn matches; they are awarded for marking eight draws when by freak chance no other person has done so. Skill in merely predicting the maximum number of drawn matches will earn the punter puny rewards; the prizes are gained by the extraneous factor that no one else has picked eight correct draws.* It is, therefore, not surprising that the people who have won prizes of £200,000 and above are generally not

* In proper forecasting it is irrelevant how many people arrive at the same appraisal of the future—the only criterion is whether the forecast is proved to be accurate or not. In football pool predictions accuracy is a subordinate consideration, if one seeks to win the top prize.

experts in football. They employed no scientific techniques, but picked numbers out of a hat or marked the draws in accordance with their birthday. I do not draw attention to football pool predictions in order to debunk the improper use of the word 'forecasting' by the commercial promoters, but because it is an instance where the desired future event is most successfully foreseen by pure guesswork. There are a few charlatans who similarly predict GNP growth by guestimating it. The only thing to be said in defence of this ignoble activity is that these GNP predictions are frequently no less erroneous than those arrived at by computerized economic 'scientists'.

II

There is a kind of guestimating which deserves to be classified separately. It arises in situations in which a 'working assumption', concerning the future, must be made even when based only on more or less arbitrary considerations. A potential manufacturer of fibres in Ireland may have no sound basis for estimating his sales two years hence; yet, a decision concerning the future must be arrived at in order to plan the size of the plant and supply contracts. In 1939 the government of the UK instructed its departments to act on the assumption that the war would last for three years. In both of these two examples, it was necessary to formulate arbitrary expectations concerning the future though it would clearly be wrong to describe them as 'forecasting'.

III

Perhaps the most common way of outlining expected events is to make forward projections from the past. This can be done by assuming that next year's performance will be identical with last year's, or that past trends (say, an average growth of 2 per cent. over the preceding ten years) will continue.

Unpublished extrapolations of Britain's national income are calculated every four months by Treasury officials who also draw on the advice of other economic ministries. Basically, these are pure projections founded on past trends. Brittan (73) criticizes the procedure of building up projections that are bound by the rule of not being 'mixed up with policy'. This, he implies, is a wasteful exercise because 'no prediction can be made without some assumptions about government policy'. Actually things are not quite as black as Brittan's strictures would have us believe, because the Treasury economists do not claim to be forecasting. Having made their projection-appraisals for the Chancellor of the Exchequer, the latter then decides what policies ought to be adopted in view of the GNP performance that is to be expected if government policies were to remain unchanged. During his term of office at the Treasury, Callaghan was subjected to strong pressure from the financial press and the Conservative Party to publish these secret projections and the government's expectations of how its policies would alter the charted course of events. The reasons advanced by the advocates of publication have convinced me that it would be a mistake to change the present practice. It is suggested that publication (of the projections together with the government assumptions about the likely impact of any new policies) would help the public at large to gain a more intelligible glimpse of the future. Whilst I do not believe in the ability of government policy to *determine* the future GNP—though clearly they can influence its shape and volume—many business men do not fully share this scepticism. The requested publication of these, now secret, projections would disseminate the illusion that the government is sharing *knowledge* of the future national product with the public. Callaghan is alleged to have opposed publication of the amended Treasury projections.* He is said to have been afraid that, if the predictions were proved wrong by subsequent events, his political opponents might then gloat and sneer at his putative failure to predict the future GNP. Callaghan should have been proud of this fear!† It is a recognition that GNP projections, even when amended by the probable influence flowing from government measures, cannot be forecasts. Until such time as the public is educated as to the difference between forecasts

* The issue as to whether to compute forward projections or not is quite separate from the demand to publish them. I agree with what Thorneycroft, a former Chancellor, wrote: 'The fact that our economic prospects cannot be assessed in advance with precision does not lessen my responsibility for exercising the best judgement I can in the light of the information and forecasts available to me' (80). (Naturally I should have preferred 'predictions' to forecasts in this context.)

† Callaghan's successor, Roy Jenkins, told Parliament in February 1968 that he was giving 'serious and sympathetic consideration' to publishing the Treasury's projections.

and conjectural assumptions concerning the future, it is wise not to dare the devil and publish these predictions.

Projections are in one sense the most 'scientific' manner of helping to portray the future. If the statistician knows enough about the past to establish reliable data on the performance and trends of preceding years, he can project forward without using any value judgement—it becomes merely a matter of looking up the right logarithms. Projections are not forecasts but honest appraisals of the future calculated by openly divulged criteria without hocus-pocus.

IV

Treasury extrapolations of the UK national income may bring about a change of government policy if the Chancellor, reading his officials' projections, wishes to steer the economic ship away from its charted course. If they remain unpublished, they cannot lead to a reaction from the public. The publishing of forward projections, which the public believes to be an informed and honest appraisal of the direction in which the economy is moving, is an invitation to an almost certain backlash. This feedback effect will by itself change the future and invalidate what might otherwise have been a valid prediction. Business men, convinced by the published extrapolations that the GNP will grow by 4 per cent., may expand production and expedite investments thus perhaps bringing about a 5 per cent. rate; alternatively, the publication of an anticipated 1 per cent. fall in the national product may so depress them as to worsen matters and induce a drop of 2 per cent.

Dishonest economists or politically-inspired civil servants can exploit the feedback mentality for nefarious purposes. Although their unpublished calculations show that the extrapolated GNP would rise in the coming year by 3 per cent., they may publish predictions for a 5 per cent. growth. Having painted a rosy picture in the hope that the public will believe their (false) predictions to be based on substantive indications, they pray for a reaction that will lead to growth of at least 4 per cent. If they achieve this aim, they congratulate themselves on having hoodwinked their public. Whilst the technique of categories (III) and (IV) both evoke feedback effects, the latter is clearly not an extrapolation but a Machiavellian prediction.

V

Whilst the technicians of both the above two categories privately expect a feedback, they do not publish their (honest or false) projections-cum-predictions with the comment that a reaction from the public might vary the charted course of the future. The authors of predictions, categorized under (III), may or may not be happy if history does not confirm their projections. It has been noted that those of category (IV) definitely would rejoice if their published prophecies turn out to be wrong (in the desired direction). Despite the differences between the two categories, they nevertheless have in common that their published figures give the impression of being definitive predictions. This is in sharp contrast to yet another category of economic prophecies, but this time one which openly invites a backlash. R. J. Ball and T. Burns, of the London Business School, periodically predict the future performance of the U K economy. Like the authors of category (III) they publish extrapolations which they honestly believe would prevail if conditions remained unchanged. They openly express, however, the hope that the publication of their, and other economists', predictions will lead to changes in the business climate and government policy, and thus prove their predictions wrong. They ask that their prediction be not 'judged as useful or not purely in terms of some narrowly defined numerical criterion of accuracy. The critical question is whether they provide adequate general signals for appropriate changes in policy' (89). Clearly this is a novel approach, a rejection of accuracy as a criterion for outlining the future national product. The authors, to my mind, do not seek the accolade awarded to competent forecasters but rather see themselves as political animals who flash signal lights. They are agitators in academic garb, and their predictions might be aptly described as contingent views of the future.

VI

To paint the future with target figures can sometimes be a rewarding activity. No harm need necessarily result from formulating the size of the GNP that could in theory be attained in the coming years. There is surely nothing wrong in setting physical targets for the economy as a whole, or sectors of it, and pouring out one's heart about the desirability of achieving a targeted GNP growth rate of x per cent. I have seen several such exercises and the ones I like best are those that are phrased in homiletic terms, such as 'Japan and Timbuctoo managed to do it...therefore it follows that we can do it too'.

Still one must keep some sense of proportion about the significance of target exercises. To suggest as PEP did—in a publication applauded by Labour and Tory politicians—that one of the reasons for the inadequate rate of growth of the British economy was 'that there has never been an objective of growth to aim at' (144) does not strike me as a very sound analysis. PEP then goes on to say that 'the mere publication of an estimate of the possible achievement of the economy for a few years ahead...may in itself be a potent force making for success'. I remember at school that targets set for our house spurred some boys on to greater efforts, and I understand that corporate sales targets sometimes have a beneficial impact upon the productivity of unintelligent salesmen. But to suggest that 'the mere publication' of GNP targets will 'in itself' produce miracles is difficult to swallow.

Target-appraisals are condemned by those who maintain that governments ought instead to forecast the planned future. A planning enthusiast like W. Arthur Lewis is contemptuous of targeted GNPs, which he regards as dreams: '...the very word "target" has become a laughing stock...what makes planning is not the targets, which merely express what we would like to see happen, but the action that is taken to achieve these targets' (87). Lewis's impatience with targets is of course founded on the belief that the future can be planned. Those who do not share his faith see nothing obnoxious in the setting of goals—provided always that the audience is not deluded about the true nature of the targeted future.

Britain's Iron and Steel Board has rightly been censured because its published forward projections of steel demand have proved to be very wrong indeed—with disastrous consequences on investments in the industry. These reproaches are deserved, because the Board allowed the impression to be formed that it was forecasting demand. The steel masters, to whom its reports were mainly addressed, did not care greatly for academic ifs and buts—they thought that the Board's glimpses into the future were definitive. In fact, as a stern critic of the

Board's statistics has shown in its defence, the figures published by the Iron and Steel Board relating to future demand were primarily an expression of hope coupled with 'a proselytizing exercise in growth economics addressed equally to the government and to industry' (70). Duncan has unearthed statements by the Board which make it clear that the data on anticipated demand for steel were meant to be target figures. Nevertheless, I do not absolve the Board of blame because it ought to have marked its published target exercises in large red capital letters: 'This is not a forecast.'

Many Conservative politicians, who pride themselves on being progressives, were overjoyed when the National Economic Development Council (NEDC, affectionately known as NEDDY) met for the first time in March 1962, charged *inter alia* with the specific task of exploring Britain's economic future. NEDDY started off with a pompous publication (76), which announced that the Council had 'approved the 4 per cent. growth objective'. (I do not grasp why they did not opt for 5 per cent or 3 per cent.)* The choice of the word 'approved', to be charitable, is a curious one and certainly open to misunderstanding. Of course later on these sagacious soothsayers were to say that they had neither forecast future growth nor acclaimed plans to implement this 4 per cent. target—they had merely 'approved' a desirable objective. Neddy was not abolished when the socialists took office and George Brown even went to 'consult' them about his National Plan. They met in August 1965 and had placed before them projections

* Brittan gives a fascinating account, in his book (73), of how this esoteric 4 per cent. was selected. Brittan writes as an enthusiastic supporter of Neddy, who has described the acceptance of the 4 per cent. target as the 'main triumph for the NEDC office...the insistence on a 4 per cent. growth target...was Mr Selwyn Lloyd's own greatest personal achievement as Chancellor, and right up to the time of going to press (it) is NEDC's own greatest success as well'. (Let me intrude here to say that I fail to understand how one can be triumphant in formulating targets, and why one should be praised for conjecturing that something may be achieved. I would have thought that one should reserve hosannas for actual achievements.) Brittan draws on inside information to inform his readers that Neddy had been told of the Treasury's 3 per cent. projections in the growth of industrial capacity. The Treasury had apparently been induced to raise its own 'realistic target on the basis of recent investment booms in British industry' to 3.5 per cent. The gentlemen, performing their public duty by attending the Neddy meetings, found the Treasury too unambitious. Some suggested a figure of 4.5 per cent., but this was ruled out because it would have meant too rapid acceleration at the end of the period under review. A compromise figure was therefore sought: 'Between these two limits 4 per cent seemed about right.'

pointing to a 3·8 per cent. growth. This time they were not asked for their approval, but only requested to examine and then express an opinion. This they did, saying that the National Plan was a 'valuable analysis' and the projected growth rates 'within the nation's capacity' (75).

It is now a matter of historical record that the economy developed along lines which bore little relationship to the course charted by the Neddy, or National Plan, growth rates. In late 1968 I spoke to some of the people who had worked on the preparation of these figures. Not surprisingly, I received varying replies in my interviews, but there was one thread running through all their defensive answers: 'What right do you have to call our projections "forecasts"? We have never claimed that we knew what was going to happen!' There is some justice in this, because a careful reading of the Neddy documents and the National Plan shows that their authors merely 'approved' the objectives, volunteered the thought that it was physically possible to achieve the stated goals, and (in the case of Neddy's first report) were modestly concerned only with 'the implications of the faster national growth rate for the seventeen industries covered'. Nevertheless, I tend to regard this as an ingenious line of defence because I have the nasty suspicion that some of the planning-minded people in Neddy and the Department of Economic Affairs did at the time really believe that they were forecasting. One has to be charitable to accept that it was never their intention to forecast, and that their ambition was limited to the formulation of targets. In any case, it remains an historical fact that the wider British public* were sold these figures as definitive data relating to the immediate development of the economy. Anyone who doubts this ought to look at the press coverage and the radio and television scripts on the days following the publication of the Neddy reports and the National Plan. It is probably true that those not versed in economics are naturally gullible when it comes to simplified GNP reportages. Perhaps the reporters and commentators on the written, spoken and visual mass media were guilty of imputing forecasting to people who were not really so definitive. Yet this is precisely the danger underlying predictions which look like forecasts, unless one reads the small print and discovers that they could also be interpreted as targeted objectives. The authors of the Neddy and National Plan

* The National Plan was also successfully merchandised outside the UK as a blueprint of the future British economy. Many non-British economists were sufficiently uncritical to accept it as the basis for their UK forecasts.

projections have no right to be indignant about having been misunderstood. They could have corrected these misunderstandings. Perhaps some did, but if so their denials were never given the same publicity as the forecasting reports.

Ronald Edwards, in those days chairman of the Electricity Council, was and is no fool; yet he thought that the Neddy and National Plan figures were more than just targets. The trouble is that action was taken with displeasing results, on the assumption that they were definitive forecasts. In two revealing publications (74) and (179), Edwards hints at the fact that he had expanded electricity capacity on the assumption that the Neddy and National Plan targets were realistic forecasts. Reading, however, between the lines one receives the impression that perhaps Edwards did not really believe that they were necessarily realistic assessments of the future. He makes it plain that as the head of a nationalized corporation he had no alternative but to act on these official projections. Consequently excess capacity was created to serve an official forecast demand for electricity that of course failed to materialize. Edwards and his colleagues were not victims of an act of God; they suffered the fate of executives in state-owned corporations who were and are expected to take seriously the soothsaying pronouncements of official prophets. There is perhaps less justification for such an attitude in the private sector yet some of the biggest companies did in fact swallow, partly or wholly, the numerate growth rates propagated as future assessments by Neddy and the authors of the National Plan. Thus Courtaulds' representative told a parliamentary committee that their corporate glimpses into the future of the GNP, and individual industries in which they have a special interest, 'have been influenced upward' by the National Plan (44). A postscript was written when Neddy met under the chairmanship of the Prime Minister on a cold Sunday, the 15th December of 1968. Apparently they had burned their fingers too severely in previous years, for that evening F. Catherwood, NEDC's director-general, told an astonished press conference that their prepared blueprint on Britain's economic future until 1972 (which had been the subject of the conference) would not be released to the public. He did, however, mention the GNP growth rate for the next year. On the following morning the *Financial Times* opened its front page with a bold headline: 'Growth Rate of 3 per cent. Agreed for 1969.' It went on to say, in heavy print, that 'Britain's economic growth rate in the coming year will be fixed at a level of 3 per cent'. Only the assiduous reader, who proceeded to read the less prominently displayed news, learned that NEDC had agreed on 'the 3 per cent. growth target'. It seems that NEDC was back to its old game of 'fixing' the future, and 'agreeing' to pre-determined national accounts. Were they forecasting? Or were they setting out a target? Or are the copy editors of the *Financial Times* to blame?

There is a lesson to be learned. If people wish to play around with economic targets for industries or whole economies they ought to do so quietly at home. If they have the urge to publish them, they must be very careful to explain the rules of the game—and if the authors are backed by the majestic powers of the state, all warning lights ought to be switched on.

VII

The world houses many learned institutions in which econometric research into the future is carried out through the construction of computerized working models serviced by a multitude of inputs and outputs. (In Britain the best known team works at Cambridge under the leadership of R. Stone and A. Brown.) This is a highly innocuous activity that is only marred when the popular press fails to understand this spectacle and attributes to it 'breaking new ground in investigating the economic future'. The good people concerned are engaged in purely theoretical work since they feed the computer with arbitrarily chosen assumptions. The machine is asked to come up with answers as to what would happen if, say, the GNP grew by x per cent., employment fell by y per cent. and the external exchange rate was revalued by z per cent. The computer has no compunctions about giving different answers if it is served with other assumptions. I feel sure that computerized econometrics is good training for advanced mathematics, and the builders of economic models probably get a lot of fun out of their work. The one certainty is that the computer cannot tell what the size of the 1970 GNP will be.*

---

* According to Leser (204), a well-known econometrician is alleged to have replied, when challenged with poor forecasting results of his model: 'It is not the model which is at fault; it is the American economy which is wrong.'

VIII

'Conditional Forecasting' is the bread-and-butter of hundreds of business economists. It consists of making predictions hedged against major occurrences, enabling their authors to affirm when the predictions do not come true: Our prognosis was right but things have turned out differently because the underlying facts have changed. The intellectual dishonesty of this type of economic prophecy is as blatant as it is useless to business men seeking practical guidelines. It is a semantic fraud to call this 'forecasting'.

In the absence of registered trade union rules for GNP soothsayers, Butler and Kavesh have performed a useful task in collating the techniques employed by many of the US economists who speculate on the future. (As the title of their book – *How Business Economists Forecast* – indicates, the surveyed economists, basking in their self-importance, do not think of themselves as guestimators but call themselves 'forecasters'.) Butler-Kavesh have revealed how these alchemists set to work on their annual predictions. The authors (53) explain that the analysts – the name is meant to imbue their work with a pseudo-scientific flavour – proceed as follows:

'First and foremost before setting down any figures the economist must state his basic, underlying assumptions... Thus, in setting up the forecast for a year ahead, the analyst will ordinarily assume that

(a) No major war or heating up of international tensions will occur.

(b) Relationships between government and the business community will not be sharply altered.

(c) Crippling strikes will, by and large, be averted.

(d) Socio-cultural patterns will not produce inordinate strains.

(e) Taxes will not be raised or lowered in any significant fashion.'

And in case all these ifs and buts are not enough to create an alibi for the inevitable failure to predict correctly, the authors add: 'To these could be added any number of reasonable assumptions relating to the external environment in which business activity would be taking place.'

These then are the rules, summarized so succinctly by Butler-Kavesh, for a game which is played by highly paid economic 'scientists' employed by the world's largest corporations. The players are not agitators advocating changes in government policy nor political civil servants seeking to influence business climate by mendacious predictions; they are also not professors who build toy models in academic seclusion. Their services are bought by business men who impatiently await a single-figure prediction. The business economists are supposed to stick out their necks and give a definitive answer. They do not. Instead they sell goods with no quality guarantees. In fact they boast that their intellectual output can only be put to use if life next year proceeds according to rules that are unlikely to apply in the real world. These soothsayers are like tipsters predicting that horse A will win provided horse B breaks its neck, the day is not dull, the wind velocity does not rise above its average monthly level and horse C is not doped. On second thoughts, these business astrologers are not really like tipsters because nobody would buy a tip from a man whose predictions depended on 'assumptions relating to the external environment'. These people, calling themselves GNP forecasters, are able to collect large fees from gullible buyers for their hedged predictions. They sneer at the unscientific nature of economic auguries which predict commercial developments by the rise and fall in the water levels of the Great Lakes, the volume of parimutuel bets on the Kentucky Derby, the average size of bills at luxury restaurants, the cycles of Jupiter-Saturn, etc. (142). The business economists laugh at quacks because their offbeat indices often prove wrong, whilst they themselves can never be wrong thanks to the dishonest insurance policies which they have taken out.

In a self-searching analysis of the accuracy of the GNP predictions, regularly published by the National Institute of Economic and Social Research, R. R. Neild (49) explains that the Institute's projections differ from actual events 'partly due to Government measures introduced during the interval. *The Review* always assesses what will happen if policy remains unchanged...'. I assert dogmatically that there always will be changes in government policy and consequently the Institute's predictions — which they describe as forecasts — must always turn out to be wrong. It does not necessarily follow that the Institute should cease its main activity of taking a glimpse into the future. What is urgent, however, is that when they issue summarized press releases of their predicted GNP data, they ought to underline the proviso made by Neild.

Though after the last war the Dutch shed many of the traditional free enterprise features of their economy, the country never became regimented enough to enable its planners to determine the future', and thus they never became competent to make forecasts rather than predictions. C. A. Van den Beld, who used to head the Short-Term Planning division of the Netherlands Central Planning Bureau, has felt the urge publicly to defend himself and his colleagues against the implicit charge that their GNP predictions have proved to be so abysmally wrong despite all their sharpened econometric tools:

'In a number of cases the forecasts, as they stand, and the observed data of the relevant year are not directly comparable because of unforeseen policy changes. The revaluation of the guilder in March 1961 is a good example of a change that was not envisaged in the Central Economic Plan for 1961' (29).

This is a poor defence by people whose implied omniscience fitted them to regiment the Dutch economy, which was not to be left to the wild forces of private initiative. The US business economists plead that their predictions are destined to be wrong because they cannot foresee events like the murder of President Kennedy, the Korean conflict (or the death of Jane Mansfield). Van den Beld claims that policy changes cannot be foreseen. Indeed they cannot, but if this is so it should be recognized that Dutch governmental forecasts are only miserable conditional predictions, and this in turn raises doubts as to the competence of the Dutch planners to control their national economy.

IX

I have left to the end the most ludicrous category of predictions that are passed off as forecasts. Whatever the failings of the other eight categories, there is an inherent logic in each of them. There is, however, nothing logical or virtuous about eclectic statements on the future which are an admixture of hopes, plans and conjectures. Thomas Wilson has brilliantly characterized such hybrids as 'those leaden documents that now fall endlessly from the official printing presses of the world... In part, they are really plans; that is to say they are affirmations of what the governments are resolved to achieve within the limitation of their power. In part, however, they are forecasts of an elusive future' (40).

This offensive description is too mild to characterize George Brown's National Plan. As a biting PEP analysis (62) has shown, the National Plan was not the offspring of just two different species, but of a hotch-potch of ingredients; 'projections', 'forecasts', 'plans', etc., are used as though they were synonyms.

The Accuracy of Economic Predictions

'Already General de Gaulle has told the country that the deficit for 1969 would be reduced to less than 6,500 million; today I am telling the Assembly that it will be exactly 6,354 million.'

COUVE DE MURVILLE*

The cocksureness with which the captains of nationalized corporations publish forecasts is unparalleled in British industry. Several aspects of their disastrous soothsayings are traced in appendix IV. In at least one case some good has come of it. Ronald Edwards, when still chairman of the Electricity Council, managed to assimilate a wholesome lesson from his corporation's wildly inaccurate estimate of the future, which had cost the consumers dearly. In a devastating attack on the putative capacity to forecast with econometrics and computing technology, he concluded that what is needed above all is 'humility... Anyone who doubts this should study the history of energy forecasts, littered as it is with error... Knowing that we don't know is the beginning of wisdom' (74). These are fine sentiments and the facts underlying them are unassailable, but I doubt very much whether central government planners and those imbued with a sound socialist faith are likely to learn from history what Edwards has already learned: the limited human capacity to forecast. The beginning of this chapter will deal with some methodological features bearing upon the measuring of the economic future, followed by examples of erroneous forecasting. These examples are not important by themselves; they are intended only as instances to prop the thesis that most economic forecasts can be shown to have been highly inaccurate. It would be absurd to predict that forecasting exercises in the years to come will be as erroneous as most of those in the past have been. Nevertheless, the examples cited would seem to establish a prima facie case for such a contention. If this is unacceptable to the

* The French Prime Minister, predicting in November 1968, how his austerity programme would affect the 1969 budget.

present members of the forecasting profession, they should explain to the laymen—duped so often in the past—why their predecessors were guilty of an incompetence they do not confess to.

WHY NOT A RANGE?

Predictors would look a great deal less silly if they quoted their predictions in terms of a range of figures, say an expected surge of exports by 4–6 per cent., a rise in engineering output by 5–8 per cent., etc. This sensible course is not followed because the use of a span does not allow the prophets to appear 'scientific'—and they often wish to give such an impression. A more credible reason is that the buyers of so-called forecasts frequently do not wish to be sold a range of figures. Thus Becker reports that there is a desk sign in the Pentagon warning the staff that 'the boss wants a single figure—not a range' (45).

In an expensively-priced publication, circulated privately by a consultancy firm to top US executives, its readers are informed that the GNP of India in 1985 will exceed that of 1965 by 107·8 per cent. The Economic Planning Agency of Japan predicts that its country's GNP will in that same period rise to $361·1 billion. (Note the decimal points!) In view of the high fees which they charge for their services, I do not suppose that these eminent forecasters are writing this nonsense with their tongues in their blushing cheeks. If they were, one could at least forgive them for displaying a puckish sense of humour but, alas, they expect to be taken seriously and one can thus only marvel at their intellectual arrogance. Or should one condemn the affluent business leaders for their stupidity in buying the decimal points?

BENCH-MARK INACCURACIES

There is a sound statistical reason why numerate estimates for the subsequent year are unavoidably built on an unproven foundation. Most GNP predictions for 1970 were made in the summer, or at latest the autumn, of 1969, but at those times a 1970 projection could only be based on a guessed estimate of the 1969 GNP. Annual GNP extrapolations are therefore inevitably unreliable. Zarnowitz (79) has calculated the average mistake in US GNP forecasts to be $10 billion; he allocates

$1·8 billion of this to estimating errors in the level of the base (and the remaining $8·2 billion to wrong predictions).*

One other example: in April 1968, Treasury estimates of the 1968 UK's balance of payments were circulated. In many speeches and articles these 1968 extrapolations were contrasted with the dismal record of 1967 which, allegedly, showed a Current Account deficit in that year of £514 Mn. In August of 1969 this particular deficit of 1967 was officially amended to £283 Mn. In the present context I am not concerned to draw the obvious lesson that persons who cannot ex post estimate accurately the balance of payment are hardly likely to inspire confidence with ex ante proclamations. My purpose here is only to show that any 1968 forecasts made in April of that year must have been erroneously framed, because they are now known to have had the wrong benchmark.

THE MEASUREMENT OF GNP INACCURACIES

Academics, politicians and journalists almost invariably describe as a 1 per cent. error the disparity between an actual growth rate of 4 per cent. and a predicted rate of 5 per cent. Such a numerical relationship seems extremely plausible to uninstructed laymen, and not only to them. In lecturing on the craft of economic forecasting, I have often quoted from a survey of hundreds of US national accounts predictions (79), which shows a mean error of 2 per cent. in GNP projections and of 2·7 per cent in predictions for industrial output. My audiences were usually favourably impressed with these apparently small errors; many thought it remarkable that such a complicated concept as the US GNP could be predicted with what they generously thought was a high degree of accuracy. This is precisely what the unincorporated union of soothsayers is constantly saying: errors of only 2 per cent. are a remarkable achievement; one ought to be grateful that—thanks to mathematical

---

* Zarnowitz has computed the error, caused by an unsound base period, in accordance with the earliest recorded estimates of the past year's national accounts, i.e. the correct level of the 1969 GNP is assumed to be the estimate published in April 1970. As I have shown in Appendix II, the GNP ex post data are being constantly revised and years pass before a figure can be considered as definitive. This, therefore, suggests that the real percentage error, which is attributable to a wrong bench-mark, may in fact be considerably greater than the Zarnowitz numeral.

equations, sophisticated computers, multifarious surveys and the devoted research efforts of Ph.D. economists—such glorious statistical success stories are written year in year out.

Such praise helps to camouflage a ruse with which the uninitiated are befooled. In the first half of this century violent annual fluctuations in the size of the national accounts were recorded. The Department of Commerce has estimated that between 1940 and 1941 the US GNP rose by no less than 25 per cent.; between 1931 and 1932 the American national product fell dramatically by 23 per cent. (and the volumes of exports and imports dropped by 32 per cent. and 33 per cent. respectively). In those days of extreme GNP volatility a 2 per cent. forecasting error would indeed have earned an economic prophet the laurels, which one must refuse to award today, in an era of relative stability, to prognosticators with a 2 per cent. error. Reverting to the British scene, I have calculated—from data in (145)—that the post-war annual average fluctuation of the UK GNP (1948–67) was 3 per cent. If we round off the figures* of the actual growth rates to the nearest full digit, the annual growth rates of Britain's GNP were either 1 per cent., 2 per cent., 3 per cent., 4 per cent. or 5 per cent. Forecasters may work with the reasonable certainty that Britain's GNP growth in the near future is very likely also to fall within this range. Let me exemplify this: If the GNP is forecast to be 1 per cent. or 5 per cent. but in fact turns out to be 3 per cent., then convention would have it that the forecasters are only 2 per cent. out. I submit that it is more logical to say that they are two percentage *points* out, and 100 per cent. wrong, whilst those who had forecast a 2 per cent. or 4 per cent. rise are one percentage point out and 50 per cent. wrong. Another illustration: If one predicts a 5 per cent. rise, and the actual rate is 1 per cent., I would say that one is 100 per cent. wrong; if one predicts a 4 per cent. rise then one is to be adjudged 75 per cent. wrong; if one had foreseen a 3 per cent. or 2 per cent. rise one is 50 per cent. or 25 per cent. wrong respectively. People, marvelling at the economist soothsayers who are seemingly only 1 per cent. wrong, forget that the range of the likely future GNP does not stretch from zero to infinity, and that in our age only minor annual

---

* They refer to calculations of the gross national product at 1958 market prices. Of the 19 rates in this period, all indicate a positive growth fluctuation, except in 1952 when the GNP fell by 0·6 per cent. In order to simplify matters, I have excluded from the generalization in the main text above this negative growth rate and also the extraordinarily large rise of 5·9 per cent. in 1964, so that my conclusions only apply to 90 per cent. of the post-war situation.

adjustments in the size of the national cake take place. In this sense, a 1 percentage point error is a large error, a 2 percentage point error a very large error!

INACCURATE—BUT NOT CONTRITE

In the coming pages I hope to deliver some convincing proof of the grave inaccuracies of economic forecasters. As to myself, I have erred so widely and been wrong so often that self-interest dictates that I should be compassionate when I behold the mote in my forecasting brothers' eyes. Should false prophets, repenting their errors, be forgiven? My reply is in the affirmative. But should one also show mercy to sinners who are not repentant but actually glory in their past misleading prophecies?

No big nation has had such a consistently fast GNP growth rate as Japan, and none as great a failure rate in its official GNP forecasts.* What conclusions can be drawn from this failure? According to one source (29), there is no need to be upset or sorry, because these enormous blunders merely prove that the Japanese economy cannot be regimented by government planners. A fair conclusion! But does it not also suggest that when the Japanese Economic Planning Agency sounds its forecasting trumpets again, one should not take it too seriously?

The well-informed intelligence department of the First National City Bank of New York is naturally briefed about the errors of American forecasters. Do they consequently debunk them, and alert business men to be vigilant when digesting their pronouncements? The learned economists of this leading New York bank clearly feel that such a sentence would be too harsh. They still take their hats off to economic forecasters, merely noting that these tend to substantially 'underestimate', and are inclined to be conservatively biased and sensitive to bearish elements (146). Fine words! Only I wonder whether all the readers of the bank's Economic Letter understand that this really implies that the forecasters are wrong, and that one cannot rely on their judgement.

* In 1955 the government predicted that in their fourth National Plan the GNP would grow annually by 5 per cent. — in fact it rose twice as fast (1955: 10.3 per cent.; 1956: 9.0 per cent; 1957: 7.9 per cent.; 1958: 3.2 per cent. and 1959: 17.9 per cent.).

An anonymous critic in the journal of the Confederation of British Industry, who had examined the forecasts of the National Institute of Economic and Social Research, came to the conclusion that they were so invariably wrong as to raise the question of whether it was worth while publishing them. He opined that because they laid claim to reliability and scientific precision, they were harmfully misleading. Yet, he thought that overall it was worth while to continue publishing them, because they at least indicated 'how one particularly influential group of economists is thinking' (147). I can think of no greater insult to economic forecasters.

In his evidence before a parliamentary commission, W. A. H. Godley (a senior Treasury official) made an amazing revelation. He suggested — politely of course — that ministries were guilty (inadvertently) of publishing inaccurate forecasts and contradictory ex post national accounts data. There are not many people in Whitehall who know so well as Godley how true these charges are, and no one has ever come up with a more ingenious answer. This Treasury representative went on to tell the inquisitive members of the House of Commons (44), that by looking at the figures of quantitative forecasts one cannot obtain a proper assessment of the future; he insisted that one ought to look at the text and not at the figures. He left his listeners in no doubt that numerical accuracy in Treasury projections was an irrelevancy: '...the real criterion of a forecast, the only criterion in my opinion, is whether or not in retrospect you can say that it did or did not give the general character of the year and more particularly whether or not it did not give the basis for the correct advice.' Well, if the verbal tracing of a trend is the purpose of forecasts, why then use figures at all?

When a forecast does not turn out to be right, the forecaster is plainly wrong. I deal elsewhere with that despicable behaviour which entails making a dishonest prediction for some noble or nefarious purpose. Unless the forecaster claims after the event that he had deliberately misled his public, he must be considered — I intentionally repeat this truism — either right or wrong. Apologias, such as 'I have been over-optimistic' or 'I am delighted to have underestimated the growth', are part of the defence mechanism of economists who are not prepared to be adjudged by the only criterion applicable to predictions. It is specious to write that 'nothing pleases shareholders so much as to learn that their chairman's uninspiring forecast turns out to be unduly pessimistic' (148), or that 'Imperial Chemical Industries got its forecast joyfully wrong' (153). The Chancellor of the Exchequer used the full authority, and statistical resources, of his office to publish export forecasts that were proved wrong by a substantial margin a few months after the solemn prophecy had been made. Was he sorry about his failure? Immaculately dressed for the occasion, Roy Jenkins told the bankers and merchants of the City of London at the annual Lord Mayor's dinner: 'I am very glad to have been proved wrong' (149). I surmise that they greeted this exhilarating declamation with applause without considering that their cheers were really boos for the Treasury's forecasters.

When Ridsdale, a Conservative Member of Parliament, suggested that the Department of Economic Affairs ought to be liquidated because its predictive assessments were 'hundreds of millions of pounds wrong', the following reply was given by Shore, the then boss of the laminated DEA: 'The important part is which side of the forecast we are likely to be wrong. (Laughter.) It is possible to take a more optimistic view' (194).

The Economist really caps them all. Their numerate glimpses of the future are awfully inaccurate—and with hindsight they tell their readers about it, adding however that 'being wrong doesn't invalidate the quantitative exercise'* (92). A strange admission: I cannot think what else invalidates quantitative predictions. Their real alibi, however, is more delicately expressed. 'We erred in imposing company.' (This is a reference to the National Institute of Economic and Social Research, whose forecasts were equally wrong.) And as to those foreigners in Paris...well, the editors boast, the forecasts of the European Economic Commission for the GNPs of Continental European countries were even wider of the mark than *The Economist*'s forecast for the UK GNP!

SOME PROSAIC EXAMPLES

When Cairncross, director of the Treasury's Economic Section, was asked whether he was capable of predicting the accuracy of future forecasting exercises, he replied: 'I would not be able to do that unless I

---

* Did they get this nonsense from the other side of the Atlantic? This is what one American economist wrote: 'Errors in forecasting may have nothing to do with the validity of the underlying theories. There are some economists who made more accurate predictions with other methods, but...these more accurate predictions do not prove that their methods are superior to those that failed' (162).

knew how accurate they had been since the war. Perhaps we should do a study of that kind that more often. It is a very chastening experience' (44). I hope that the three British examples which I shall be quoting below may help Cairncross and others to note the quantitative dimensions of past failures. But lest unreliable economic soothsaying be seen as a *maladie anglaise*, I am citing first two specimens from outside the British Isles.

I

Critics have suggested that one ought not to be too beastly to Indian economists by highlighting their GNP forecasting failures, and consequently I restrict myself here to examining their predictive powers in a much simpler field, budget estimates. In a sixteen-year period (1949–64) the projected revenue in the Central Government of India's annual budget showed an average error of 11·2 per cent., and of 8·5 per cent. for expenditure (50). This proves to the hilt the charge laid by Klein (150) and many other observers, that 'neither the absolute data nor the index numbers issued by the Indian government warrant confidence with respect to their accuracy...' One is urged to be charitable and excuse this on the grounds that the Indian authorities are only beginning to establish statistical services. Yet the Indian government is so intoned with Socialist ideas that it thinks itself competent to plan its economy in minute detail many years ahead. Little (48), for example, is not very reproachful about the imperfect Indian numerate data, but he cannot help noting that these cast a shadow on the reliability of the Five-Year Plans. If budget estimates are so far out, ought not the planners to be chary about the quantitative assumptions underlying their detailed national plans and projections? Apparently not in India! 'It is extraordinary what little fuss the Planning Commission makes about the poverty of Indian statistics.'

II

Under the auspices of the National Bureau of Economic Affairs in New York, Zarnowitz and his colleagues have scrutinized the GNP predictions of leading government, business and academic forecasters (79).

In the 1953–63 period the US GNP was about $500 billion, and the annual average GNP fluctuation $22 billion. If, therefore, one had not bothered to research future changes but had just presumed that the subsequent year's national accounts would be identical with the current year's, one would on average have been wrong by $22 billion, i.e. 4·4 percentage points. If those glimpsing into the future had been not sophisticated forecasters but just ordinary mortals, who had lazily extrapolated past GNP changes and mechanically calculated GNP predictions from the trend established in previous years, they would have been wrong by $12 billion dollars, i.e. 2·4 percentage points. The National Bureau's sample, however, showed that erudite prophecy is superior. By how much? On an average the professional economists were $10 billion out, i.e. guilty of a 2 percentage point error. It is surely significant that econometric, and other, techniques gave the self-designated experts only a minute edge over those who just extrapolated past trends. Yet the performance of the experts is in one sense even less laudable than the 2 percentage point error—bad as it is—would suggest. Whilst the National Bureau, for this analysis, lumped together all major US forecasters, the layman wishing to feel the pulse of the US economy is unlikely to consult all of them and then strike an average of the annual forecasting Derby. If one breaks down the national average, it will be found that the $10 billion errors year-by-year ranged from $4 billion to $20 billion in individual forecasts. As there is no consistency in accurate predicting by individual forecasters, the layman cannot pick experts with recognized credentials. If, therefore, business men opt to rely on a handful of forecasters only (and not on the average of all the forecasters), they may sometimes be buying predictions which are far wider of the mark than any back-of-envelope calculations made at home.

But perhaps the US soothsayers are improving their technique? Since the formation of the National Association of Business Economists, the average predictive efforts of the group are pooled and published annually as 'the consensus of the forecast group.' In the autumn of 1968 the consensus opinion on the current-price growth of the 1969 US GNP was publicized as 5·4 per cent. Already by September 1969 the president of the Association had thrown in the sponge: 'I am chagrined to reveal that the consensus forecasts made last year at this time for the year 1969 are best forgotten' (195). The 1969 GNP has in fact gone up by 7·8 per cent., i.e. a 2·4 percentage point forecasting error was perpetrated—

a discrepancy of over $21 billion. And this despite the advance in computer technology and econometrics!

III

I do not think that James Callaghan deserves Kenneth Fleet's biting quip that as an economic prophet he would not have made the Old Testament charts (151).* During his term of office as Chancellor of the Exchequer, he repeatedly stated that he had no such ambitions. In fact, when challenged in Parliament to publish forecasts, he refused (in December 1966) to do so, 'for the very good reason...that the forecasts are always wrong'. *The Economist* blasted this as a 'deplorable speech', but Callaghan stuck to his guns. When he rose to speak in the House of Commons on the 11th April 1967, however, he left all his good forecasting principles at home:

'...the overall balance of payments should improve again substantially between 1966 and 1967. We should move from last year's deficit of £189 Mn to a surplus in 1967 as a whole with an even bigger one in 1968.'

And now for the hard facts. The projected surplus for 1967 has turned out to be a deficit of £417 Mn, and the anticipated 'even bigger surplus' in 1968 is now known to have been a deficit of £407 Mn. (Callaghan's failure to predict correctly was enhanced by the fact that his estimate of a £189 Mn deficit in 1966 was an overstatement; in the light of new evidence it is believed to have been only £48 Mn.)

In a memorable television confrontation between the ex-Chancellor and David Frost (18th October 1968), the former confessed that he had resigned his office because he had deliberately misled the House of Commons, one month before the November 1967 devaluation, when he had denied that the Treasury was about to alter the external exchange parity of sterling. He asked the country's forgiveness for having lied, but pleaded that he had lied for Britain's sake. Callaghan claimed that when he had made this admittedly false statement to Parliament, he was knowingly sacrificing his reputation. I mention this confession in order to pose the question, whether Callaghan had perhaps also lied in April

* I have the greatest respect for Kenneth Fleet's output as a financial journalist but I challenge his theological credentials. Were the biblical prophecies really more accurate than the Treasury officials' GNP predictions? Did the Old Testament prophets intend their so-called forecasts to come true?

1967—only a few months before the government finally devalued—'for the country's sake' in order to generate a euphoric atmosphere which just conceivably might have induced the holders of hot money to switch into sterling and thus stave off devaluation. I do not know the answer to this question, but I shall suggest one. I strongly suspect that Callaghan was not lying in April 1967 when he made his rash balance of payments predictions. Probably the unflattering truth is that the Chancellor honestly believed that these projections were based on a realistic appraisal.* Where did he get his data from? He relied of course on the professional economists and forecasters in his office. If my conjecture that Callaghan was not telling a deliberate lie is correct, then in April 1967 the experts concluded that by December there would be a surplus on the yearly 1967 balance of payments; it is worth repeating that in fact the year threw up a deficit of £417 Mn. Unless the contrary is proved, I shall consider this stupendous blunder to reflect not on Callaghan's veracity but on his faith in the ability of the Treasury to make definitive forecasts.

IV

There is one good thing to be said for the British soothsayers, particularly the non-government ones: their predictions are terribly wrong but when this is shown to be so, they poke fun at themselves for their past misdemeanours and tell their readers about it. (Many of the GNP specialists in under-developed countries might benefit from acquiring both a sense of humour and a willingness to publicize their failures.)

The following—not untypical—example of fallacious GNP predicting is culled from *The Economist*, whose published explorations of the economic future have a far-reaching circulation. Not the magnitude of the error, but the element of timing, is in this instance particularly significant. If predicting is not just guestimating but the result of research and informed thinking, one would reasonably expect predictions to become progressively more accurate as one comes nearer (in time) to the specified future period. In December 1965 *The Economist* informed

---

* The cited balance of payment forecast for 1967 was not the personal whim of James Callaghan, but the considered view of the government. On the 7th February 1967, the Prime Minister also announced that the country was facing a prospective surplus in that year.

the world that in its judgement the 1966 UK GNP would grow by 1·25 per cent. On the last day of 1966, the editors self-reproachingly beat a retreat and divulged that 'now it looks more like only ½ per cent' (93). The uninitiated might have thought it easier to guestimate the 1966 national accounts in December 1966 than in December 1965. Alas, this is not always so, because when the official 1966 data were published, they exhibited a 1·7 per cent growth rate (145), i.e. the first (the earlier) prediction of *The Economist* was less erroneous than the second.

V

The National Institute of Economic and Social Research (NIESR) is probably the most influential forecasting body in the UK. It is easy to test this by studying the press for seven days after the quarterly press releases of the Institute. The contents of the NIESR predictions make headlines; many papers write editorials evaluating afresh the economy in the light of these revealed glimpses into the future; financial correspondents covering the stock exchange and foreign exchange markets attribute—probably justly—fluctuations to the NIESR news. The Institute's reputation is unmerited. There is not the slightest foundation for the (mythical) belief, which is admittedly widely held, that NIESR predictions are more reliable than those of the government,* *The Economist* or any of several academic sources: on balance the NIESR's record is actually slightly worse. Like most British prognosticators, the Institute usually miscalculates the UK GNP's real growth rates by an average error of 1 to 2 percentage points. Sometimes the NIESR's failure is particularly blatant. One of its biggest failures was the prediction in January 1959 that the gross domestic product would rise by 1 per cent., and industrial production by 3 per cent., between the last quarters of 1958 and 1959. The actual changes were 5 per cent. and 9 per cent. respectively (49).

There is an unfortunate tendency by the NIESR to justify predictive failures on the grounds that they cannot foresee 'radical policy changes', devaluation, deflationary measures, etc. Reading between the lines, one receives the impression that they think the world is quite

* The NIESR soothsayers gain more credence because they are not tarnished by the suspicious undertones imputed to governmental estimates of future happenings.

unfair because it upsets their predictions—which presuppose normal conditions—by introducing abnormal economic unheavals. At one stage (90), they even said explicitly that in view of 'a radical policy change', which turned their predictions topsy-turvy, a post mortem on its wrong forecasts would not be particularly instructive. Despite such occasionally smug apologias, the NIESR does often publish post mortems on its mistakes. This alone is enough to secure a place in heaven for their false prophets. And if there are foolish gnomes in Zurich who take the NIESR quarterly publications seriously enough to guide them in their sterling trading—who cares?

The Single Firm and the GNP

'A pox on prognosticators! May their tribe decrease and may their followers return to tea leaves and the lunar tides. And may business recover from its case of economic hypochondria!'

E. B. WEISS

So far I have only considered GNP predictions in relation to the economy as a whole. Evidence suggests that whilst capitalist and communist governments can sometimes *influence* the direction of economic development by tax changes, fiscal manipulations, devaluations, etc., they are unable to plan with reasonable chances of success a finite quantitative growth of the national product, and therefore cannot forecast correctly future GNP magnitudes. It is said that GNP predictions do not only serve macro-economic purposes, but are also of direct use to single firms. Many GNP soothsayers boast that their games can be put to good use by private entrepreneurs. This indeed is widely accepted and consequently many business firms subsidize the preparation of national accounts predictions, which they read with assiduous attention. Some firms even charge their staff economists with the computation of independent GNP forecasts before tackling product projections. As two American enthusiasts put it:

'In corporate work, GNP becomes the starting point; from there the analyst can narrow his focus more sharply to the industry and, ultimately, to his firm. To be sure a given industry or firm may well prosper while the economy dips, but this is the exception and not the rule. Thus knowledge of general trends represents a firm foundation upon which to build a sales or profit forecast' (53).

I challenge strongly the assumption, made by these apologists, that GNP figures are useful guides for individual businesses. It is not too difficult to demonstrate that reliance by individual firms on GNP predictions is not merely silly but actually dangerous.

The grave errors in GNP predictions, which I outlined in the previous chapter, still underscore the extent of the incompetence of econometric prophets. If one asks for their worksheet, one discovers that these gentlemen calculate hundreds and thousands of individual expenditure and income items and then add them up to arrive at the height, length and width of the national cake. Erroneous as their macro-economic predictions are, these are still much less faulty than their estimates of component categories. The overall results, which are less inaccurate than they deserve to be, are improved by the fortuitous reconciliation of many errors. GNP predictions, therefore, contain a spurious element of accuracy, because of the automatic obliteration of individual errors when the all-embracing average is struck.

Unknown to the vast mass of GNP users, the Central Statistical Office warns that the reliability of the annual national accounts at current price is ± less than 3 per cent. (105). The CSO goes on to say that the reliability of the major constituents is ± 3–10 per cent., and in some cases ± more than 10 per cent. The seeming success of overall GNP predictions, being out by only 1–2 percentage points, owes much to the mutual cancellation of many other predictions which are vastly more faulty.

Governments are usually interested in the general trend of the economy and lean on the single figure of a projected GNP growth, whilst the individual firm ordinarily focuses its attention on components of the GNP. The variation in the degree of inaccuracy—of the whole and of its parts—is therefore crucial to firms which hope to derive meaningful guidance from estimates of the national accounts.*

For the rest of this chapter the working assumption will apply that overall forecasts of the GNP can be both meaningful and accurate. On this hypothesis, I shall examine the question of whether an accurate

* 1968 jolted socialist planning morale in the UK. Consumer expenditure is the largest single item in the GNP, accounting for about 70 per cent. If the government cannot control its size, what hopes are there of successfully planning lesser categories? In the first quarter of 1968 the Chancellor of the Exchequer forecast a decrease in consumer expenditure for the current year. His ambition was very limited: he did not project what consumer expenditure would be cut down and what social class would contribute to this objective—he merely ventured to say that total national consumer expenditure in 1968 would drop by 1 per cent. Roy Jenkins assured Britain's foreign creditors that he was not merely conjecturing, but in fact making a forecast based upon the inexorable logic of certain fiscal and tax measures he was introducing. The facts are now known: consumer expenditure far from dropping actually went up by 2.4 per cent. To Jenkins (and perhaps the gnomes of Zurich) this must be proof of how undisciplined the UK consumer is, how unwilling he is to react in a prescribed manner to governmental steps. The British people frustrated Jenkins's forecast by heavy dissaving, and I rejoice that they thereby demonstrated how difficult it is to regiment a free people.

GNP projection can be helpful to the individual entrepreneur. It is fair to set aside possible fluctuations in the GNP by, say, 25 per cent. as were experienced in the pre-war years, and to restrict our inquiry to the sort of GNP growth rates the Anglo-Saxon countries have had in the last decade, i.e. average movements of 3 per cent. Is there a decisive meaningful correlation between the GNP growth rate and the development of economic categories? (Later on I shall argue that the fate of the individual firm has very little to do, certainly over the span of years, with the growth of the larger industry group to which it belongs.)

Perhaps it is best to start with some very general indicators. In the quotation above it is asserted fatuously that the profit forecast of a firm is built upon the foundation of the overall trend established by the movement of the GNP volume. Anyone who does not live in Cloud Cuckoo Land knows that not only is an individual firm's profit margin hardly affected by the GNP growth rate, but even industrial profits as a whole are determined far more by other elements, such as changes in taxation, price and wage controls, and other government interventions.

In the summer of 1964 the Treasury explained that UK export forecasts to North America are fairly closely related to the trend of the US GNP (154). There is no denying that a study of the projections of the American national product will prove of some assistance in estimating British exports, but anyone who relied in his corporate plans mainly on this element would be building on shifting sand. Of far greater significance than a possible 2-4 per cent. rise in the US GNP is an evaluation of the US tariff policy, the production costs of German and Japanese competitors, and the level of the (open or disguised) export subsidies available to UK manufacturers—all these are independent variables quite unrelated to an assessment of the US GNP. Events in 1968-9 proved that the sales volume of British exports to North America in the preceding three years had been determined decisively by a non-GNP factor: the overvaluation of sterling.

Leaving aside profit margins and export sales, is there an industry group which can anticipate changes in its output that are the direct consequence of an accurately predicted GNP growth? All the available evidence suggests that there is no such correlation and that the performance of single industries is not ordinarily related to GNP movements in any discernible pattern—cf, for example, the detailed analysis by the NIESR (90). British history is littered with instances of how some industries in one downward cycle reduced output faster than the GNP contracted, but years later in another downward cycle, managed to swim against the GNP stream by actually augmenting output. There is no established statistical relationship, holding true over a number of years, that allows one to predict how a 1 per cent. GNP growth influences industry A or B. Credit squeezes affecting stockholding, consumer anticipations concerning the stability of purchasing power, taxes, taxes and taxes again, savings habits, controls of a general or industry-specific nature, instalment credit regulations, exchange controls and import levies — all these, and other factors, play havoc with any attempt to relate a GNP prediction to the future performance of one industry. To return again to our quotation at the beginning of this chapter: facts just do not bear out the presumptuous assertion that only in exceptional cases do industries or firms develop in the opposite direction to that of the GNP. In trying to sell GNP predictions as a handy tool for business decisions, the authors must have been leaning on pre-war history. In the world of today, the fluctuations of the GNP influence single industries very little or, put in another way, other factors are much more powerful.*

It is necessary to at least mention in this context that product innovation is the single most important element, which — over the span of years — determines the differential growth of industries. If the leaders of the British cinema industry had been idiotic enough in 1948 to plan investments in accordance with projections of the UK GNP, they would have landed in the bankruptcy court. The size of disposable consumer expenditure — or even the estimated portion thereof likely to be devoted to entertainment — was and is almost irrelevant to them, because clearly the growth or decline of cinema audiences is decided largely by television. What does the industry manufacturing rubber contraceptives care about the future GNP? If they are at all interested in predictions, they are concerned to know how many Roman Catholics will obey the Pope's ruling on birth control. But their real worry is how far the industry's growth will be stunted by the pharmaceutical industry's success in selling the Pill. The captains of the steel industry had better not study the projections for the UK GNP in 1975, even if they think that it can be ascertained accurately. They should employ

* 'I would regard the country's overall rate of growth as having little bearing on the likely trend of demand for the product of my industry and still less bearing on my company's sales. And before anyone suggests that the industry I work in — the newspaper industry — is atypical, perhaps he would care to name a typical one' (1).

their thinking time more profitably by assessing the inroads which aluminium and other metals may or may not make on their traditional markets.*

There is only one economic sector the products of which have such a wide application as to link it directly to the national level of economic activity; I am referring to the fuel industry group. In September 1960 the NIESR published an energy forecast which it based on two variables: changes in fuel efficiency and the growth of the gross domestic product. The predicted consumption for 1965 was 282 Mn tons (coal equivalent) as against an actual consumption of 294 Mn (155).† The financial press hailed this forecasting exercise as a great success and, for the moment, I shall ignore the overall error of this energy projection. This leaves, however, wide open the question of what practical use such a general energy forecast could be to UK fuel producers and importers. A breakdown of the NIESR analysis shows that in predicting the consumption of *specific* fuels, its forecasting errors were several times greater than the overall error. The consumption of oil went up much faster than had been predicted, whilst coal consumption lagged far behind the estimates; the boom in central heating was not accurately assessed, and the phenomenal rise of the fuel needs of the expanding road transport industry was not anticipated. Petrol for lorries, coal for heating homes by open fires, coal for the generation of electricity, gas for central heating—these are all 'energy' to the prophets of total fuel consumption. Adding up the various forms of energy output and consumption—with errors in different directions cancelling one another out—produced a forecasting discrepancy of 'about 4 per cent'. However, the person charged with planning coal output, the company considering investments in petrol stations, the business man conjecturing on the volume of demand for gas appliances—why should they be interested in the overall demand for energy? It is the anticipated requirements for specific products which leaven their actions. Their product interests diverge sufficiently to make it highly unprofitable for them to speculate on the overall growth of the wider group to which they belong.

* Edward Lewis, chairman of Decca: 'A forecast of overall demand for electronic capital goods in 1970 is only of marginal interest to us. We have to decide what the demand for quite specific types of equipment will be, what our competitors will be producing...' (101).
† Later the NIESR was to say that this reflects a forecasting error of 'about 4 per cent'. It is a strange way of describing a forecast that projected an annual growth of 5·7 Mn which turned out to be 7·5 Mn.

To pay attention to comprehensive energy forecasts can actually be harmful, because the growing demand for one type of fuel may be primarily conditioned by the decline of demand for another type — gas and coal are commercial enemies. Yet myths do not fade away. As late as March 1968, the Permanent Under-Secretary of the Department of Economic Affairs said that it was possible to make long-term demand forecasts for fuel, because it was a 'homogeneous product' (172).

Another striking example comes from the NIESR stable. In 1960 they produced a forecast for the sales of four electrical consumer durables during the 1959–65 period (155). This was a much more specialized demand study than that on energy and seemingly provided interested companies (some of which produced all of these articles) with a lucid projected forecast of their output. The NIESR conjectured an annual rise in total sales of 2·5–5·0 per cent. — in fact sales dropped by 1·2 per cent. per annum. The forecast suggested that by 1965 sales would be £378–437 Mn whilst in fact only goods to the amount of £304 Mn were sold; the forecast thus deviated by 24–44 per cent. from actual performance. Yet, of greater significance to the firms was the ex post finding that there is no such thing as a homogeneous demand for electrical consumer durables. This is shown by the varying proportions in which the forecasts for single product items fell short of actual sales: the sales of washing machines in the 1959–65 period were 18 per cent. less than the forecast had suggested; those of vacuum cleaners 23 per cent., television sets 35 per cent. and refrigerators 9 per cent.

In the context of this chapter it is fascinating to read the NIESR's confession as to why they had gone wrong. In their frank appraisal they admit to have estimated wrongly certain volatile elements that proved highly determinant, such as changes in stockbuilding, fall in unit prices, product improvements, replacement demand, the saturation factor and 'a considerable rise in the demand for other electrical appliances'. On their own admission, the most grievous sin was to tie up the likely demand for these electrical durables with the anticipated movements of the national product or disposable consumer income.* Their fault was to depend to an unwarranted degree upon a causal rela-

---

* The NIESR rightly claim that had they automatically extrapolated the past demand for these four appliances as a function of the GNP, their forecast errors would have been even bigger.

tion between consumer demand for washing machines, refrigerators, etc., and the size of the projected GNP, and thereby underplay the other complex extraneous—but in practice more influential—factors, that make the British housewife buy appliances irrespective of whether the GNP in that year is rising or falling by 2 per cent.

When a company serves the whole national market, there is at least a presumption that it might be interested in the predicted growth of the national product. Many producers of goods and services, however, depend entirely on local or regional demand for their output. I have argued that there is no significant correlation between the aggregate national future demand for British hairdressing and the predicted growth of the British GNP. Even were someone to discover the statistical existence of such a link, this would be useless information to the owners of hairdressing establishments in Aberdeen and Cardiff who depend entirely on locally generated demand. For most purposes national indicators are not reflections of regional developments. The Deputy Commercial Adviser to such a sophisticated body as the Electricity Council relates (198) how his principals attempted to incorporate national economic growth considerations, particularly those of Neddy, in their specific forecasts for electricity demand. As, however, national demand for energy is unrelated to regional demands—which still determine many regional production and distribution activities of the electricity industry—the GNP and national fuel predictions have not proved very helpful.

In the absence of cartel arrangements, and excluding industries dominated by one firm (such as Pilkington Brothers or British Oxygen), the demand schedule of one industry is not identical with that of its component single firms. There is a healthy tug-of-war within many industries that often leads within the space of a few years to a fundamental realignment of the market. Under free enterprise, a market leader can quickly lose his dominant position to an aggressive competitor.

What should the corporate planners at Cadbury's do when they read of a conjectured GNP growth of 2 per cent. in the coming year? I suggest that they ought to ignore it. What if the chocolate industry has commissioned a group market research study which projects a 3 per cent. growth in chocolate consumption in each of the following five years? I suppose that this might guide Cadbury's in its decisions for the subsequent year. After five years the market forces in the chocolate industry are likely to have changed. Surely dynamic Cadbury's must consider the possibility that a general 16 per cent. increase in demand could be translated into an increase of 24 per cent. for the sales of its products, provided it pushes some competitors into a corner?

In 1967 the British Electrical and Allied Manufacturers' Association issued dismal reports about the decline of consumer demand, recording an 8·5 per cent. drop in 1966 in the industry's output of refrigerators. One company (LEC Refrigeration), however, had increased its turnover by 9·5 per cent. and expanded its share of the UK market. Clearly, if LEC had reacted in 1965 to forecasts predicting a fall in consumer buying of refrigerators by cutting back its production, it would have acted foolishly. Instead, its management decided that, despite the projected general decline in the demand for refrigerators, it would step up its output and carve out for itself a larger portion of the industry's sales.

The *Financial Times* (156) has reported an interesting forecasting-planning exercise by the Peek Frean company, which embarked on a £3·5 Mn modernization scheme at one of its factories. To justify this expenditure, it had to be shown that the investment could still be profitably operated in 1980 and beyond. It appears that these corporate planners did not consult George Brown's National Plan and do not seem to have concerned themselves unduly with NIESR extrapolations pointing to the UK's likely GNP in fifteen years' time. Peek Frean commissioned a market research study with the brief that its future sales prospects should not be assessed merely by projecting the possible demand for its existing range of biscuits. The remarkable marketing director of the company conjectured that fifteen years hence the tastes of the British housewife will have altered, and that other goods *then* in vogue might have greater growth opportunities than the traditional products Peek Frean was selling successfully in the sixties. The study threw up several possible new products but, as Peek Frean was not obsessed with the idea that it can compel the consumer to buy its products or that it can predict with certainty what the consumer will want in 1980, it opted to plan for a relatively uncertain future. The one thing it was certain of was its inability to plan rigidly now its output in fifteen years hence. Consequently the factory was designed in a manner that would not restrict its productive potential to the present goods. The flexibility of the new machinery will enable it to be changed to handle new varieties, which might in future years come on to the commercial scene. Peek Frean is not the only company in the UK which does its planning in relation to as yet unknown innovations rather than in accordance with forecasts for its existing products.

There are devout socialists who draw sustenance from such flexible corporate planning to vindicate rigid government planning and forecasting. Michael Shanks agitated forcibly for a National Plan when the Labour Party was still in opposition; he was also a member of its preparatory commission which designed administrative and economic schemes that were put into operation when Harold Wilson became Prime Minister in the autumn of 1964. Shanks had the rare fortune of being called upon to implement his ideas when he was appointed to a senior post in the newly-formed planning ministry, the Department of Economic Affairs, which now Rests in Peace. After the failure of George Brown's National Plan, he left government service but he has not yet produced, as some of his erstwhile colleagues have, an essay on The God That Failed—in fact Shanks has remained loyal to his old ideas and bemoans the fate of British planners who are now, so it seems to him, unjustifiably maligned. He defends them by counter-attacking the business critics of central planning: 'Why then, if corporate planning is good, should national planning...be bad?' (103). This is an impressive question and tells much about the reasons for the demise of the National Plan. It demonstrates that some Whitehall strategists do not grasp why flexible planning and forecasting by single firms makes sense, whilst government plans to regiment the whole economy in pre-conceived patterns are destined to fail.

Some Forecasters Cheat

'Beware of false prophets, which come to you in sheep's clothing,
but inwardly they are ravening wolves.'

ST. MATTHEW

Even simpletons know that many honest economic predictions turn out
to be wrong, but surprisingly few people are aware how much 'forecasting' has become a craft practised by villains and knaves, model
builders and idealistic rogues. This chapter presents some source
material that may enlighten the gullible as to the motivations of many
who catch the headlines with their 'scientific' glimpses of the future.
First two methodological aspects are considered which highlight the
techniques employed to make predictions seem credible; then some
types of misleading forecasting are categorized, and finally two detailed
examples (one each from the US and the UK) are cited.

Not only governments but also private individuals make deliberately
false announcements concerning the future, yet few of the forecasting
impostors seek to swindle the public for personal gain. Most are imbued
with the noble aim of influencing events in a manner which will ultimately prove beneficial to the group or national interest they set out to
serve. Moralists will no doubt establish a gulf between those who de-
fraud for narrow material purposes, and those who deliberately lie for
what they consider is the common good. So be it — I merely seek to show
that both are guilty of deception.

They seem to me highly irrelevant, but still — for the record — I
report that there are flourishing contradictory, psycho-analytical com-
mentaries to elucidate the mental forces, which impel prophets to
publicize wrong accounts of the future. Thus, Edwards (74) believes
that forecasters and planners have an unconscious bias towards the
agreeable rather than the disagreeable and that this explains their
excessively optimistic predictions. On the other hand there are those
who have searched the souls of economists and found many of them to
be excessively conservative and subject to pessimistic bias (68), (146).

HOW TO INSPIRE CONFIDENCE

This age of public relations officers and psychological warriors has made a generally cynical public circumspect when government spokesmen pronounce on weighty matters. Under these circumstances a published forecast, even from a country's president or prime minister, which foreshadows a 5 per cent. growth in the economy during the coming three years, does not necessarily inspire confidence in its truthfulness. If the public (and, in this connection, the business community in particular) is to be propelled to believe in the impending 5 per cent. upsurge, then this prediction must be part of a seemingly comprehensive analysis of the economy. It helps if the forecast is backed by several volumes of descriptive and statistical matter, if complicated tables with intricate details are published, if supporting charts (preferably in colour) are prepared, and if many important organizations and luminaries are cited as suppliers of the source material.

One of the first to recognize the scope offered by a statistical dramatization of objectives was Robert Nathan, who during the Second World War helped to formulate several government programmes, and as a member of the Planning Committee of the War Production Board succeeded in selling to the American public some major policy decisions. Nathan's technical tools of analysis were remarkably weak, and yet this planner was extremely successful in his public relations exercises. In a remarkable review of Nathan's strategy (written more than twenty years after the events) Gross (28) observes tauntingly that Nathan's ability was 'to clothe ambitious goals with the "number magic" of concrete statistics'.

C. A. Blyth, of the National Institute of Economic and Social Research, makes the following point in an erudite paper read to an international conference of forecasters (191): 'It is very important to know whether the way in which the forecast is presented—its journalistic qualities—makes some policies more likely to be adopted than others and whether this bias in presentation is deliberate on the part of the forecaster. One suspects this is the more likely the closer the relationship between forecaster and policy maker.' E. F. Schumacher learned about the fallacies of forecasting from his long spell as the chief economist of the National Coal Board. He has now arrived at the bitter conclusion that all long-term forecasting is somewhat presumptuous and absurd;

as to short-term forecasting he has become convinced that refined techniques rarely produce significantly different results from those obtained by crude approximations. (The latter is a euphemism for guest-imating, i.e. predicting without hiring econometricians and computers.) Yet, Schumacher — cited in (70) — can think of a reason why a detailed prediction may after all be preferred:

'...if a refined technique is used a picture may be presented which through its precision and verisimilitude carries conviction, so that the "tenuous character" of the forecast is concealed. People are unduly impressed by the appearance of thoroughness and the fact that everything "adds up".'

A piece of first-hand evidence has been supplied by Samuel Brittan, who served with the Department of Economic Affairs during the momentous days when the National Plan was drawn up and marketed. Headlining his report: 'A Virtuous Confidence Trick?' (157), he discusses the influence of expectations upon growth:

'...a "National Plan" in an advanced industrial country is at the bottom a confidence trick for inducing a favourable view of the future... The main justification for including in a "Plan" large numbers of industry-by-industry projections interspersed with copious prose is that a short paper expressed in terms of the total GDP, with a few other broad aggregates, would strike most industrialists (and many business economists) as too abstract and insufficiently detailed... There is also the more cynical observation that a big document full of figures is more likely (even if unread) to carry conviction than a short statement of objectives.'

Now we know.

SOME LIES ALWAYS CARRY CONVICTION

An economist told me the following story: 'In the course of a consultancy assignment for a small, developing country, I submitted an evaluation of a proposed policy change. In my report I outlined that it was economically harmful, and added in a postscript that I also thought it unfair to the people affected. I was called to a personal session with the Minister of Finance. Flanked by the senior officials of his department, he told me that whilst his government had hired me as a putatively competent economist, they were now forced to deduce that I was not very suitable, because I was apparently compelled to introduce moral considerations to prop my economic recommendations.' I have no means of knowing whether this indeed was the real reason for his dismissal, but I do know that the story illuminates a prevalent tendency to divorce the expediency of government policies from ethical considerations.

There is a weighty literature on the measurable impact of The Law of Forecast Feedback, most of which is written in such objective language as not to raise the principled issue of whether governments are entitled cynically to disregard the truth and make deliberately wild and inaccurate predictions with the aim of bringing about a better GNP growth. Some writers on the subject ignore altogether the implicit lack of morality, whilst others formulate some cursory codicil to show that they are at least aware of the existence of the problem. Kemp (15) recognizes that to governments 'announced forecasts are merely means to ends', and that consequently they are 'not directly interested in the accuracy of forecasts'. Knowing what he does, it seems to me rather mild to add 'This evidently raises ethical issues...' Indeed, it does!

The most brilliant analysis of the effects of contrived forecasts that I have seen is that by Chiang (158). When he finished his job, he must have had an inner urge to stand up and be counted on the moral implications. Yet his only relevant comment is: 'Still the above has dealt only with the question of feasibility, and feasibility is by no means a synonym for desirability. One may indeed wish to rule out artificial forecasts altogether on moral or other grounds. To consider such factors, however, would take us beyond the scope of this paper.' First, one ought to comment on the delicate word 'artificial' which sounds so innocuous though it is meant to describe lying and swindling. Secondly, I wish to make it plain that to me the probity of governmental declarations is of far greater importance than the technical implications. I shall now touch upon the question of whether fraudulent GNP statements can always retain at least some degree of credibility.

The Bank of England hides and distorts data without — so it seems — its directors losing any sleep over it. In publishing the monthly reserves, it has been known to issue loss figures that were subsequently proved to have been more than seven times bigger in reality (159). Its figures are so obviously untrue that financial journals comment on a drop of £15 Mn by asking: 'Why £15 Mn? Why not £14 Mn or £19 M or even £15– Mn?' The Earl of Cromer, former Governor of the Bank of England, told the House of Lords (193) that at present we do not have 'true and accurate reserve figures published monthly'. In that curious speech, he asserted that although there was no 'intention to mislead on the figures'...it is widely recognized, and he agreed with this, that 'the reserve figures...in their present form...are...meaningless'. But lest the noble Lords become frightened, he comforted them by describing it as something perfectly proper, a 'tactical arrangement'. The gnomes of Zurich must have been wondering whether their command of English is sufficient to appreciate the nuances of this apologia. Less exalted people might have sympathized if the 'tactical arrangement' had consisted of the complete suppression of the publication of these reserve figures. To, however, deliberately publish untrue figures—under the imprint of a governmental agency—raises some moral issues, at least for simple minds.

Yet, though the Bank of England's deplorable habit of releasing untrue reserve figures is universally known, it does not follow that the monthly trickeries do not sometimes work. It is intriguing, but apparently correct, that the regular publication of the Bank of England reserve figures—which are known to be inaccurate—has not proved entirely self-defeating. People in close touch with the money market claim that the discredited Bank of England releases actually influence the operators, and that the money market still (however slightly) reacts to any newly announced figures.

If despite consistent* misrepresentations, the aura of the Bank of England is still pervasive enough to emanate some credence in the accuracy of its announced foreign reserves, it is no wonder that governments with a consistent record of wrong predictions should also continue to be believed. Kemp rather naïvely suggests that lying governments face a technical dilemma: 'To achieve economic objectives it may be necessary to repeatedly hoodwink the public; but the possibility of hoodwinking derives from gullibility, and even the most gullible will not be deceived indefinitely by the same confidence trick' (15).

I very much fear that Kemp is wrong. The already cited article by Chiang (158) examines how the public reacts to wrong economic forecasting. He shows persuasively that, although the 'acceptance weight' deteriorates with each re-discovery that the forecasters are untruthful

---

* Should my language seem too crude, perhaps the reader would prefer that of *The Economist*. The writers of this journal are not prone to describe untruths as lies; hence they say: 'On Tuesday the Treasury picked a figure out of a hat and solemnly announced that Britain's reserves had fallen by £15 Mn' (159).

and/or incompetent, this does not entirely impair public faith in government forecasts—the 'acceptance weight' never drops to zero.

It seems as if the myth enveloping government oracles is too potent to be destroyed completely. The way British business men reacted to the National Plan in 1965 is a further proof for this surprising phenomenon. A good socialist like Joan Mitchell, who idolizes central government planning of the economy, has given us one reasoned exposition: 'There is little doubt that government forecasts must be better informed than private ones' (42). Obviously this is a convincing explanation when one sincerely believes (as she does) in the implied erudition and competence of civil servants.* It is, however, difficult to comprehend how people who do not share Joan Mitchell's touching faith in governmental wisdom continue to pay attention to government economic forecasts and somehow react to them. Whatever the reasons, the evidence I have managed to sift points to Chiang's thesis being right and Kemp's wrong. It appears to be a fact that governmental predictions always have some repercussion on economic behaviour.

WHY PUBLISH THE TRUTH?

Weather forecasts by the Meteorological Office are frequently attacked for being wrong. The M.P. Gresham Cooke has even carried the fight into parliament, where he has denounced the government for unpredicted foggy weather. He has also castigated the Meteorological Office for forecasting sunshine on a Whit Monday, when the celestial powers decided unexpectedly upon a rain force which developed suddenly over the Atlantic and was blown over the British Isles by a high-speed airstream, thus spoiling the holiday for millions by turning it into a wet and cold day.

---

* Decisions, how much plant and production to plan, imply a substantial element of risk-taking. In an exhilaratingly brilliant article on statistical magic, Ely Devons scrutinizes the widespread view that the central government, the nationalized boards, and their servants in Whitehall, have some special knowledge which enables them to narrow these risks very substantially, if not to eliminate them altogether. Indeed, this imputed superior knowledge has frequently been put forward as an argument in favour of nationalization or public control, because by utilizing it the state can allegedly plan efficaciously output and investment instead of having them determined accidentally by the vagaries of market forces. With a sledge, forged out of examples from British post-war history, Devons smashes this illusory belief in Whitehall's 'special knowledge' (71).

Gresham Cooke's complaint may be frivolous but it has none of the anti-social implications of a resolution passed by the National Chamber of Trade at its autumn conference in 1966 (78). The motion expressed 'concern at the damaging effects that adverse weather forecasts can have on the business of traders in seaside towns'. One can brush aside the demagogic remarks of one speaker that 'the weather forecasters took a sadistic delight in predicting bad weather', and pass over the dubious request of the conference that 'the meteorological experts are urged to take a brighter outlook...', to consider their main complaint. The delegates sponsoring the motion mostly came from seaside towns, where traders depend for their livelihood upon an annual peak period of eighteen weeks. It is factually correct that adverse weather forecasts on radio and television seriously deter people from visiting the seaside, with trading suffering as a result. Their displeasure, however, was not directed at the accuracy or inaccuracy of the forecasts. No one actually said that in the interests of encouraging trade, the Meteorological Office should broadcast false news of sunny weather, but it was implicitly demanded that news of likely bad weather ought not to be *publicly* forecast during the holiday season.

Meteorological predictions have proved much more accurate than economic ones, and there are promising signs that the statistical accuracy of weather forecasts will reach near-perfection in our lifetime. But, some people say, expertise in forecasting does not necessarily justify publishing them. There is a difference between telling a lie and omitting to broadcast the truth. Adults are responsible for the consequences of their actions, and this includes the reasonably anticipated impact of spoken and written statements concerning future events. The seaside traders are not concerned with adverse weather (for which they can hardly blame the meteorological civil servants) but with the damaging effect resulting from a widely disseminated prediction of bad weather.

The publishing of a weather forecast does not affect the predicted weather outcome, though it can have an injurious effect (as was noted above) or a beneficial one (when it warns people to have their raincoats ready). On balance there is probably no case for suppressing forecasts of this kind. The situation, however, is different on the economic scene and a much stronger case can be stated for suppressing honestly calculated stock exchange or GNP predictions. There are economists who believe in the human capacity to make meaningful predictions, but yet think it dangerous to publish them because such predictions can change events and affect the predicted outcome.

The rest of this chapter will be mainly concerned with the ramifications of the Law of Forecast Feedback, that separates weather prophets from GNP soothsayers; the latter (unlike the former) can create an impact which may self-validate, enhance or nullify predictions.

All those who disseminate dishonest predictions, dishonest in the sense that at the time they broadcast them there was no reason to believe in their validity, seek to exploit the possibility of a significant feedback. Actually they do not hope for 'a' feedback, but for a feedback in a particular direction. In a paper read to the American Statistical Association, G. C. Smith warned prognosticators—who think it possible to bring about *specified* reactions—that, whilst the Law of Forecast Feedback always hovers over economic predictions, the *feedback affects the outcome in an unpredictable manner* (67). Dishonest predicting is censurable on moral grounds, but one can add that even for reasons of expediency a government should think twice before hoodwinking its business men. It is almost certain that an authoritative forecast will always successfully displace the economic ship from its set path, but forecasters ought to be made aware that they cannot determine where it will drift to.

THE CROOKS

In order that predictions may leave their marks on human behaviour, the predictors must enjoy an acceptable authority. Unlike GNP forecasts emanating from government offices or academic institutions, those formulated by stockbrokers or individual business men carry almost no weight. In any case the crooks, who engage in dishonest predicting to seek material gain for themselves, have no interest to publicize dishonest GNP projections because any resultant feedback will not line their pockets. The scope of forecasting crooks is therefore strictly limited to predicting such matters as mineral or oil discoveries or the future profits of company A or B. Today, corrupt financial journalists are a rarity in the Western world and an extinct breed in the UK. The wings of unscrupulous share pushers and fraudulent company promoters have been vigorously clipped. Racketeering forecasting, for strictly personal gain, only seems to flourish nowadays in some of the shady private investment letters, but these have a low acceptance credibility.

Economists and accountants who are employed by, or work for, private corporations and banks are sometimes induced to prepare for publication forecasts that are intended to produce a feedback which would advance their principals' interests. Livingston (68) has written about such deplorable behaviour in America and implied that to evaluate predictions one must look to where 'a business economist's bread is buttered'. This seems an unwarranted generalization for not all privately employed forecasters are guilty of such conduct; nevertheless it is reasonable to assume that few private companies (and particularly banks) would allow their staff to broadcast predictions that might damage their profits. Since 1960 a new type of unsavoury forecasting has reared its ugly head on the British scene. In many contested takeover battles, corporations have employed outsiders, or made use of inside staff, to manufacture forecasting ammunition, which after a short time (sometimes only a few months) is proved to have been widely of the mark. When these predictions are exposed as false, the predictors are often defended as 'honest but incompetent'. The new U K regulations that are now being prepared to stop these abuses indicate that 'incompetent' is not always the right word to describe the authors of such forecasts.

The most persistent form of blatantly dishonest forecasting emerges from the printing presses of governments which are ready to tailor projections to impress the donors of economic aid. International agencies and many of the rich countries like to think that their aid will be used in a manner which—in their thinking—will prove most beneficial to the recipients. Many of the receiving counteries are willing to pay homage to the donors' criteria by falsifying existing statistical records and preparing bogus plans in order to maximize the inflow of unrequited funds. As the donors love to see a high proportion of the GNP devoted to 'investments', governments (that have no scruples about issuing fraudulent forecasts) are happy to oblige by predicting accordingly the development of their economies.*

'When the Marshall Plan was being introduced, one of the chief European figures in its administration...told me: "We shall produce any

* There are of course enough experts in the donor countries to uncover these crooked forecasts. International agencies and the rich nations, however, are wary of openly denouncing false predictions, when these bear the imprint of governmental planning bodies; they fear to hurt the susceptibilities of sovereign nations.

statistic that we think will help us to get as much money out of the United States as we can. Statistics which we do not have, but which we need to justify our demands, we will simply fabricate*... In underdeveloped areas there is often an important element of "boasting", besides a general desire to give the questioner the kind of answer he would like to hear, however remote it might be from the truth' (16).

'In both India and Pakistan, the national plans have increasingly become a foundation on which to negotiate for increased external aid. In many Latin American countries, national planning efforts have originated through the insistence of the US, the Alliance for Progress, and the World Bank that plans be developed as a condition for receiving assistance...' (28).

TARGETS DRESSED UP AS FORECASTS

The majority of dishonest forecasts are not proclaimed to impress rich foreign governments but to cajole the indigenous population. False GNP predictions then become weapons in a psychological war waged by governments eager to induce an economic atmosphere which, hopefully, will reverberate the desired repercussions. The predictors elect, according to circumstances, to broadcast either unjustified pessimism or unreasonable optimism. Mosak-Nathan foresaw a US economy doomed to mass unemployment; twenty years later Beckerman and his team painted an exaggeratedly rosy future for the UK economy. Both groups treat their kind of forecasting as virtuous because it aims to impel a faster GNP growth; it is noteworthy that their respective signposts to the future point in opposite directions.

On p. 104 targeting is described as a respectable activity provided it is not cloaked as forecasting. The setting out of economic targets, which describe physically achievable aims, is of no use to the dishonest prognosticator who banks on producing an intended backlash, because this can come about only if business men believe that the predictors have definite foreknowledge of what will happen (and are not merely targeting something that could conceivably happen). Opinions differ about how to spur people on to greater effort and induce a climate of expansion: is the future to be represented in optimistic or pessimistic colours?†

* Some underdeveloped countries with dishonest rulers have the incentive to paint the picture blacker than it is, to predict gloom and to underestimate their future economic growth—in order to attract more international charitable aid.
† To falsely predict economic stagnation may frighten off potential private investors, but many of these governments are willing to take this risk if it will enhance the flow of unrequited assistance given on a non-commercial basis.

There are suggestions to the effect that Americans regard low targets, dressed up as forecasts, as a springboard from which to bounce in order to exceed the seemingly certain future. Other nations, it is said, react best to an unrealistically high GNP prediction; they are not dejected when the predicted goal is not reached (58).

Dishonest pessimistic predictions can also serve another Machiavellian objective, as is illustrated by the following corporate and electoral specimens. In some diversified corporations, divisional heads are sometimes encouraged – at the annual budget sessions – to present their sales targets as definitive predictions. These managers face the dilemma of how to lie. If a division has pending, before the main board, applications for salary increases, augmented advertising appropriations or capital allocations for new plant, it may be expedient to ensure the success of these applications by exaggerating the demand existing for the division's products. By forecasting buoyant sales the expansion plans of the division may be furthered, but simultaneously the responsible manager risks his standing in the company when the false forecasting chickens come home to roost. If, however, the above cogent reasons for misrepresenting the anticipated future sales in an exaggeratedly optimistic fashion do not prevail, the departmental head may opt to cheat in the reverse direction. I have already alluded to the unfortunate tendency not to evaluate predictions by the degree of accuracy. Experience has taught many executives who live in the jungle of intra-corporate jealousies that to exceed their own sales forecasts does not lower their prestige. The opposite is more likely. They will not be denounced as incompetent predictors but instead bask in the glory of having beaten – due to extraordinary efforts – an allegedly reasonable and realistic forecast.*

The party managers of electoral campaigns may face a similar dilemma. A secretly commissioned public opinion poll indicates that the two chief contestants are running neck-and-neck. To publicize this is regarded as inexpedient and to deceive the public is considered praiseworthy if it helps the party to win. Should the voters be told that, according to reliable information gathered, the party faces certain victory

---

* 'One of the most successful men I know is renowned for the gloominess of his views on the prospects – any prospects. There is I believe an element of cynical calculation in the line he takes. Cheerful forecasts, he believes, are bitterly remembered if they are wrong, and not remembered if correct. Gloomy forecasts, on the other hand, are not remembered if wrong because everyone is so relieved. Consistent gloom, therefore, brings a reputation for wisdom' (196).

or defeat? If victory is forecast, this may lull supporters into a state of false euphoria, but it may also induce cliffhangers to climb on to an apparently winning bandwagon. If defeat is prognosticated, this will lower the spirits of supporters but may also prod them to increased activity to avert the prediction coming true. Political leaders in Britain evaluate the mentality of the British people to be such that desired repercussions are best evoked by making predictions which err on the side of optimism.

On the economic scene it is thought more rewarding to forecast as high a growth rate as the gullible will swallow. Those who are engaged in what may uncharitably be connoted as cheating do not of course discuss this in television interviews and their techniques are often only discernible in private conversations or by reading between the lines of official communiqués. Most financial journalists, however, have few illusions about the forecasting character of the government's published plans. In a penetrating analysis of a new National Plan, that the discredited DEA planners were hatching in the summer of 1967, the *Sunday Times* found it more to the point to inquire about the 'usefulness of a 1967–72 plan for inspiring growth psychology' than about the accuracy of the figures it was to contain (88). This cynicism was of course well founded on the deceptive forecasting contents of the first National Plan; its promoters had claimed that it was an exercise based upon the expectations of corporate leaders in the private and public sectors. It was presented to the business world as a forecast which was grounded on the collective wisdom of hundreds of decision-makers who had given the government the benefit of their sectional anticipations. As PEP (62) put it so unkindly:

'It is in fact clear that an upward bias, dictated by political considerations, was a prime feature of the DEA's exercise, since a single rate of growth well in excess of what had previously been achieved was decided on before any information had been assembled from industry...'

As *The Economist* does not like mendacious predictions by foreigners, it has spoken disparagingly of 'the common Jugoslav habit of announcing news before it happens in the hope of increasing the chances of its happening...' (160). Are its own recipes for Britain so different? When the UK faced a new budget in April 1963, the editors felt called upon to give the Chancellor their advice. Some of it was in the form of monetary measures and tax changes, but *The Economist* reserved its *pièce de résistance* for the psychological guns that it wanted the government to shoot with:

'Britain looks to the Chancellor next week for an ambitious target for expansion; he should go for 8 rather than 4 per cent... It would therefore be entirely responsible (indeed almost conservative) to set the minimum target this year at some 6 or 7 per cent. above present levels... Mr Maudling will have failed, both politically and economically, if by the time he sits down next Wednesday he has not burned some new target figure for this year's growth into the nation's consciousness' (161).

The misleading words 'target figures' should be ignored because the editors were not really interested in target calculations which informed business men how many tons of steel could or ought to be produced. What *The Economist* wanted was an authoritative statement by one of Her Majesty's senior ministers that in 1963 the economy was about to expand at a very rapid rate. It hoped that when this forecast had been burned into the psyches and hearts of corporate executives, it would trigger off a backlash of sufficient potency to validate the original target-prediction. Maudling did not seem to think too much of psychological warfare of this kind, but his successors clearly heeded the spirit of *The Economist*'s editorial injunction.

WASHINGTON... AT THE END OF THE LAST WAR

Between the summer of 1944 and the spring of 1946, the American business world had showered upon it predictions of gloom that were to afflict, according to the prognosticators, the US economy as soon as demobilization had been completed. These forecasts were not only read privately by the government but were broadcast throughout the nation. (Press headlines declared: 'Government economists predict 8 million unemployed by 1946.') The bearers of these sad economic tidings were primarily concerned to ring alarm bells about future prospects. Although they all belonged to the economic discipline, they acted as agitators who hoped for a political backlash that would ensue. One large research organization foresaw one third of the total labour force unemployed. The research units of some trade unions projected a post-war unemployment of 20 million. Perhaps the most interesting and influential predictors were the academically trained economists who were serving in the government, amongst whom Jacob Mosak and Robert

Nathan were the most vocal. Even when Mosak's first gloomy messages, delivered in the autumn of 1944, had already become disproved, he continued unrepentantly to propagate his pessimistic prognosis. As late as March 1946, he published an article in which he said that 'the models relating to the national budget show that the American economy faces a threat of severe depression in the post-transitional years, unless the federal government assumes responsibility to maintain stable full employment' (34). Nathan was deputy director and chief economist of the Office of War Mobilization and Reconversion, which also disseminated, seemingly authoritative, despondency. Two of his staff members (E. E. Hagen and N. Kirkpatrick) advised the government in the summer of 1945 and publicized in November of that year, a departmental estimate that the number of the then one million unemployed would swell to 8·1 million by the first quarter of 1946, and that the GNP (calculated on an annual basis) would in that period be merely $161·8 billion. (The arrogance of these decimal points is shattering.) The facts are now easy to establish. The predictors were fundamentally wrong; their anticipated deflation did not materialize but inflation did; the number of unemployed was 4–6 million less than predicted; the GNP and other macro-economic indicators diverged radically from the alarming forecasts—and all this without the requested government interventions. The table below—source (51)—compares these prophecies with the

INDICATORS	Hagen-Kirkpatrick Forecasts	Actual Figures	% Discrepancies
Unemployed (Mn)			
4th quarter 1945	6·3	2·0	215
1st quarter 1946	8·1	2·7	200
GNP (annual) $ *billion*			
4th quarter 1945	164·6	179·1	9
1st quarter 1946	161·8	174·4	8
Disposable Income (annual) $ billion			
4th quarter 1945	119·9	135·1	13
1st quarter 1946	120·9	135·7	12

actual performances of the economy as reported a year later by the statisticians of the Department of Commerce. The GNP and Disposable Income data are seasonally adjusted and given in constant-price dollars (based on first-half-of-1945 prices). To me the most astonishing feature of this *débâcle* is that the projections were made in the summer of 1945 and published for public consumption in the middle of the last 1945 quarter, i.e. only a few weeks before the relevant predicted period ended.

Some economists rallied to the defence of Mosak-Nathan when their erudite glimpses into the future had been disowned by history. Klein, for example, exonerated them from blame because 'errors in forecasting have nothing to do with the validity of many of the underlying theories' (162). Indeed Mosak, Nathan and other fellow prophets-of-doom found that their careers had not suffered by serving up erroneous national accounts estimates.*

There were others, however, who thought that one could not just shrug off this mass wave of wrong predictions that had damaged the public standing of economists and affected the prestige of the US government departments which had publicized them: 'The false economic forecasts should be listed among the major calamities that have befallen this nation in recent years' (163). The Mosaks and Nathans were not put in the pillory, because most business men were just pleasantly surprised that the prophecies of a depression had not materialized. Here and there articles appeared poking fun at the disowned prophets with the sting usually directed at their competence to forecast. This seems to me to miss the main point. The false economic prophets knew their jobs extremely well and many of them were highly skilled technicians. As will be noted below, the reasons for their publishing wrong predictions were deeply embedded in their political philosophy.

Is it fair to deride now with hindsight Mosak-Nathan for making what have turned out to be wrong predictions? In my view, it is proper to do so, because there were at the time other economists busy debunking the hysteria of gloom. They arrived at opposite conclusions not because they were professionally more able, but because they operated

---

* I have found no reference to Mosak expiating publicly his forecasting sins. After retiring as chief of Economic Analysis and Forecasting in the Office of Price Administration, he became a respected professor of economics and later also director of the Bureau of General Economic Research and Policies in the UN secretariat. In the latter capacity, he turned his attention to teaching the under-developed countries how to forecast. He was appointed as chairman of a group of nine UN experts, who published in 1964 'Studies in Long-term Economic Projections for the World Economy'.

with contrasting political guidelines.* (Here is one more instance of the close link between faith in state planning and, what may be termed, the ideology of forecasting.) One of the forecasting heretics was Hahn who explained as early as January 1945 why some American prophets did not trust the economy to adjust itself after the war, and therefore called upon the government to prevent a depression. Hahn stigmatized them as Jeremiahs who describe 'postwar mass unemployment as something that follows more or less perforce from the working of the capitalist system' (36). Backed as the soothsayers were with the authority of the government departments which employed them, few paid attention to Hahn's question:

'How much weight should be attached to these predictions? Unlike Communist and fascist economies, a free economy is directed not by government orders but by the calculations, hopes and fear of millions of people; the objective conditions with which these people will have to reckon, and—even more—their subjective reactions are as unpredictable as the future in general. Therefore estimates of future billions of working hours, of the national income, and of the goods to be produced are nothing but toying with figures.'

Why did so many economic predictions at the end of the last war contain such pessimistic tidings? Was there a purpose behind them? Mosak, Nathan and others were New Deal enthusiasts who operated state controls during the war and conceived it their duty to press for continued state intervention after the war. Although they sincerely believed this to be in the public interest, they were also aware that the majority of the US public, and certainly the business community, rejected these views. Their strategy was to shock the American people with the prospects of mass unemployment in order to create a feedback from their prognostications, and thus bring about a backlash that would permit considerable state intervention in the running of the economy. Mosak said so explicitly when he referred to the threatening dragon of a severe depression. It will come 'unless the federal government assumes responsibility to maintain stable full employment' (34). Livingstone spelt it out:

* Woytinsky makes the point that nearly all wrong forecasts were made by prominent proponents of the Keynesian theory, whilst the predictors from the other schools opposing the prognoses of doom-unless-the-government-steps-in turned out to be right. He concludes that 'the probability that this distribution of errors is unrelated to theoretical differences is extremely small indeed' (163).

'The Robert Nathan forecast of eight million unemployed in 1945 could also have had political roots. Mr Nathan and most of his associates wanted a Full Employment Act, increased Social Security benefits, and a higher minimum wage. To get the cure, they promised the disease' (68).

Woytinsky said of the union projections of twenty million unemployed, that these were disseminated because the labour leaders were 'crusading for full employment through deficit spending' (163). Another American observer said of the theories of gloom that they were 'apparently designed to prove that the job was too big for private industry and that government spending on a vast scale would be necessary to avoid serious unemployment' (38).

Undoubtedly the New Deal economists genuinely thought that some kind of a depression was in the offing, a belief conditioned by their un-belief in the viability of private enterprise. But there are also some sub-stantive suggestions that they exaggerated the quantitative dimensions of their already distorted view of the economic future in order to strengthen the role of the state.* It so happened that their predictions did not produce—though not for lack of trying—the desired backlash and still the forecast depression did not come. As Newbury put it:

'Fortunately for the American people, the business community made its own assumptions and forecasts based on its own separate individual judgements. Business men ignored or discounted pessimistic predictions. The American consumer went ahead and spent his money in fortunate ignorance of what these pessimistic forecasters had expected him to do' (38).

BECKERMAN BUILDS A TOY MODEL

The magnum opus of British forecasters-cum-planners was penned by Beckerman and his associates (9): 655 closely printed pages prepared under the auspices of the NIESR and published by an illustrious university press—it certainly beats the National Plan in size, time dimensions, and the quality of printing. Statistically it is an overawing tome which covers everything from a projection of the billion net ton-

* In a lecture at Harvard in 1944, Mosak asserted dogmatically: 'Only the government is in a position to provide positive assurance of full employment.' He went on to explain that certain private investments ought to be subsidized by the state, the government should establish a price-and-wage policy and broaden the social security programme, etc. (64).

miles of coal and coke to be carried in 1975 by road to the housewife's expenditure in that year on bread and cereal (calculated by the diligent authors in accordance with the expenditure elasticity for various other food items extant in 1960).

Should our political masters and municipal busmen handle this ambitious bundle of printed paper and flick through its pages,* they will say modestly that, whilst they do not understand its esoteric language and are unable to comprehend the mathematical formulas, 'this is good sound scientific stuff'. It has taken Beckerman years to compose this futurist discourse. To what use will it be put? Is it politically motivated? Does Beckerman think of his forecasting as a game? C. T. Saunders wrote the introduction:

'We are not attempting a forecast of what is most likely to happen; it is impossible to make meaningful forecasts for a period of ten years or so, except by assuming that past trends in human behaviour, in policy, and in technical progress, simply continue. That would have been possible, but it is not what we set out to do. We have, on the contrary, assumed that productivity will grow faster than in the past and that British industry will become more competitive in international trade. We believe that we as a community have it in our power to realize these assumptions; we have tried to express them in numbers and to apply them in some details.'

It appears that the Beckerman team selected a 'hypothetical growth rate' to construct a model of what the UK economy should look like in 1975. They chose 3·8 per cent. Because of the size of the book, it is a time-absorbing process to discover why that figure was chosen, but the reasons are cardinal for an understanding of the implicit motivations of the authors. From Saunders's introduction and other comments in the book it seems that the hypothetical rate was selected because it was considered physically possible to achieve this target. ('We have it in our power to realize...') Other remarks indicate that the UK ought to achieve this future projection because other countries have proved such growth rates to be feasible. Having chosen a hypothetical rate, all that can be justly claimed for the numerous tables is that they are 'relevant to the

---

* I am reminded of a group visit organized to celebrate the opening of a new factory. Amongst my companions was an 80-year-old engineer who remarked benignly: 'I notice that most of you are admiring the intricate nature of the machinery of which you understand nothing and are becoming enthusiastic about the aesthetic beauty of the building – I am concerned with the serviceability of the installed plant. You all allow yourselves, so smugly, to be photographed with this seemingly magnificent industrial edifice in the background – will it help you to discover that this plant is technically inefficient?'

solution of problems that will arise within the context of a growth rate such as that we have projected'. No one can quarrel with a game, which is based upon an admittedly theoretical growth assumption and does not pretend to indicate what life will really be like in the mid-seventies.

Authors are ambitious animals. Whether they concede it or not, they want their books to be read and, in socio-economic fields, also to have some influence. Clearly Beckerman and his team are no exception. They are under no illusion that many people will actually read their book. Yet they must surely fear that the few readers who examine it because they are interested in the quantities of the listed end-products (tons of coal, numbers of workers in Scotland, consumption of butter) will ultimately discover the assumptions underlying the numerate portrait of the future. If they find out that the growth rate is a theoretical one, and the calculations based on relatively static premises, they may conclude that the study is of little practical value.

There is nothing explicit in the book to suggest that Beckerman wears the uniform of a soldier in a psychological warfare unit. Nevertheless, it is clear that Beckerman has homiletic ambitions. He wants to create a feedback and, one cannot but conclude this from the coming quotation, wishes to influence the direction of the economy. He does not seek merely to describe the economic future but wants to help shape it. To conjecture the intellectual background of this massive book, the following sentences deserve careful attention:

'In an economy that has been growing slowly, it is difficult to expect acceleration if future growth expectations are simply extrapolations of the past. Persuading the community that a 4 per cent. growth rate will be achieved may not, alone, ensure that it is achieved, but persuading them that only 2·8 per cent. will be achieved is a fairly safe way of ensuring that 2·8 per cent. will not be exceeded.'

The above could be interpreted to mean that Beckerman is not convinced that the average 3·8 per cent. growth will in fact be achieved in the 1963–75 period, but that he believes it to be virtuous and patriotic to use such a relatively high rate for detailed predictions. This is clearly a subjective decipherment, but there can be no controversy about the misleading name of the book. The unambiguous title is: *The British Economy in 1975*. It does not say that a model has been constructed which is founded on a growth rate, that the authors have decided to choose — perhaps for psychological reasons to prod the British businessmen? — without believing that it will necessarily be the actual growth rate of the period. The ifs and buts in the text elucidate that Beckerman does not want his glimpses into the future to be treated as a forecast but he must surely be aware that many naïve readers will nevertheless regard it as such. If I am right in my suspicion that the 3·8 per cent. rate was selected *inter alia* in order to produce a feedback effect, then of course it is vital that the business community should be made to think of the predictions as definitive realistic forecasts. The designation of the book leads one to imagine that its contents tell about what Britain *will* be like in 1975 rather than what it *ought* to, or *could*, be like on certain hypothetical assumptions.

Is Predicting the Economists' Main Function?

'The prophets prophesy falsely, and the priests bear rule by their means; and my people love to have it so.'

JEREMIAH

Most economists do not suffer from self-delusions and few seek solace on the psychiatric couch. Unlike the many business men who talk seriously about GNP forecasts during their luncheons economists know how inaccurate and meaningless (or downright deceitful) national accounts forecasts are. Then why practise this magic craft? Samuelson has an ingenious answer: 'Economists cannot forecast well, but experience shows they forecast the economy better than any other group thus far discovered' (4). This is a euphemistic way of saying that non-economists are marginally worse forecasters than economists. On an island in the Hebrides, where there is no qualified dentist, sufferers from severe toothache turn in the last resort to the local hairdresser who pulls out teeth in a much less clumsy manner than the plumber. Just because the plumber is even less competent, this surely does not provide the hairdresser with the boastful qualification of being a competent dentist. Samuelson's implied defence of forecasting by economists constitutes a weak case, and therefore more powerful arguments deserve to be examined before one can finally conclude that magic and sooth-saying ought to be divorced from the economic discipline.

There are extremists, such as A. Hahn, who argue that as economists (like others) cannot make accurate predictions they should leave it alone altogether. Milton Friedman is in the other corner of the ring; to him the present incompetence to predict accurately ought not to obscure the fact that the advance of economics depends on the ability to predict. Lutz (26) puts forward narrow expediency to support Friedman. Having enumerated a multitude of wrong predictions by leading economists, he comes to the sad judgement that however incompetent economists are at foreshadowing accurately future events, they have professionally no alternative but to continue with prognosticating; otherwise they abdicate their most important function: to act as economic-political advisers.

Some economists dolefully admit that they practise this magic art because they are compelled to do so by their clients. When the City Editor of a London paper writes that 'an economist without a forecast to his name is a sad thing to contemplate' (164), he merely repeats what many business men expect of their hired economists. I can attest from personal experience that economists are often pressed to guess the likely outcome of commercial decisions.

An economist may glimpse into the future and then expound that a, b, or c could happen if a certain course is followed, but he ought to add that external circumstances, uncontrolled by the individual firm, may determine which shall prevail. If bullied to express an opinion as to future macro-economic conditions, he should only open his mouth after he has made it plain that this sort of intelligent guessing is a separate activity, which he is carrying out without the skill that has guided his analytical work and the construction of micro-economic models. Yet such a cautious attitude will frequently condemn him as a useless consultant. If he wants to be cheered, he must follow the after-dinner speaker who arrogantly proclaims himself as a one-armed economist. After contemptuous references to the type of economist who says 'on the one hand...and on the other hand', he declares his practical talents: 'I stick out my neck to predict that the GNP will rise next year by 4·4 per cent.' This will gain him general adulation. He usually sleeps soundly in the knowledge that most of the audience will not remember his prophecy the following year and that consequently nobody will wring his neck.

Academic economists may not be under similar pressures but they have other reasons for soothsaying.* Many of them are adamant that economics is a science, and that the essence of every science is inextricably linked with foresight in its particular territory. This is not the place to discuss the vaunted assertion that economics is a science, but rather to raise the objection that predicting is not a regular attribute of every science. (What did Darwin predict?)

* Jewkes, after moving during a long distinguished working life amongst hundreds of academic economists, reports with a heavy heart how coldly he used to be received when he warned his colleagues that they should not claim for the economic discipline the power to predict (24).

Daniel Bell (47) offers yet another explanation for this hysterical pre-occupation with forecasting. The dominion of science has made econo-mists (and others) secure in the belief that nothing is unknowable. If there are no inherent secrets in the universe, then the future can be predicted with certainty provided one applies oneself to this task with the right scientific methods.

Even in these secular days enough people in the Western world remember how God called on Jonah to rise and go to Nineveh to pro-claim its destruction because of the wickedness therein. At first the prophet refused to carry out this task and only after passing through the belly of a great fish was he persuaded to implement his forecasting mission. When he finally entered that depraved city, he cried out unto the citizens: 'Yet forty days, and Nineveh shall be overthrown.' It is a matter of record that God turned away from His fierce anger after the people of Nineveh had proclaimed a fast and covered themselves with sackcloth 'from the greatest of them even to the least of them'. But this displeased Jonah—and who could blame him? After all he had staked his professional prestige on forecasting something that God had ordained. Jonah relates that at first he did not believe that a gracious and merciful deity would really want to do something so dreadful as to destroy a whole town; yet God compelled him to come round to the view that indeed wickedness must be severely punished. Jonah lamented his fate to have been proved a false prophet.* Of course there was a happy end to this story because God later persuaded Jonah that he ought to be content to have made a wrong forecast. The false prophet recognized that rather than assuage his offended *amour propre*, he should give thanks to God for having spared Nineveh 'that great city, wherein are more than six score thousand persons that cannot discern between their right hand and their left hand; and also much cattle'. The Old Testament does not relate what, I suspect, finally brought Jonah to his reluctant acceptance of God's *volte face*: he probably said to himself that but for his wrong forecast, the iniquity of Nineveh's population

---

* Had God instructed Jonah to go to these evil people in order to *threaten* them with extermination if they did not mend their ways, this would not have con-stituted a forecast. As is known, Jonah obediently made a definite assertion that the town would be destroyed. Perhaps the Lord understood well what a feedback effect is. Had Jonah merely prognosticated the possibility of punishment, the people of Nineveh might not have repented as sincerely as they did when they thought they faced inevitable death. Forecasting, rather than conditional pre-dicting, obviously generates a stronger backlash!

would never have been turned into repentance and a return to righteousness.

Those who are still naïve enough to think that economists have demonstrated a capacity to predict the future with a high degree of accuracy can be referred to the statistical evidence which proves the contrary. It is, however, useless to propose such a course of study to Lutz, because he has already convinced himself of this (and published numerous instances to disabuse the immature of their credulity in the predictive powers of economists). Lutz (26) drags Jonah into his apologia for economic forecasting. He suggests that economists forecasting a crisis which does not come about ought to give thanks, like Jonah, rather than pity themselves for having disgraced their discipline. If the lesson to be learned from Jonah's heart-breaking adventures is that statistical failings are not a criterion by which the forecasting craft is to be judged, if professionals find glory in having been proved wrong, if fallacious forecasting becomes respectable and even virtuous when it generates a pleasing feedback effect – if economists wish to have their work evaluated by these standards, then truly they must deepen their working attachment to broadcasting the shape of the future.*

When he was Chancellor of the Exchequer, Harold Macmillan complained that 'some of our statistics are too late to be as useful as they ought to be. We are always, as it were, looking up a train in last year's Bradshaw.' Macmillan probably intended it as a light-hearted aphorism and did not conceive at the time that it would be remembered for many years thereafter, to be quoted and underlined by those who agitated for a greater allocation of state funds for economic forecasting. This makes it the more urgent to analyse the political implications of this short pithy maxim.

* G. C. Smith probably related the following story to illustrate the benefits to be derived from wrong forecasting – despite the abuse heaped on to the shoulders of the persecuted predictor: 'An economist...in preparing a sales forecast... carefully estimated the customary seasonal drop in January, according to past experience... A new sales manager, anxious to get off to a good start, determined to eliminate the January drop, and instituted an intensive incentive campaign... Instead of a January decline, there was a boomlet. The company president, naturally, berated the economist for a poor forecast. When the economist explained what had happened, the president said, "You should have expected that, and taken it into account." "But sir," said the economist, "if I had taken it into account, the forecast would have been much higher, and the sales manager would not have put on the campaign, and the sales would have been lower, and I would have been wrong again." "As usual," said the president.' (67).

Only railway historians filed past issues of Bradshaw time-tables. For all others, interest centred on the current issues of Bradshaw (when it was still published), because these recorded future time schedules. In contrast, current issues of serious economic statistical journals tell us about past events; they do not foreshadow future schedules of the consumption of instant coffee, labour redundancies in Newcastle or steel exports to Peru—if they attempt these impossible tasks they prove to be very unreliable. There is a streak of political philosophy underlying the comparison of Bradshaw to economic statistics. Published train schedules can reasonably be given in great detail, and are likely to be highly accurate, because the railway authorities have the power to make their forecasts come true (within very narrow margins of error). The economic statisticians cannot determine the future; they can guestimate it or dream about it but unlike the railway technicians they are impotent to forecast it accurately because of the volatility of market forces and the whims of the undisciplined British consumer.

I attach great value to the collation of economic statistics (indicators of past performance), because these expedient tools can helpfully guide corporations and governments to quantify some of their future actions. The plea to hasten the publication of past statistics—in order to bring about a situation in which the current issues of economic statistical journals tell us of last year's happenings rather than of those two years ago—deserves to be heeded. Macmillan almost certainly had this in mind when he quipped about 'last year's Bradshaw'. His saying, however, is now being exploited by planners with predicting ambitions who seek to justify the publication of detailed economic forecasts. They draw sustenance from the Bradshaw analogy to spread the illusion that, because British Rail has enough foreknowledge to publish its future schedules, the state ought also to be deemed prescient enough to discern the exact patterns of the future economy.

When forecasts are exposed as fallacious, the perpetrators of the errors can be exculpated on the shifty ground that the techniques employed were imperfect but that at least valuable lessons have been learned. With more money, more technicians, more computers* one can

* The Westinghouse Electric Company knows much about computers, but they have also learned the hard way, after an expensive four-year comprehensive study of sales forecasting problems in their industry, how useless they are for predicting accurately matters that are ultimately determined by the freely arrived at decisions of unpredictable mortals. Westinghouse started off by dreaming of better sales forecasting methods, based on modern computer techniques,

make certain that next time near-perfection will be reached. I reject this approach empirically by comparing the GNP forecasting errors of twenty years ago with today's to find that there has been little systematic advance. But there is a more fundamental reason for rejecting the notion that in time more refined statistical techniques will make accurate national accounts predictions possible. Being an optimist by nature, I like to think that my grandchildren will not live in a society of automatons. If life remains relatively free and dynamic, it will throw spanners into computers and frustrate any efforts to forecast the coming year's GNP in the same meticulous details with which the Bradshaw tables outlined the future movements of inanimate trains.

The planning ideologist recounts forecasting failures in order to recruit resources for the construction of better divining models. My purpose in setting out the inaccuracies of economic forecasts is naturally different:

I

I must admit that some element of *Schadenfreude*, which is perhaps not a very noble motivation, has influenced me. It is a counterpart to the cocksureness with which people like Myrdal sell their planning recipes to underdeveloped countries; it is a reprisal for the contempt shown by George Brown and his staff to critics of his National Plan when it was launched.

II

When one scrutinizes the economic predictions of celebrities and finds them to have been consistently off the mark, one becomes better equipped to evaluate their current forecasts that have not yet been tested by time. To show that economic magicians have been wrong in the past does not

---

which would lead to Utopian results for production planning and inventory management. They are now expert enough to tell the American Statistical Association: 'The layman erroneously attributes forecasting powers to modern computers. The professional knows better, but he can be criticized for aiding and abetting the lay beliefs' (165).

prove that these same people will again be wrong in the future, but it at least raises healthy scepticism.

III

According to Bauer, 'a great upsurge of interest in forecasting is usually evidence of an unhealthy state of mind, especially of a readiness to welcome panaceas' (8). A society which worships predictors and oracles loses its critical outlook. In an age which worships soothsayers, the emergent credulity threatens to drown rational appraisals that take account of present life with all its sordid and agreeable revelations.

IV

Anti-forecasting blasts may also help to restore the economic discipline to its proper place: to explain the past and the present, to analyse the consequences flowing from an interplay of given factors, and to help laymen to understand trends that *may* shape the future. An over-indulgence in predicting deflects the economist from playing a role in those fields of knowledge where he can make a skilled contribution.

V

Economists, using the tools of their trade, express the future in terms of GNP, sales, hours of work, imports, etc. It is, however, a dangerous delusion to deduce that because certain phenomena are depicted in economic language, their quantitative and qualitative dimensions are necessarily determined by economic causes. The egalitarian British Welfare State, Hitler's confiscation of Jewish shops, the Kenyan land-laws – all these may be considered as appropriate subjects for economic evaluation. Though now part of economic history, they were clearly not brought about by causal factors which are within the economist's professional orbit. To expose the fallacies in forecasting by economists helps to establish that the economic future is as elusive to economists as it is to other mortals, because it is so largely determined by the intrusion of non-economic elements. Economists treat these interferences with 'normal' economic behaviour as 'irrational'. There is a great deal of haughtiness in their assessment of the behaviour of real human beings. Of course it is true that much of life is shaped by the volatile — often deplorable — conduct of adults who refuse to behave in a manner that would maximise their own welfare. If economists wish to call this 'irrational', I have no complaint except to remind them that the prevalence of unpredictable human behaviour disqualifies them from acting as 'rational' forecasters.

Part III

The Virtues of Economic State Planning

Planning has Two Meanings

'While...almost everyone enjoys being a planner, no-one wants to be planned.'

RICHARD LYNN

Planning has become an emotive subject and Adam Smith had better be left out of it. Taxpayers' money for the dental inspection of school children does not necessarily set a precedent for providing adults with free wigs. To preserve the countryside may be a good thing whilst subsidizing the installation of central heating in municipally-owned houses may not be. Free primary school education is socially not identical with awarding companies a grant to establish a factory in Inverness. Arbitrarily fixed emoluments for soldiers are not precepts for the state regulating the salaries of computer operators.

Modern British socialism, seeking to regulate the economy by centralized planning, does not rely on forced labour camps in the Hebrides or the nationalization of all sweet shops. No longer is the legal ownership of assets employed in production, distribution and finance a decisive criterion. It is also possible so to arrange matters that state-owned enterprises, like the railways and the post office, are run on independent economic lines; this depends on whether their managers are given sufficient commercial and financial autonomy. On the other hand, if the government so chooses, it can effectively determine the policies of privately-owned companies and make them operate on pre-determined uneconomic lines.*

* I am referring here to the power of a socialist government to obtain parliamentary approval for measures which tell private corporations how to run their affairs. This is not the same as company executives voluntarily obeying the 'wishes' of the government to carry out policies opposed to the interests of their customers, employees and shareholders. The strange behaviour of most large UK companies in the 1965–69 period, which 'voluntarily' allowed themselves to be dictated to by Whitehall, is a fascinating subject that will undoubtedly be traced in future studies by political scientists; they will need the assistance of sociologists but economists will hardly be of much help in elucidating this non-economic behaviour.

The nature and extent of Western planning depends in the last resort on the political philosophy embraced, however inarticulately, by the majority of voters. The competence and integrity of the civil service, the ownership of assets, the economic performance of nationalized bodies — all these are of subordinate importance to the subjective decisions of the voters as to how intensely they wish their lives to be regulated by the state. Economic theory has little to contribute to this, an essentially political, discussion. Economists had better stop posing as experts, who can make an objective contribution to the planning dilemma of Western society.

Just as in my dissection of the other sacred cows, I shall begin with a conceptual definition. In the case of the GNP it proved helpful to clarify right at the start that it does not deal with all human efforts in the pursuit of happiness but merely with those goods and services that can be valued in monetary prices. A seemingly pedantic discussion, in the introductory chapter of Part II, established that it is worth while to differentiate terminologically between conditional and certain predicting; the word 'forecasting' was reserved for the latter notion. A similar job must now be done for 'planning' in order to clear the decks and get rid of double-talk. So many different things are connoted as planning, that a definition of its nature and scope is a prior condition for deciding how much to love this creature.

At the outset project and corporate planning must be removed from the scene because neither is relevant to the political issues that will be raised. Corporate planning, carried out by company executives, can mean product strategy or the building up of the corporate unit through diversification or other growth techniques; neither depends on political decision-making by the legislators.

Project planning involves the achievement of a specific end in either the private or the public sector. To plan the construction of a £100 Mn nylon plant may be part of, but is not necessarily identical with, corporate planning. If ICI executives are adamant in carrying through such a project planning, they stand a greater chance of achieving physical success than with comprehensive corporate planning. Similarly with the government: attempts to shape the economy in order to produce a 6 per cent. increase in the GNP is a well nigh impossible task. Project planning, however, such as the limited aim of building 1,000 new schools in two years, is within its capability and can be brought to a successful fruition.

'Planning' is of course derived from the word 'plan' and this is where the conceptual difficulties in defining the former begins. 'Plans' can mean many things. According to Brittan, a national plan in an advanced industrial country 'is at the bottom a confidence trick for inducing a favourable view of the future' (157). George Brown's *National Plan* (75) is described by its authors as 'a guide to action'. In Part II of this book I gave several instances of how plans may be (genuine or cheating) predicting exercises. Some plans contrive to formulate targets. One distinct meaning of planning is to draw up plans and involve the economic strategists in 'indicative planning'. Planning in this sense need not frighten people who are concerned with their individual liberties. Of course it is often wholesome to debunk the nature of such planning by exposing the true character of the so-called indicative plans, but basically this type of exercise concerns drafting and not executing. This is neither dangerous nor very expensive. Certainly it is not a government activity which would induce me to man the barricades. Men who wish to remain free need not shoot draughtsmen who prepare conjectural blueprints for new prisons; they ought to reserve their bullets for the eventuality when builders actually construct such an edifice and policemen discharge the orders of imprisonment.

Edward Boyle—who made a touching speech in support of Labour's National Plan (11)—quotes approvingly Dow's definition of planning as 'organized, mutual discussion by private firms and public corporations' (166). *The Economist* similarly opines that the 'virtue of economic planning lies not in the arithmetic of the target figures but in the discussion about growth that they promote' (167). How innocuous it all sounds! Well, that indeed is *one* meaning of planning.

Political passions, however, are not aroused by blueprinting, amicable debating and the mutual exchange of conjectural thoughts. A much more sinister type of planning consists of moulding the economy in accordance with the ideas (and sometimes, but not always, the pre-conceived designs) of administrators able to implement them.* This alternative definition of planning separates the men from the boys. Boyle's

---

* I am drawing a thick black line between people who only propose a course of action and those (having powers to do so) who choose to act. It does not follow, however, that action necessarily achieves the aims the men of deeds intend to attain.

wishy-washy exposition is not politically explosive and leads to the beloved maxim that 'we are all planners now'. Planning, in the terms defined above, highlights the controversial issue of state intervention in economic life. George Brown does not wish to be remembered primarily for his discussions with Neddy and the schemes for Britain's future that his ministry designed. He rightly lays claim to have been a planner in the sense of someone who does things—such as keeping the wages of bakers down, bringing industrial plants to a distressed area, expending public money to keep alive a bankrupt shipyard, etc. When, after the Michael Stewart interlude, a successor had to be found to George Brown, as the ministerial head of the Department of Economic Affairs, the choice fell on a politician who epitomized this disparity between the two main conceptual definitions of planning. Peter Shore had spent most of his working life drawing up plans for the future; he had guided and counselled but had never been able to put into practice his ideas of what was good in the public interest. His first pronouncement on taking over the DEA (that served as the economic planning ministry) was to make it plain to the business world that he was not mainly concerned with planning by discussion and exhortation: 'I'm an interventionist.'

Let there be no doubt that the Labour Party engaged in planning by treating it as a political function of active interventionism. Nationalizations, grants, prohibitions, subsidies, differential taxation, playing around with exchange rates—this is how they accomplished economic facts. When still in opposition, and eager not to frighten the electors overmuch with the intention to forcibly create life conformably to their socialist notions, the Labour Party used to emphasize that it would encourage this, and discourage that, it would steer industry... All this proved largely a play with words. Harold Wilson sent nobody to Siberia and did not even introduce labour mobilization through a resuscitation of the wartime Essential Works Orders. He had other planning tools and they were diligently employed. Nobody was actually forced to buy Welsh coal but production in non-economic pits was artificially maintained through a ban on the use of cheaper coal from abroad and appropriate taxes on imported oil. When three shipyards refused to merge consonant to a Whitehall edict, the Labour planners did not despair: the recalcitrant companies were informed that, unlike other more obedient British shipyards, they would not receive the government credits needed to attract orders from British shipping companies; no policemen were sent out but at the end of the day the companies did obey. At a time when the UK clearing banks had to pay 6 per cent. and more for time deposits, the Bank of England urged them 'voluntarily' to take upon themselves real losses by subsidizing UK exporters with 5·5 per cent. credits, whenever the state-owned Exports Credits Guarantee Department ruled that they should. There are various theories as to how the government was able to accomplish this particular planning; the one known fact is that without chopping off anybody's head the privately-owned banks were made to toe the line.* The Board of Trade found it unnecessary to ask Parliament to pass a Bill, prohibiting new aluminium smelters from having an annual output in excess of 100,000 tons. Yet, in a deal with a foreign company and the Norwegian government, the UK authorities had undertaken so to limit the aluminium output of privately owned companies in Britain. They were able to guarantee this by planning both the location and the uneconomically low output ceiling of new smelters through the simple expedient of telling the potential UK aluminium investors that unless they complied they would not receive state-subsidized fuel — the planning was successful.

The producers of the *National Plan* (75) laconically speak of government 'influence on the use of resources'. State planning, whether for desirable or nefarious purposes, does not influence — it forces and prohibits, constructs and destroys.

Planning, in the sense of the government (directly or indirectly) ordering individuals or corporate managements to pursue specified economic policies (or to desist from doing what they would otherwise have done), is of course far removed from that meaning of planning which refers to the mere preparation of plans. The former is sometimes called 'coercive planning', which thereby attaches a pejorative connotation to the concept. It is, in my view, fatuous to discuss in the abstract whether one is for or against planning. The real question is surely where and how the state is to engage in planning.† Douglas Allen, one of Britain's leading

* The Prime Minister expressed it elegantly: '...we have persuaded the banks to offer...a very favourable rate of interest lending to the export firms' (190).

† From a formalistic standpoint, Western governments are interventionists over a very broad front. Laws appertaining to washrooms on factory premises, fraudulent labelling of merchandise, hygiene in restaurants, employment of infants, etc., restrict managerial freedom. It is, however, nonsense to argue that these interventions constitute centralized planning. They are fringe phenomena which restrict individual liberty to a minute extent only and do not basically weaken the underlying competitive forces of a free enterprise economy.

state planners, would have it that planning is 'a developing science in industry and government' (172). One school of thought maintains that — in so far as certain economic activities are, and others are not, intrinsically suitable for centralized planning — the scope of planning is ascertainable by factual technical reasoning. I reject these so-called objective approaches to the subject, because I consider that all major planning decisions are sustained by the political philosophy of those who hold the reins of state power.*

Unless a government is run by a dictator or an oligarchy who exploit society for their own gains (which need not necessarily be material ones), the motivation for state intervention is always that it enhances the wider public interest. This implies that the government, as the collective agent of the people, makes decisions that seek to adduce greater happiness than would otherwise have been generated by the citizens' individual decisions. There are a number of fields in which centralized planning indeed achieves this welfare objective. One must, however, be quite explicit that every (good or bad) planning activity negates the free working of market forces, i.e. it infers a rejection of individual discretion in production and/or consumption.

Modern state intervention in the economy is advocated on account of social reasons, the interdependence of several branches of economic life, and/or the attainment of economies of scale. In the first two categories, state planning implies the abrogation of the economic calculus of relative money prices as a managerial criterion.†

---

* There are obvious infrastructure exceptions, such as sewage, street lighting, fire services. Individuals ought not to be left to decide personally how much to contribute for the maintenance of the fire brigade. This is a technical issue because the nature of fire hazards is such that flames in my neighbour's house are likely to affect my security and property. But this has nothing to do with the state regulating cotton imports or controlling steel production.

† Let it be assumed that the government of country A, say because of a potential military blockade, plans its farming sector so that all wheat is grown at home. If economists then demonstrate that country A is worse off by this policy than when it had previously manufactured machine tools that were sold to the low-cost wheat producing country B in exchange for wheat, they are introducing irrelevant price calculations. The wheat-planning scheme is inspired by a political consideration; if the people of A accept it as valid, they have deliberately opted for relatively dearer wheat.

I

For a variety of reasons it is undesirable to price certain goods or services in accordance with the willingness or ability of the individual consumer to pay for them. If I am knocked down by a drunken driver, my willingness to pay an extortionate price for transporation to hospital ought not to determine the charge for an ambulance.

Depending on the country's social climate, production and consumption in certain sensitive areas (such as gambling, alcoholic drinks, addictive drugs, military weapons) may be considered matters that ought to be planned by the state. The decision of the Labour government to ban the sale of arms to South Africa is an apt example of such a type of state intervention. It interfered with the economic freedom of U K companies to manufacture goods for willing buyers, it created unemployment, and led to a loss of foreign currency earnings but these economic consequences clearly did not influence a decision which was made to assuage the social conscience of (what was assumed to be) the majority of British people.

II

British Rail is centrally planned by Whitehall and its managers are instructed to operate in a manner, and on a scale, which does not provide for costs to be matched by the charges to rail users. The public is, in part, prevented from freely choosing the services of either road or rail transport, because the government stifles such competition. The State prohibits the unbridled use of road transport; in addition certain measures have been taken which are deliberately aimed at raising its price level (relative to the under-pricing of rail charges). This policy is motivated by the ideology of planning transport as a comprehensive industry. British, German and other interventionists claim that in order to retain the railways at an artificially inflated economic level, they are compelled to plan the competing road transport branch as well. The objective, to maintain a larger railway net than could be justified by the willingness of the public to use it at the charges that would have to be imposed to cover costs, is of course linked with the social consideration of preventing augmented congestion on the roads that would follow a

decline in rail transport. This may or may not be a valid reason to subsidize the railways. The point to note in this context is that in order to
plan the railways and force unwilling consumers to partake of its service
which they would otherwise have disdained, another economic activity
must also be planned; in this case it takes the form of artificially restrict-
ing the expansion of road transport.

Until the discovery of North Sea gas, the nationalized gas industry
was planned by Whitehall to become a stagnant branch. Its managers
were not allowed to expand as fast as they could have done. Its biggest
handicap, which was deliberately imposed on the industry, was the
ban on the manufacture of gas by the cheapest method; they were compelled to use coal when this was no longer economically the most expedient input. Even in 1970 the gas (and electricity) boards are under
Whitehall duress to purchase millions of tons of coal they would otherwise not have bought. The Gas Council has been ordered to desist from
its intention to sell natural gas to the electricity generating boards. The
Labour government went even further by clamping down on commercial efforts of the gas (and electricity) industries to persuade coal users to
switch to the more modern fuels. The gas industry was thus placed into
two straitjackets. The planners justified this by reasoning that their
intervention in the gas industry was linked to the state planning of the
coal industry. Hence, because of the interdependence of gas and coal,
and the (alleged) social desirability of bolstering the production of coal,
the gas industry was planned in a restrictive direction.

III

The economy-of-scale motivation for planning is based on economic,
and not social, reasoning. It is argued that if planners succeed in concentrating the production of all stockings in one large factory, to replace
hitherto 'wasteful' manufacturing in ten small plants, output can be
cheapened and the consumer blessed with lower prices. The same spirit
permeates a planning edict which prohibits the manufacture or import
of more than three types of stoves; this will cheapen servicing and cut
down on the need to stock a large range of spare parts. By forcibly con-
solidating output, the planners also hope to do away with squandering
funds on sales promotion.

This sort of planning can be adjudicated by three criteria: is it indeed a method which brings about cheaper and larger output? Even if the answer is in the affirmative, is the consumer better off with lower prices but without the option to select his purchases from a large variety of goods? To plan calls for the inevitable interference by state officials — even if this can produce a relatively larger output, would society not on balance be happier with a smaller output and less constraint?

State planning for specific objectives, or the regimentation of single or complementary industries, calls for detailed instruction from the government. 'Functional planning' is said to be another breed altogether because, allegedly, it differs from the former type of planning on two fundamental counts: (a) functional planning ordinarily does not involve the planners in a political value judgement as its sacrosanct objectives are said to be accepted by all parties, and (b) its general character influences economic behaviour indirectly and thus obviates the necessity to issue specific, detailed orders from above. I challenge these assertions that functional planning is basically distinct from other types of state interventionism.

Six years of Labour rule have evinced that the logic of functional planning leads inexorably to specific directives. As to its so-called acceptable objectives, one can only concede that planners often succeed in convincing their victims that sacred economic cows are divinely bred and are not a matter of party politics. I do not know of a single broad economic objective which is served by state interventionism (through the use of the multifarious powers of the state to create money, tax, control wages-prices-credit-dividends, regulate import-export, etc.) and does not involve the planners in a political value judgement. Reduce consumption to aid investments...penalize imports to spurt exports... deflate incomes to keep the value of money stable...redistribute incomes to fight poverty...reward companies and unions for amalgamating... maintain the external exchange rate of the currency. The Wilson government sincerely believed that they could call upon economists to render technical advice on how best to implement these aims. British socialists regarded them as objectives which are in their view not only in the public interest but are accepted as such by all responsible, honest and patriotic citizens. It is therefore not surprising that critics, contesting the social desirability of these ends, are treated as traitors, almost akin to the vendors of military secrets to an enemy in war time. In reality the subject matters of functional planning do not revolve round the technical skill of economists and administrators, but on the political validity of the objectives. For example, ridicule for the retention of an antiquated exchange rate may be nurtured by the roots of the same political tree that throws doubts on the benefits to be derived from the nationalization of the steel and stocking industries.

Below are some instances of functional planning. Originally investment *per se* was something virtuous in the UK, but this general state-sponsored ideal underwent a gradual statutory metamorphosis. Investment in selected locations then became particularly desirable. Soon afterwards certain investment goods were condemned as parasitical. Finally a sophisticated points system for rewarding investors – according to location, industry, type of goods, etc. – was established with the state awarding money prizes for the points. (If an investor was especially astute he could earn extra points by individual negotiations.)

Initially all overseas investment was regarded as equally harmful to the balance of payments. Then the planners thought again and began to work with specific instructions that entailed a sliding scale of penalties or prohibitions. Investment in the US was especially bad, in Australia medium, and in India good (and the last was therefore encouraged). Overseas investment by insurance societies was bad, by corporate investors half-bad, and by individuals (building up foreign portfolios) good. The plans have become ever more tailored to individual industries and companies, until today overseas investment planning according to published rules is rarely possible; most cases are considered on their merits by the government.

At one time there was the idea that wage increases should be kept down to defined percentage ceilings which were to be determined by omniscient gentlemen in London. Then the rules were varied to take account of bogus productivity pacts, level of earnings, etc. Finally expediency gained ground and the criterion became whether the economy could afford a strike – consequently busmen and dons were treated harshly and the planners gave in to the dockers and railwaymen.

At first all purchases of foreign goods and services were thought to be bad. Then it was decided that some categories were worse than others; thus to spend a holiday in Italy was wicked (and therefore circumscribed) but to purchase an Italian car was less bad (and therefore unrestricted). The planners opined that the import of Hong Kong toys (to take but one example) must be clamped down on and made subject to an interest-free loan by the importers to the Treasury, whilst – by the use of another arbitrary yardstick—fresh South African peaches could be imported without penalties.

Once the state blessed all mergers. Then it decided that mergers with foreign-owned companies should be subject to planning directives. Afterwards it was concluded that even the amalgamation of British companies ought to be directed in such a manner that the state would decide which were to marry one another. When in the summer of 1968 Rank was about to obtain the voluntary agreement of the shareholders of Cambridge Instruments to a merger of the two companies, the government's merchant bank (the Industrial Reorganization Corporation) did not agree. Rank—perhaps surprisingly in view of the general acquiescence of British companies to the wishes of the Whitehall planners—did not allow itself to be coerced. Rank was told of the Government's wish that its competitor, George Kent, should take over Cambridge Instruments but Rank still would not obey. But, of course, once the IRC threw state funds into the battle, it was able to settle the issue in favour of George Kent. A principle had become established: the general government injunction to British industry to amalgamate is subordinate to the rule that if the planners have a preference for a certain corporate marriage, it is that which must prevail.

Despite the above examples to the contrary, much of British functional planning is still to some extent of a general character. It is when one goes to the under-developed countries that most of planning is found to be in terms of individual treatment for every substantial economic unit.

Many Labour theoreticians have expounded the thesis that planning and competition are twins that can comfortably slumber in one cot. The record of Harold Wilson's administration has helped to prove that competition is anathema to planning.

The most supple planning technique is of course provided by nationalization. British nationalized bodies have sometimes thrown up directors who rebel against encroachments on their autonomy—two troublesome governors at the Bank of England, an independent Beeching at British Rail, a defiant Robens at the Coal Board—but of course such persons can always be sacked and in any case the Treasury holds the purse strings to smother any real autonomous nonsense. On the whole Whitehall has found the nationalized corporations pliant in adjusting output, prices and wages in accordance with instructions.

Thus any highfaluting notions about competition between nationalized corporations are actively discouraged in the cause of comprehensive fuel or transport planning.

It is easiest to regulate state-owned companies; the next most convenient planning receptacle is the privately-owned company which is a monopolist, or enjoys a decisive market domination, in its field. This is why the Labour Party has so enthusiastically supported the merging of large corporations into even bigger octopuses. Monopolists, or near-monopolists, are administratively relatively easy to control and be made to obey the government's will—by carrots of grants and protection from foreign competitors, and/or the threatened stick of differential taxes and references to the Monopolies Commission.

If it is not possible to plan through nationalized corporations or private monopolies, then Whitehall shows its enthusiasm for government-sponsored cartels. Instead of enthusiastically prosecuting firms under the existing legislation governing restrictive trade practices, the Labour Party has exhibited deliberate laxity; there have even been ministerial hints that cartels are not such a bad thing provided they operate to further government aims. Whitehall has not so far succeeded in making compulsory employer membership in the Confederation of British Industry, nor is a union card as yet a statutory condition of employment. Yet many planners think that such measures may ultimately have to be applied to back national collective agreements and state control over wages.

White and Coloured Planning

'One Norwegian newspaper remarked…when a Norwegian econometrician was picked under the United Nations Technical Assistance Scheme to go to India to help work out a better methodology of economic planning, that Norway could have done India a much better service by sending her a fishing boat.'

R. FRISCH

In 1964 T. Balogh reached the British summit of a political economist's ambition: Prime Minister Wilson appointed him to a key position in 10 Downing Street to rescue backward centralized planning in the UK from the inferior status the Conservatives had accorded it in Whitehall. The appointment was most pertinent because, only a short time before acceding to power, Balogh had blasted the Tories in an arrogant— though not untypical—outburst for letting British economic planning reach a stage which placed it twenty years behind that of India. Balogh seemed to imply that the cause of this failure was lack of support from the Tory Prime Minister. The stupendous Indian success, wrote Balogh, was to an appreciable extent due to her leading planner (P. C. Mahalonobia) 'carrying with him the Prime Minister and other political leaders' (12).

One's first reaction to this incongruous flattery of socialist India—or was it meant as a denigration of capitalist Britain?—is to assert that state planning cannot be condemned more sharply than by this comparison. As India's socialists have brought their country to the brink of economic disaster with excessive state interventionism, one ought to give thanks to the Tories for their backward planning which at least assured Britain a slow but steady advance in welfare.

Yet there is much truth in Balogh's suggestion that the Indian leaders were in love with planning. I believe that there is no other country in the world—certainly no Afro-Asian economy—which has given birth to so many books in so short a time on its national planning. It has already been pointed out that the competence of the Indian planners is low indeed, just as the forecasts for that country's GNP and the measurements of its published statistics are deplorably inaccurate. I am well aware that to forecast national accounts in India or prepare meaningful statistics in an under-developed economy are hard tasks. To publicize Indian planning failures may add salt to already sore wounds, but this is unfortunately necessary when so prominent a socialist economist as Balogh foolishly asks India to raise its planning head proudly above the shoulders of the implicitly retrograde British planners. In any case, four years after Balogh's eulogy was written, the Indian government in despair postponed the publication of the 4th five-year plan, and downgraded the once holy Planning Commission to an emasculated advisory body.

There are important features that differentiate state planning in under-developed countries from that in the rich world. Enough experience has accumulated to demonstrate the latent failures of transplanting modern Western techniques of rationing, controls and sophisticated taxes into economies that are neither culturally nor economically ready for them. Marx thought that socialism would be embraced first by developed countries, for only these possessed the preconditions of an industrial and literate society which alone would enable central planning to work smoothly.* As compared with the West, most under-developed countries lack a large staff of trained bureaucrats, a literate population, an uncorrupt civil service and a social acceptance of state laws. Another essential ingredient for comprehensive state planning is the existence of large industrial enterprises; in the Afro-Asian and Latin American countries only a small part of the GNP is produced by (relatively easily controlled) big companies. The output of 100,000 ICI workers can be planned much more efficaciously by Whitehall than the Rangoon administration can plan the crops planted by 100,000 Burmese peasants.

The other main difference has to do with political morality. In the West, socialist and other politicians who practise centralized planning have been elected to do this. Harold Wilson did not outline to the British electorate that he would introduce legislation to control wages-prices-dividends, but the voters knew that the Labour Party stood for more state interventionism and less private enterprise. In a way they opted for state planning—but they also had the chance at the next election to express their disapproval by displacing the party devoted to

---

* Today everyone knows that Marx was wrong. What is, however, even more tragi-comic is that as the Comecon countries are frantically seeking to raise themselves to the cultural and industrial level of Western Europe, they are beginning to turn away from comprehensive central planning.

planning. In the vast majority of under-developed countries the electors are not given an opportunity to make this meaningful choice and are stuck with centralized planning whether they understand and like it or not. They can only resist encroachments on their liberties by frustrating the planners in ways that we, in the West, would regard as improper.

I have had many talks with international civil servants who genuinely believe it to be their mission to help impose state planning on under-developed countries; in their opinion these economies need it more than the West because they are at a lower cultural and economic level. This mirrors an interesting clash between what international agencies deem necessary and what facts show to be feasible. Myrdal (6) has given expression to these sentiments that appear to be a hotch-potch of Western paternalism, ethnic superiority and intellectual snobbery—and show a complete disregard for the economic and cultural substructure that must first be formed before planning can be attempted. (This is said on the assumption that one wishes the presently under-developed countries to become victims of the scourge of planning once they have reached a higher stage of development):

'Economists now generally endorse the opinion that the under-developed countries need much more planning and state intervention if, under very much more difficult conditions than the now-developed countries ever faced, they are to have any chance of engendering economic development.'

Myrdal is a leading exponent of theories that outline the benefits awaiting all mankind through state planning. He is entitled to express these views, though he has no right to the pretentious assertion that all members of the economic discipline accept planning as a sacred cow. Highly significant is his phrase that under-developed countries need 'much more planning'—much more than what countries? More than Sweden needed when it first built the Stockholm University? More than Sweden needs now?

There is something reprehensible in the sentiments expressed by people who are devoted advocates of free enterprise for Chicago, Stockholm and London, that the poorer nations of the world need the authoritarian directive of state planning (aided by international funds). Quite apart from the objective difficulties to which I have already alluded, this seems to smack of an economic racialism, according to which the West can do without the whip of centralized planners while the poorer, mainly coloured, people of the world need it badly.

The Ten Facets of the
Planning Gem

'What rotten planners, who make no allowance for the unexpected and make no allowance even for the misfortunes which they themselves have engineered.'

ANON.

PRESTIGE

Individuals, corporations and unions all have their pride and adorn themselves with prestige symbols. None like to admit to failures, but there is a limit to their self-indulgence. Even when a pet objective fails to live up to the planned expectations of its promoter, there are usually means to continue for some time and hope for the best. Yet there is always a day of reckoning: it comes when the individual cannot borrow any more, the shareholders of the company scream about the loss-making venture, and union members threaten to unseat the responsible officials. Then begins the painful procedure of cutting one's losses. It is a humiliating process to be forced to admit that one was wrong, and in the private sector people can lose their managerial jobs for having been bad planners. One of the merits of the large US corporation is that, having invested in what turns out to be a bad project, managements are quick to liquidate their ill-conceived ventures. But sooner or later, all individuals and non-state bodies are compelled to change course when their original planning has gone awry. Although many would like to continue stubbornly with discredited plans, without subsidies from the public purse they often have no choice but to drop loss-making operations.* Some must even sell prestigious office buildings to avoid bankruptcy!

* Although post-war Britain did not need an expanded coal industry, state resources were made freely (and cheaply) available to the National Coal Board. Once a policy of heavy capital investment in modernizing pits had been decided upon, it was a formidable job to halt this planning enthusiasm even after it had become apparent that the British people did not want or need coal as their main fuel. The cardinal question to ask is whether the coal industry in private hands would have been able to attract capital for the modernization of the mines at a

Governments seem to feel the need for external prestige symbols in inverse proportion to their countries' wealth. Ostentatious and luxurious living standards for the ministers and civil servants of countries in receipt of substantial foreign charity is not uncommon. The large limousines in which the diplomatic representatives of poor nations drive in the Western capitals to finance ministries and international agencies to ask for more aid have been the subject of wide and acrimonious publicity. Nevertheless, such shameless behaviour — which according to Western apologists is conditioned by the emergence of healthy nationalism — is not of any economic significance. It may be censured as politically unhygienic but obviously does not entail the misuse of any but a minute part of resources available to under-developed countries. What is truly damaging is the expenditure of funds (mainly aid) on economic prestige symbols, the purpose of which is to beget the coveted 'international demonstration effect'. The formation of national shipping companies and airlines, the magnificent conference halls for international gatherings, the underutilized nuclear reactors, motorways and ports — Nkrumah's Ghana was not at all exceptional! Milton Friedman, who was one of the first to call attention to this construction of economic monuments, has pertinently pointed out that these paradises flourish because the planners are aided and abetted by the relative over-supply of financial resources in the hands of governments, which do not have to explain to any meeting of shareholders the profitability of their past and future planning (66).*

The Report of the Estimates Committee dealing with overseas aid, and particularly the minutes of the evidence, constitutes a valuable document, illuminating the state of mind of the senior administrators in the recipient and donor countries (18). The witnesses went out of their way to say that whilst one 'could also, of course' make out a very good economic case for prestige projects, one ought not really to be concerned with prestige but with what is best for the under-developed

---

* Oscar Niemeyer is a famous architect and Marxist. He does not like working for private clients because 'they are always changing my plans for economy's sake'. His critics say that he sometimes ignores construction problems and has been known to forget things like kitchen windows in private dwellings. Under the circumstances one readily accepts that he 'is happier with the freedom he enjoys on large-scale government projects' (169).

---

time when the future profitability of the industry was so precarious. If the answer is in the negative, it would indicate that the private ownership of the mines could have prevented a tremendous volume of misinvestment.

country. Yet their evidence points clearly to the vital role played by the public relations perspective. The High Commissioner in Pakistan: '...a piece of project aid like the electrification of Lahore Railways is an identifiable project which is identified with Britain from the general public relations point of view. That has certain advantages. On the other hand, nobody happens to notice that a few marine diesels for fishing boats happen to have come on aid.' The following is taken from the questioning of the representative of the Treasury who deals with the finance of overseas aid:

'What is the view of the Treasury about project aid?' 'There was undoubtedly about ten years ago an era of big projects in India and elsewhere, big steel works, big dams, projects which the developing countries thought brought prestige to them as well as opening up the prospect of tremendous advance, and which also was thought to bring prestige to the donor countries.' 'Do you think the donor countries looked on these big projects as being valuable from a prestige point of view?' 'Without doubt both donor and recipient countries did.'

Planning by the state suffers from the severe handicap that it is often irreversible (or at least difficult to rectify) when the original plans are shown with hindsight to have been wrongly conceived, or to demand fundamental alterations because of a change in circumstances. The haughtier the political leaders of a country, the less prone are they to admit in public that they have planned wrongly. Planning by the state is also particularly dangerous in that the government can frequently find finance to continue with processes that represent a wasteful allocation of resources. The private sector, unless bailed out by benevolent state planners, has to back its judgement with money which yields a profit to the lender. Of course the prestige of private planners is also blemished when investments prove a failure; yet, unless they can find fools to throw good money into a bad pot, the stark reality of commercial duress forces them to desist from continuing with a silly venture. Governments, who know that their standing with the people would suffer from a confession of failure, often find ways and means of persisting in a folly that ought to have been stopped.

Although these strictures on state planning apply universally, there is a relevant schism dividing the majority of under-developed countries from the parliamentary democracies of the West. The presence of a free press and parliament, that publicize misinvestments and scorn the planning extravagances of civil servants, limits the scope of stubborn state planning agencies. When the Attlee government used taxpayers' money on a grandiose groundnuts scheme in Africa, the misadventure was stopped because of articulate public criticism. This planning only cost the UK a few million pounds. Had the Labour Party not had to reckon with the democratic structure of Britain, the socialist groundnuts would probably have entailed a loss of tens of millions. However perilous all centralized planning is, the hazards are much smaller in a democracy. The citizens of Indonesia have more to lose from the rashness of their planners than the people of Britain have cause to fear the bureaucrats in Whitehall.

PATRONAGE

Planning, in the sense of doing as opposed to the mere drawing up of plans, is implemented by a bureaucracy which regulates the economy by awarding material prizes (grants, tax favours, guaranteed government purchases) to the obedient, and which heaps penalties (levies, extra taxes, or outright prohibitions) on the disobedient. The more refined the planning, the greater the freedom of the bureaucrats to hand out prizes and penalties tailored to each individual case.* This is the source of corruption, the widespread nature of which in Latin America and the Afro-Asian continents is known to everyone who wishes to know. Most of it enriches the pockets of the bureaucrats but some of the graft is destined for the coffers of the ruling political party. Although in many cases it is just a way of augmenting their own income, improper behaviour by the providers of state patronage may also take the form of awarding unrequited favours to friends, relatives and members of ethnic, tribal or political groups to which the officials belong.

Planning an economy is rationally defended as a technique to augment the volume of welfare beyond the level it would reach by the free interplay of economic forces. In practice this aim may be frustrated when the

---

* Western planning is supposed to be conducted along publicized lines that make it unnecessary for state officials to judge individual cases. As a generalization this is true when compared with most Afro-Asian planning, but there are vast commercial terrains in Western countries where the bureaucrats can and do discriminate between applicants by the use of indeterminate yardsticks. Anyone who has dealt with the Board of Trade or the exchange control authorities of the Bank of England knows that in certain important fields there are few fixed rules. The applicant is at the mercy of what the officials think (or are told by their political masters to think) is in the public interest.

moral fibres of a society are attacked by the virus of corruption. Economically it may prove damaging when planning decisions are formulated with an eye on the spoils that can be secured by the planners, when the size of the bribe (rather than the public interest) determines the bureaucratic judgements. In December 1968 the United National Independence Party won the general election in Zambia with the slogan: 'It pays to belong to UNIP.' President Kaunda ordered that trading licences should only be issued to members of his party. Such methods proved successful expedients in rigging the election. Were they an equally good expedient for the economic welfare of Zambia?

Except in some municipal areas, corruption of this kind hardly exists in the Western countries. The French planning expert who arranges subsidized state credit for an electronic firm, the Dutch official who makes an investment grant available to an American investor, the Board of Trade inspector who allows a merger to go through — none of them receives a 'cut' in a secret Swiss banking account. This absence of personal (or political party) corruption in the West contrasts sharply with the practices in under-developed countries. Contrary to Myrdal's assertion (p. 181), this is a vital factor underlining why backward economies can ill afford the luxury of planning.

A different type of state patronage, prevalent in the West, is fed by the (partly) discretionary powers of the personally incorrupt planners. It often leads to a misallocation of resources, which is no less severe than that brought about by mercenary corruption in the less developed economies. When planning takes the form of controlling the private sector, the state apparatus bullies firms to act in a manner which negates economic expediency but serves the (real or imagined) public interest, or the cause of the political party in power. The techniques of the Whitehall planners are not to be found in any published manual but are nevertheless highly effective. Merchant banks depend on the good will of the Bank of England and sometimes accept hints on how to act even when this does not help their customers. Corporations who sell most of their products to the nationalized corporations feel themselves (often erroneously) subject to Whitehall pressure. Some private companies calculate that by obeying the non-statutory wishes of the planning bureaucracy, they may escape possible adverse treatment or, even better, become known as 'good boys' who deserve a cream cake to be supplied by the taxpayer at the behest of well-disposed civil servants and ministers. After all, the state has much to offer: cheap credit, permission to borrow while this is refused to others, discretionary grants, the setting aside of anti-monopoly and cartel regulations, subsidies, exemptions from exchange controls which are applied to competitors, bent price controls, and many other bountiful gifts. In their turn companies may be expected to comply with requests to export at a loss, acquire bankrupt competitors, desist from making foreign purchases, buy from designated sources, invest in certain regions (in the home country) or under-developed countries as may suit government policy, charge government buyers less than private customers, institute a closed union shop, continue with uneconomic production in order not to embarrass the government with labour redundancies, etc. All of these, and other elements, are reported from the U K; in some other non-communist countries planners have even stronger fists than have their British confrères.

Certainly the private U K sector is not regimented enough to react always, or even predominantly, with respect to edicts from Whitehall. A good example is provided by the doubtful custom of British companies (168) to make contributions, without their shareholders' explicit consent, to the Conservative Party. The Labour government enacted a Bill which made such contributions public knowledge. Its hope that this would turn off the tap was dashed because, unlike several U S corporations with U K businesses that had previously contributed to the Conservative funds, many British companies refused to be intimidated by possible reprisals from Whitehall or the procurement officers of nationalized corporations. The socialist planners therefore still have a long way to go before they can impose their will upon the whole private sector of the U K economy. Clearly, the bigger the scale of the public sector, the easier it will prove to plan the remaining privately-owned firms.

Regional political considerations play an important role in swaying state officials from applying their authority to maximize the national interest. Free enterprise U S A is the country which exemplifies, par excellence, the location of federal state projects and the expenditure of federal funds in accordance with the pressure that state senators and congressmen are able to exert by blackmail and the barter of their votes. It is significant that some British government subventions have been geared, for reasons of electoral expediency, to the establishment of *several* production units in different development areas of the country when *one* large viable unit ought to have been built. In many other countries the uneconomic multiplication of publicly supported ventures is the price that has to be paid for government interventionism. The planning of nationalized corporations is particularly prone to the influence of regional considerations. It is much easier to compel the managers of state-owned corporations than private firms, which have to be rewarded or severely bullied, to keep uneconomic production running in areas of high unemployment. The leaders of the Labour Party in the distressed Cumberland area once begged the Wilson government that, if it was unable to force private companies to establish factories in their area, it ought at least to compel the nationalized corporations to do so. Not all such appeals are heeded by the Whitehall planners, but the artificial siting of many government offices and factories bears witness that local party officials, and not economic logic, do often determine the location of new ventures.*

THE DISGUISED PLANNING COSTS

Planners act in what they think is the public interest. When they cover a nationalized corporation's losses or subsidize a deserving private company, they do so in the declared belief that the resultant expenditure of taxpayers' money buys national welfare. In some cases this is true. Yet if planning, as I have repeatedly argued, is a political decision then the electorate ought to be allowed to evaluate the specific worthwhileness of large slices of state intervention. This it can only do if the true individual costs are calculated and the information disseminated. In many underdeveloped countries planners do not need popular consent, but in Western democracies planners indirectly depend on it. They consequently have an incentive to ensure that the public is given a distorted picture of the costs of state planning. E. Rolph is both an economist and wedded to the democratic rule of government, which explains why he holds the unpopular view that

'...in a democratic society, people should be aware of what their government is costing them. Such information is indispensable for intelligent judgement about the desirability of expanding or contracting particular government functions... Public accounting should ideally provide the cost information in an unambiguous manner' (102).

* U. Tun Wai—cited in (7)—has this to say: 'Another aspect of planning in Burma was that projects were at times included either for political considerations such as obtaining votes in an election or because of the personal preferences of one or more ministers.'

One hears a great deal about the social benefits accruing to the British people from the maintenance of an inflated coal industry and a commercially over-extended railway net. Officially it is said that the magnitude of these social costs can be ascertained from the size of the published deficits of the National Coal Board and British Rail. In fact, however, the full costs are considerably higher because in addition to allocating tax revenue for covering the deficits, the economy also has to bear relatively higher fuel and transport charges which result from the planners' interventions in road transport and the non-coal fuel branches.

The planners' smokescreen, that the deficit of British Rail is due to social considerations aimed at preventing congestion on the roads, deserves to be scrutinized critically. Undoubtedly this element exists and may well form the basis for a socially justified subsidy to rail transport, but in the present accountancy atmosphere surrounding public corporations social considerations are deliberately mixed up with commercial factors which produce a loss for non-social reasons. The social benefit argument is often an alibi for the uneconomic running of an industry. In many parts of the world private air, shipping, rail and postal carriers receive a defined subvention from the state coffers for performing an uneconomic, but socially desirable, function. In those cases, however, the measure of the cost of the social benefit is clearly discernible from a reading of the public accounts.

All over the world planners have evolved means to disguise the cost of planning. Where multiple exchange rates abound, it is easy to give favoured importers and government bodies allocations of foreign currency at a low exchange rate (in terms of the local currency) and charge others a high rate. 'Tax Forgiveness' exempts state corporations from levies imposed on the private sector, or enables them to recruit funds at an effectively lower interest rate because of partial or complete exemption from direct taxes. Banks are compelled to make loans at low charges to certain (public and private) corporations or for favoured causes, and told to recoup their losses by collecting relatively higher charges from other borrowers. These are only some of the many ways to hide from the public gaze the comprehensive cost structure of centralized state planning.*

* It is not uncommon in the English-speaking countries for governments and municipalities to be allowed to recruit funds through the trickery of offering bonds, the interest on which is tax-free. In 1969 the new Socialist Chancellor thought it morally justified to charge 30–45 per cent. (long-term) capital gains tax on the disposal of capital assets but to exempt certain government securities.

THE INVESTMENT MANIA

Is there a greater negation of socio-economic liberty than to deprive adults of the freedom to choose between consumption and saving? The power of planning bodies to decide the proportions of the national product that are to be saved-invested or currently consumed has far-reaching social and economic repercussions. This type of state interventionism cannot be justified on grounds of social costs, or economies of scale, or for any of the other reasons that are usually given for nationalization and the payment of subsidies. The investment cult is based on an arrogant paternalism which asserts that people must delay enjoying some of the fruits of their labour in order that they or their children may have a better life ten, twenty, thirty years hence. It is part of Western tradition that a responsible person should set aside some of his current earnings in order to create a nest-egg for emergencies, the welfare of his children, and old age. The decision to do so, and to what extent, ought—in my value judgement—to be a personal one. Socialists disagree, because they see it as a function of the state to decide upon the dimensions of the national volume of savings. Socialists are not frantically interested in voluntary savings because they know that the state can always create forced national savings.

The Labour government followed the precedent set by its Tory precursors to tax income derived from savings at a higher rate than that charged on income derived from work.* It would be fallacious to attribute this discrimination to some fiscal technicality; it is in fact part of a political ideology which treats the fruits of private savings as socially less desirable than the proceeds of work. Modern Western society—not only the UK which however excels at the game—deprecates savings that have been made by the voluntary decision of the individual. High income taxes, capital levies, prohibitive inheritance duties...all teach the individual that freedom to save does not connote freedom to enjoy the full benefits of his savings. Some of the social legislation in the UK pointedly punishes an older man for having saved in his younger days.

* To tax so-called earned and unearned income at different rates strikes at the root of equity implicit in a progressive income tax. The British system adds insult to injury by applying this discrimination only to those who are not rich. Income derived from savings is only taxed at a higher rate than income from work if the latter does not exceed £10,000 per annum—beyond that range the tax rates are equal.

There are no limits to the collective savings approach propounded by the planners. Companies can be statutorily compelled to withhold the distribution of profits and individuals made to accept some of their emoluments in 'forced savings'. High taxes are of course the favourite method to divert consumer income into investment funds, which are then placed at the disposal of sagacious state officials. Business men are enamoured of tax reductions (when investment allowances are given) or of open subsidies (when outright grants are made); in both cases the government finances these subventions by imposing higher taxes than would otherwise be necessary and thus again reduces the disposable income available to individuals to opt voluntarily for consumption or saving. Governments in the West do not raise all their investment funds through taxation. They also borrow money and if state investments do not yield enough profit to pay for the interest, then the latter is of course covered by additional taxes or borrowings.

When the Bank of England proclaims its periodic credit squeezes, it is always careful to tell banks that whilst they are expected to cut down on lending for consumer goods, and working capital for businesses, they are to encourage investments at the expense of these other, allegedly inessential, demands. Under the Tories, the corporate profits tax was regulated by the amount of retained profits, i.e. the more companies saved, the smaller their tax liabilities. When the differential profits tax was abandoned, a new type of discrimination favouring investment was introduced. Corporations were permitted to write off from their tax liabilities not only the statutory depreciation of assets but also the bonuses (called investment allowances) given by the state to reward investors. Harold Wilson's government went a step further. It was so imbued with the merits of investing that it dropped the reactionary Conservative practice of paying these bonuses only when the investments had actually yielded a taxable profit. The socialists replaced the investment allowances with investment grants which are now given for the act of investing irrespective of whether the projects have laid any golden eggs that are subject to tax. Investing is so saintly that socialists do not wish it to be blemished by irrelevant Tory considerations relating to profitability.

Why are the planners so successful in canonizing their investment ideal? Why does it prove a relatively easy task to put people into a savings straitjacket with talk of a sweeter life to come? My feeling is that the state planners of long-term investments are sheltered from public indignation, because the benefits or drawbacks cannot be expected to surface for a long time. When a government nationalizes the stocking industry, this measure can be adjudged by the customers within a few months; it will soon become known whether capitalist or socialist stockings are cheaper and of better quality. When an electronic monster is built and the construction period is ten years, the planners can always argue that the benefits of this investment ought to be evaluated on a long-term basis. Accountability is then successfully shelved.

At the end of the fifties, millions of pounds were invested in housing miners, infrastructure and machinery in order to raise production at pits that have since been closed down. In 1961/2 an £11 Mn Lurgi gas plant was erected in Warwickshire, when this manufacturing process, depending on low-grade coal, was already outdated; the plant was finally closed down in April 1969. To finance these investments, the British people were told at the time to tighten their belts and pay extra taxes in order that the government might assist the declining coal industry. It is obvious that the British economy would have been better off if this investment had not been made and proves that investment *per se* is not always a good thing—what matters are the right investments. But they demonstrate, in this context, an even more significant truth. When the state made these compulsory investment-savings decisions on behalf of the taxpayers, many critics pointed out that the schemes were not economically feasible.* The proof that these critics were right was delivered only many years after the damage had been done. No one has been punished because few people remember that these pit closures were not the result of divine tribulations but consequences flowing from the errors of human planners. The short memory of their victims powerfully aids state planners to channel, forcibly, present resources into seemingly attractive long-term investments.

The investment fetish strikes particularly hard at the poor in underdeveloped countries, who are deliberately made even poorer by their masters with promises of pie in the sky. The message is often sincerely intended and the prospects of ultimately delivering a baked pie for postponed consumption may be genuine; yet it is a slumming attitude of socialist paternalists that forces people to suffer for a future paradise that the poor would rather forego if they could only have some

* A parliamentary committee, appointed in November 1960, expressed its doubts about the economics of the projected Lurgi plant (69).

pottage now. Little and Clifford (13) are not hostile to planning in under-developed countries, yet they too find themselves forced to protest:

'Why, and with what possible justification, should we urge that the poverty-stricken should save more for future generations? Why should we prefer the poor to save what we give, rather than consume it? Why should visiting economists go round advising how to raise the incidence of tax in poor countries?'

Just as the rich countries give priority at home to investment goods, so are they wary about extending aid—or subsidized long-term credit— for consumer goods to the poor countries. The leaders of the latter know better than to ask their rich friends for bicycles, meat or blackboards; to the donors these are unproductive items and have none of the putative welfare features of nuclear reactors and large turbines. In most cases the governments of the under-developed countries are not averse to complying with the demand of the rich nations that aid should be used primarily for long-term investment projects rather than for the immediate alleviation of social misery, because the intellectual planners of the poor countries are also infatuated with the investment mirage. They show little readiness to allocate their own, and donated, resources for the import of consumer goods, seeds and fertilizers which would mitigate the poverty of the masses, and help their GNPs to grow with the aid of the physical capital already on the spot. Their exchange controllers prepare a red carpet for applicants who wish to bring in investment goods. When multiple exchange rates are in force, the favourably-priced rates are naturally reserved for machinery, etc.

Myrdal of course is in favour of democracy, not only for Sweden but also for the under-developed countries. Yet there is an open clash between the democratic wishes of the mass of the population in the poorer parts of the world and his advocacy of a policy of augmented savings-investments which he is selling to the political decision-makers. At least he has no doubts himself that the solution is one which negates democracy as it is understood in the West: 'Undoubtedly democracy... makes it more difficult for governments to hold down the level of consumption in the degree necessary for rapid development.' Recognizing this, Myrdal does not hesitate to propose a solution which by the choice of his word 'compulsory' epitomises the international do-gooder who is willing to ram long-term investments down the throats of hungry and unwilling people: 'There is no other road to economic development than a compulsory rise in the share of the national income which is withheld from consumption and devoted to investment' (199).

Obsession with happiness-in-the-future is a characteristic of the modern breed of planners whether they are active in poor or rich countries and it has no colour bar.

LONG LIVE INDUSTRIAL MACHINERY!

Socialists display a tendency to regard manufacturing industry as the chief source of wealth-creation, as the most productive part of the economy. This causes them to be biased against the marketing function, agriculture and the service industries. It follows from this approach that the state must give priority to industrial development at the expense of other sectors. Many policies of the UK government are inspired by this political philosophy and find expression in its formulation of credit restrictions, labour cost subventions, export subsidies, payroll taxation, etc. The socialist credo on the superiority of production in factories is also affirmed in the distribution of the massive grants given by the Board of Trade to induce investments. (According to official thinking, investment in hairdressing establishments or food shops does not merit state aid; this is reserved for industrial manufacturing.) The most luscious grants are not available just for any type of investment in manufacturing, but are reserved for the purchase of *new* fixed plant and machinery. Equipment, to qualify for grants, can be imported or made at home, but it must not be second-hand.

Several White Papers elucidate that Britain's growth can best be accelerated by the installation of new industrial equipment.* Few have dared to question the validity of this specific investment cult, and consequently state funds have been settled on many spurious projects that would never have attracted risk capital from private savers. At one

---

* This of course is an unwarranted assumption. Investment in transport, better management, and scientific research can often produce bigger eggs. Investments in retail distribution have been no less helpful in raising the British standard of living than has electronic equipment which has made car production cheaper per unit of output. The investments in Marks & Spencer merchandising and Sainsbury supermarkets, financed by private voluntary savings, have resulted in an accretion of human happiness which is as weighty as the benefits derived from improved production methods in factories that have been aided by state subsidies obtained through forced savings.

stage—as the Board of Trade foolishly boasts—the combined package of 'free depreciation' and grants meant that within two years of laying down a plant in Northern Ireland and the Development Areas the investing firm could recover—from the taxpayers—80 per cent. and 73 per cent. respectively of its capital expenditure. No university degree is needed to appreciate that when an investor need only find 20 per cent. of permanent capital to finance a new factory, with the state providing directly and indirectly 80 per cent., the economic calculus of evaluating a project by genuine standards of profitability is not called into play. Although in 1970 the state subsidies for industrial investments in these areas were 'only' 50 per cent. and 40 per cent. (plus normal depreciation), this lavish bearing of gifts still continue to distort corporate investment decisions.

But is it really always true that the welfare of the British people is best and most rapidly advanced by the state prodding private investors to buy new fixed industrial machines? Many other things often produce faster and more lasting results. A reform of the anachronistic system of apprenticeship and an abolition of the time-honoured institution of 'mates' enable production per man-hour to rise without any concomitant expenditure on machines, as has been demonstrated by companies which have overcome trade union conservatism. A reduction in direct taxes—which are in Britain particularly high, *inter alia* because of the state policy of subsidizing selected investments—could also raise production with existing resources and counter the brain drain of skilled labour from Britain. Perhaps the most inimical feature of the programme, that gives priority to the acquisition of new machines (many of which are imported), is that it militates against a full and economic utilization of existing plant. The most efficient way to raise output in industry is to work a second and third shift. Yet entrepreneurs are indirectly discouraged from doing this. When companies apply for bank credit to obtain more working capital for multi-shift operations, they are told that the credit squeeze does not allow this: available financial resources plus state subsidies must be diverted to new machinery—it sometimes proves easier to buy additional machines than to exploit existing plant more intensively.

Most British industrialists are wary about looking a gift horse in the mouth. Yet some have been willing to speak up and say that the investment subsidies have made little difference to their acquisition of new, technologically advanced, plant. It is the economically unsound projects that have truly benefited from the investment grants, for some would otherwise not have been realized.

Although unhealthy priority for industrial machinery has proved mischievous enough in the UK and other rich countries that indulge in such state planning, the damage in the under-developed countries, caused by this political infatuation, is many times more serious. The preoccupation with increased heavy industrial equipment has brought about ludicrous situations where scarce foreign currency is allocated for machinery, while none is available for the import of sufficient raw materials and spare parts to utilize it. A shining new factory in an under-developed country may actually worsen the balance of payments, because operating it may require imported materials. (The Burmese found that the machinery of a modern spinning and weaving factory was not suitable for home-grown cotton; the foreign exchange position however, did not permit the import of the needed strains of foreign cotton, and consequently the factory stood partly idle.)

Rao has described how the Indians, in their Second Plan, cut expenditure on social services and irrigation in order that resources could be

'shifted to industry; and not just industry, but basic industry: steel, cement, coal, power and oil which provide the sinews of industrial development, and machine tools, machine building, heavy engineering and heavy chemicals which give the country its growth potential in the physical sense, and will set it on the road to self-sustaining and self-accelerating economic development' (7).

The food crises in India during the sixties were officially predicted in 1959 when an Indian government report, prepared with the help of the Ford Foundation, was issued. The report was not acted upon because the Indian planners did not give top priority to the alleviation of *current* suffering. Many commentators have come to the same conclusion as the Paddock brothers (200), that the Indian socialist planners refused to be diverted by the impending food shortages from downgrading agriculture and continuing with their emphasis on industrial development at the expense of food production.

Perhaps it is true that if the Indian government devotes the major part of its own, and donated, means to 'heavy engineering and heavy chemicals...', the country may reach economic beatitude in the twenty-first century. In the meantime, there are still thirty years left of this century; tens of millions are near starvation and hundreds of millions are stagnating in abysmal poverty. The planners disdain their fate because India needs now, for the prosperity of its remote future, steel works and nuclear stations.

In 1963 Norman Kipping went to India to find that tens of millions of pounds of British aid, in the form of heavy industrial equipment, 'was not being fully utilized' – to cite the euphemism of the parliamentary Estimates Committee. Why? He discovered that the Indian government did not allocate the necessary foreign exchange to provide these plants with the imported components that they needed. He then suggested that by providing aid in the form of spare parts and materials the expensive capital projects could be put to their intended use. Kipping returned home to tell Whitehall that there were many points in the Indian economy where a penny of immediate expenditure would create a pound of production. What has become known as Kipping Aid is undoubtedly the most fruitful application of UK help to India. It, however, raises two unanswered questions: Why is the principle of Kipping Aid not applied universally? (Perhaps the world planners think that only in India is industrial investment under-utilized!) Is not the very institution of Kipping Aid a condemnation of the planners in India and the donor countries, who because of their obsession with industrial machinery had made it necessary to provide this special relief?

The emphasis on industrialization has led to the neglect of service functions, such as improvements in internal transport and storage,* and especially of agriculture. This attitude is particularly deplorable, because in most parts of Asia extra farm investment is likely to produce about twice as much output as extra industrial investment. The anti-farming bias is only modified when it comes to export crops which a state marketing board can merchandise abroad to obtain even more industrial capital goods. (Ghana, for example, pushed cocoa growing at the expense of the rest of agriculture.) Twenty years of post-war planning of industrial incongruities in the under-developed countries has produced a powerful reaction and the anti-farming trend is now being reversed. International agencies and some of the rich donors have

---

* In some of the poorer Asian countries pests and damp destroy a third of the harvested crops. (According to George Ball (201), one third of the Indian wheat crop is lost through inadequate transport and storage between the farmer and the consumer.) The storage problem could easily be solved by teaching the natives to construct bins out of local raw materials, lined with polythene. Yet it has proved more difficult to recruit a few thousand dollars for this type of investment than to obtain loans of millions of dollars to acquire nuclear reactors.

at last recognized that charity is better applied by helping poor peasants to improve their cultivation techniques than by contributing money to another steel mill.

When some members of the Estimates Committee met with the High Commissioner in Delhi, they were told that although 'so far British aid has been concerned very little with Indian agriculture...', British policy is now changing and becoming more agriculturally orientated. The Committee was however still puzzled why development aid from the UK had in the previous twenty years gone to projects like the Durgapur steel mill and not to agriculture: 'Your Committee...are surprised that it should have taken so long to reach...this [new] assessment, since dependence on agriculture was equally marked in developing countries previously.' This 'surprise' indicates political simple-mindedness on the part of the Committee. Its members probably did not fully appreciate the ideological basis on which industry was preferred at the expense of agriculture. This discrimination has now diminished, but the planners are still hopeful that the day will come when they can again concentrate on turbines and computers.

IT MUST BE BIG AND CAPITAL-INTENSIVE

Once upon a time Standard Oil, Krupp and ICI were the bad boys because socialists thought that being big was a vice in itself. Today planners (outside the United States) have gone to the other extreme. They are no longer satisfied that regular commercial forces will lead to healthy corporate amalgamations – in their view the state must push, bully and bribe big companies to become even bigger by merging. The fetish of size has also gripped the Labour government which has allowed anti-monopoly regulations to lie dormant in order to help create corporate colossi. The establishment of a state merchant bank, liberally endowed with taxpayers' money, has been justified on the grounds that willing and unwilling UK companies must be coaxed to worship at the altar of bigness.

If being big and capital-intensive is a planning panacea for industrial countries, then it is perhaps not surprising that those who seek to plan life in the underdeveloped economies sell the same remedy there – with disastrous results when measured in terms of the present welfare of the poor sufferers. When genuine near-full employment prevails, material output can indeed be expediently augmented by commissioning more capital-intensive modes of production. This is the economic vindication for bigger and bigger units in the Western world. When, however, a large part of the potential working population is unemployed and another large part is under-employed, the introduction of labour-saving devices does not necessarily help the GNP to grow, but merely generates the demoralizing effect of increased unemployment. By planting automated industrial giants on pre-industrial societies, small-scale production is stifled, local initiative impaired and the domestic private accumulation of capital slowed down. Many of the large industrial projects in the under-developed countries are on such a scale that only big foreign corporations or the state (often with foreign aid funds) can afford to finance them.

£30 Mn aid money in a heavy electrical works at Bhopal, and £70 Mn in a steel works at Durgapur, are the two main capital-intensive British government investments in India. They were meant to be prestigious showpieces, as well as levers for the Indian GNP. Yet their many deficiencies, the Indian lack of expertise to manage, and the fact that the plants are not fully utilized, have caused many headaches in Delhi and London; indeed they have produced the reverse public relations effect from that which had been in the minds of the planners. Yet some good has come from what some regard as perhaps not the ideal destination for British tax money. Now that the construction of these big projects has been more or less finished, the Treasury has gone on record as saying: 'We would now be cautious about entering into the financing of anything quite as big.' In 1967 the Indian government finally agreed that the original intention to double the capacity of the Durgapur plant should not be implemented. With proper reticence, the Treasury commented: 'We were very thankful they did come to that decision' (18).

Although the two big projects are said to be completed, the British authorities are still under constant pressure to extend further loans, and aid, to make them viable. If Britain does not accede, it might make these investment projects look like blatant failures. Not only the UK government but other donors too are similarly pressured. The Russians, in particular, are being 'requested' by the Indian government to buy some of the output of their twenty-five big aid projects, lest it be said that Russian-financed projects have turned out to be industrial white elephants.

In muted language, but nevertheless firmly the Estimates Committee consider the Durgapur aid project to have been a failure. They also touch on one of the motivating factors which had originally induced Whitehall to engage in this planning exercise. The Indian nationalized corporation, operating Durgapur, also manages two other big steel plants which were donated by the Russians and West Germans. The Committee makes the explicit charge that the British decision to finance Durgapur was decisively inspired by the wish to gain political prestige, i.e. to deprive the USSR and Germany of the halo of having been the sole donors of steel plants to India.

The former UN economic adviser to Burma and India, E. F. Schumacher, learned at first hand that the zealots of mammoth capital projects, in the poorer parts of the world, are uninterested in the promotion of small-scale schemes that are capable of quickly improving material conditions. He founded the Intermediate Technology Development Group (171), which hopes to fight poverty in the under-developed countries by advocating labour-intensive techniques suitable for agriculture and small-scale manufacturing. The group has so far failed to make much impact upon Western decision-makers, and some Indians I have spoken to in London even regard its work as an insult to Asia. Why? Schumacher and his friends think that the present stage of development calls for small, simple implements for production made mainly from local materials and for local use (not for export). This seems to offend some of the articulate leaders of the under-developed countries, who seek to obtain aid for big capital-intensive projects. The Schumacher group disseminates information on low-cost agricultural machines which they regard as suitable for farming in developing (but not necessarily in developed) economies, such as animal-drawn toolbars and hand-operated transplanters.

The founding of the Intermediate Technology Development Group is a welcome step though its members are perhaps politically a little naïve to appreciate why in the present climate they have made so little progress. The ruling philosophy of aid in the post-war years has been 'What is best for the West must be best for them'. The vocal planners of the poorer countries are irritated with the ideas of Schumacher. They say that Western imperialism owes the former colonial territories a moral debt...they do not want to receive hand-operated implements, but demand heavy capital goods so that their countries can have the largest electronic and nitrogen plants of the world. Schumacher is hard put to counter the attack that intermediate Technology is concerned to provide the poor countries with only the second best:

'For whom is it a second best? Is a bicycle a second best for someone who has got nothing? No, it is the best for him, and the gift of a car would ruin him. Is a computer the best thing for the illiterate? Certainly not. I agree that everybody should have the best, but thoughtfully chosen — that which is best for him.'

Big irrigation schemes attract photographers from all over the world. When foreign donors and indigenous planners have the chance to have their pictures taken next to an impressive dam, they are happy and look with disdain on proposals from Schumacher to import small pumps for local boreholes. One million hand-operated pumps may immediately bring more happiness to the poor peasants of India than an irrigation scheme which will take a decade to come to fruition. Planners love the future and they want it to look big.

EXPORTING IS PATRIOTIC

State planners of the United States and the USSR, interventionists in the UK and Ghana, red and blue, all love exporting. Even solid supporters of free enterprise in the Western world see nothing wrong in the state directing economic forces so as to keep imports down and exports up. Medals, tax reductions and knighthoods beckon industrial exporters. Firms manufacturing for the home market import-replacements are not praised for their efforts, yet at least they escape being castigated as enemies of society. But importers — whoever has heard of a company chairman receiving the MBE in recognition of his efficient buying of foreign goods? I know of no serious economist who is willing to argue that there is a special virtue in exports, though few publicly debunk this fetish which is revered by political leaders throughout the world.

State interference is only justified if this results in an accretion of welfare over and above that which would have accrued in the absence of such intervention. Exports only make sense if the value of the imports which are bought with their proceeds is bigger than the benefit which would have been derived from selling the exported goods in the domestic market, or from having produced something else for the local consumer. It was surely a doubtful proposition to limit the sale of Scotch whisky in the UK so that increased exports could yield foreign currency to buy abroad champagne and tinned peaches. Even more incongruous are the edicts of the Cuban and Israeli governments to ration at home sugar and oranges respectively in order to export more of these crops. Was the value of the resultant imports really greater than the lost enjoyment of these staple products in the home market? The answer is almost certainly in the negative, because planning tends to prize exports receipts above their real value.

A theoretical case can be made out for encouraging exports, even with subsidies, when these are produced by unemployed resources which would otherwise not be creating any material values. But the sacred cow of exporting is worshipped no less devoutly in countries with Full Employment, where the artificial bolstering of exports implies the non-satisfaction of home demand. When, in 1961, the British economy was hungry for workers to man its industries, the government encouraged the National Coal Board to sell coal abroad — even at a loss.* Between 1965 and 1969, the Labour government instituted what were in effect disguised multiple exchange rates by subsidizing exports (through sub-ventions, cheap credit and other means) whilst extra burdens were placed upon imports. British planners have, however, much to learn from their colleagues in the less developed parts of the world where the state sponsors exports by paying exporters huge bonuses, or gives them the privilege to use all, or part, of their foreign receipts to import goods for which no official allocation of foreign currency is otherwise available. This export madness can lead to over-invoiced exports and other illegal transactions. Ingenious, though hardly law-abiding, merchants know that if they purchase foreign currency on the black market to remit home as alleged export proceeds, they will make a good profit on the import licences awaiting patriotic exporters.

Of course British exporters are not rewarded sufficiently highly, and importers not penalized enough, to make such phantom transactions feasible. Yet, some no less bizarre export planning is concocted in Whitehall. The risk of exporting to doubtful foreign buyers is borne

---

* There are many instances where the citizens of country A import goods, manu-factured in A and sold at a loss to country B, from B. Usually these are illegal transactions.

As the people of Londonderry in Northern Ireland are in United Kingdom territory, their purchases of normally-priced English coal are not registered as export sales in the books of the National Coal Board. The sale of cheap coal to Eire, a few miles to the south of Londonderry, is rewarded with the accolade of patriotic exporting. Not surprisingly, many people in Londonderry burned English coal which they imported via Eire.

largely, and sometimes wholly, by the British taxpayer. To inflate the export statistics (and sometimes also for foreign policy considerations), British firms have been persuaded to send goods abroad, on credit, to places where default is near-certain. There is no virtue in selling goods abroad if you are not likely to be paid for them. Through state interventionism, British exporters need not, however, always think of the credit-worthiness of their customers because they know that the government will compensate them for resultant losses. Only slightly less absurd is the state support given to exports on extended credit terms, at subsidized rates and with government guarantees against default, which cover payment periods of up to fifteen years. At a time when the Bank of England is compelled to borrow foreign currency abroad at high rates of interest, the Board of Trade encourages exports that will not be paid for (if at all) until many years later. To execute these exports immediate foreign currency expenses are incurred to finance their import content. The resources employed to produce the long-term credit exports cannot manufacture goods for the home market which in turn is supplied by imports on short-term credit.

It is easy to demonstrate that in some circumstances a country gains more from exporting £100 rather than £110. Yet planners are not concerned with the national costs of exporting, nor with the interdependence of imports and exports. They feel that a country's economic performance is to be judged by the gross export figures in the trade accounts. Whether the exports are ultimately paid for or not, or at what loss of welfare they have been produced, are regarded as secondary considerations. Planners love exports and it is well known that love does not always generate rational behaviour.

THE LURE OF QUANTITIES

The GNP is represented by an overall single figure that collates the value-output of goods and services, irrespective of whether they are meant for immediate consumption or have a more lasting life. With the reservations stated on pp. 66–70, the GNP takes account of quality differences. A mini car and a Rolls Royce, though both are 'cars' in unit measurements, contribute different values to the GNP, because buyers are prepared to pay more for the latter than for the former. The manufacture of 100 disposable tissues enlarges the national cake by a smaller amount than does the production of 100 linen handkerchiefs. Quality and durability are elements that often find some place in the numerical size of the GNP.

Planning is, however, often concerned with physical targets and when this is the case quantity takes precedence over quality. Then, standardization—with no regard to the individual demands of the consumer—becomes the rule. It is one of the characteristics of communist countries that their products are frequently shoddy and have a much shorter life than similar goods made in free enterprise economies. The reason is not difficult to discern when one learns that communist managers are frequently rewarded in relation to the quantity of output and not for its soundness. This folly of quantitative planning often involves society in economic waste: a television set, produced with sixteen hours' labour and $20 of material, has an average life of two years; but using slightly better materials costing $25 and 20 hours of labour, a set can be manufactured with an average useful life of four years. Thanks to brand names and the consumer choice open to buyers in a free society, the Western consumer may elect to buy 100 per cent. extra quality by paying 25 per cent. more for the better-quality set. In a communist society, the planners' paradise, this choice is not always available; medals are distributed for the number—and not the value—of television sets assembled by Stakhanovite toilers.*

The implicit economic waste and disregard for consumers' foibles, adduced by standardized quantity production, are of course irrelevancies in certain situations. Commercial considerations would never have justified the war-time construction of the famous Californian Liberty ships that had to be sent to breakers' yards after only a few years, when they became operationally obsolete because of their rela-

---

* In theory the central communist planners could give factories detailed production orders with varying sizes, qualities and designs. As, however, this would involve specific orders for millions of different items, the state authorities plan production by aggregating heterogeneous goods into artificially homogeneous categories. Instead of planning the manufacture of x yards of blue-handkerchiefs-with-coloured-borders and y yards of green-nylon-blouses-for-oversized-women, orders are given by the top bureaucrats in terms of 'z yards of textiles'. Ellman (192) has described the bottlenecks and distortions which have arisen in the USSR as a result of this policy of aggregation. When the managers of the textile trust are told to produce 'z yards', and fully recognizing that the largest physical output is the criterion by which they will be judged, they will tend to opt for the most convenient product-mix. The most convenient product-mix from a manufacturing angle does not, however, correspond to the ideal product-mix consumers would choose if they could freely express their preferences.

tively low quality. Liberty ships were not intended to have a long life, but were vessels that could be quickly manufactured to supply tonnage for immediate military needs — quantity alone mattered and other merits were rightly put aside. One can conjecture also peace-time circumstances, such as famine and earthquakes, where similar quantity considerations are rightly given economic priority.

It is, however, inane to apply this yardstick to production in the affluent societies of the West. Yet the legend of increased productivity is often interpreted to mean that if output can be boosted by cutting out frills and variety of choice, then this is a desirable national objective. State planners pay less attention to the quality of education than to the hours of tuition, less to the thoroughness of medical examinations than to the frequency of visits to the doctor, less to the stability of the surface than to the miles of roads constructed, less to the comforts of accommodation than to the number of houses built. Housing is perhaps the best example of how interventionists waste resources in their race after numbers. When an insurance or building society is asked to risk money by granting a long-term mortgage, it does not only inquire about the present market price of the object but also about its likely value in twenty years. This is why it turns up its nose at requests to lend funds for a dwelling place without central heating or a garage, or for buildings, with flats on the fourth floor, that have no lifts. Government planners are obsessed with the *present* demand and disdain such long-term thinking. Housing programmes, financed with taxpayers' money, are adjudged by the number of units built. It follows that with given resources it is politically expedient to construct smaller and less luxurious, but the largest possible number of, houses. Undoubtedly this would be the correct policy for a housing minister in Calcutta, but in a Western country where public housing leads to improved conditions for slum dwellers (and not the taking in from the streets of people who have no roof over their heads), quality ought to play a more decisive role. By commercial criteria, it would therefore be a better investment of resources if 80,000 housing units of a high standard were built instead of 100,000 units that may meet present demand but will in a few years lag behind the standard of the time. The value of 80,000 spacious, central-heated houses may necessitate the same financial expenditure as is needed to construct 100,000 relatively low-standard houses. Planners in their craze for numbers and statistical records have a preference for the latter. It is one of their occupational diseases.

STATIC THINKING

Planners lack imagination. They believe in a future GNP consisting largely of goods and services in demand at the time when their plans are prepared.

Drawing up forward projections of what the economy will look like in five or ten years, planners can elect to make one of two types of presentation: either they merely mention general categories — e.g. disposable consumer demand will be 50 per cent. up — which are next to useless for business action, or they can refer to detailed prognostications, e.g. the demand for refrigerators will in year y be x per cent. higher than in the base year. As the National Plan was meant to be a practical guide to the future, and its promoters did not wish to waste public money on publishing only generalities, it became a document with specific forecasts. Thus, the experts in Whitehall predicted that (constant-price) earnings of British ships from tanker freights would go up from £333 Mn in 1966 to £385 Mn in 1970; in the same period the output of Portland cement would rise from 13·3 to 25 Mn tons; employment in the cotton industry would fall from 361,000 to 253,000; the export of steel would go up from 3·89 to 4·25 Mn tons, whilst UK paper imports would increase from 1,407 to 3,010 thousand tons.

There is some consistency in this childish play with numbers. The devoted men and women who drew up the National Plan presumed that the British public would consume in future the same kind of articles which they had hitherto bought. The only important modification to this assumption was that as people became more affluent, they were expected to move in a pre-conceived manner to a higher expenditure scale with concomitant — and predictable — changes in their consumption pattern. Similar static thinking also prevailed in the planners' assumptions relating to labour costs; they made allowance for a certain increase in productivity but basically extrapolated that traditional forces would continue to determine the size and mode of working of the future labour force.

What would planners have done at the end of the last war, had they then been asked to delineate Britain's economic future? They would have calculated — in those days without computers, so it would have taken rather longer — how much soap the British housewife, at a given level of income, would need to wash up her dishes. Undoubtedly this would have led to a forecast that a certain number of new soap factories would be constructed to meet this conjectured demand. The intellectually immobile planners-forecasters would of course have been proved wrong, because the production of washing-up soap has declined steeply as the result of the unexpected invention of detergents. Could even the most sagacious civil servant have guessed in 1960 that sales of electric toothbrushes would flourish in 1970? Beckerman has extrapolated from 1963 data the output of the British economy in 1975, but it is noteworthy that he has taken no account of the thousands of people who may be employed by the new tourist agencies that might have sprung up by then to promote package tours to the moon.

Corporations, speculating on their future, are now progressively turning away from estimating the demand, in ten years or more, for their existing range of products, and are concentrating on predicting (and helping to develop) the emergence of new articles. This craft is called technological forecasting; its many practitioners in the US refer to it by the initials TF. Many companies allocate a substantial portion of their Research and Development budgets to conjecturing how far as yet unborn inventions might make obsolete their present products, and aim to guestimate the resulting shifts in consumer demand. Michael Shanks, analysing in 1964 the output of ICI, concluded that half of its exports consisted of products which had not been invented when the company was formed (173). There is no reason to doubt that since 1964 advances in chemistry have played even greater havoc with the feasibility of selling in 1975 the same products as were marketed successfully in the fifties. It is not surprising therefore to learn that ICI is in 1970 much more concerned with technological futurology than with the kind of static forecasting on which the detailed National Plan was founded.

A word of sympathy for our national planners would not be out of place. They cannot walk in the footsteps of corporate planners, who confess that the one prediction which can be confidently made is that the future is unknown and that the consumer-demand structure constantly undergoes a radical metamorphosis because of altered tastes and the appearance of new products. An unpredictable economic future and rigid planning is self-contradictory. If one wishes to regiment the economy to prepare it for a *definite* future, one cannot afford to say 'I do not know'. Such an admission would obviate the wisdom of much of state interventionism. Government planners are frequently timid creatures who tend to play safe. This is why they prefer, nay are forced, to employ criteria with static gauges.

NOT BY BREAD ALONE

There is a common philosophical denominator in the unholy trinity of the GNP, economic forecasting and central planning. This again springs to the surface, when one probes the mental outlook of state planners which is largely circumscribed by the limited welfare objectives embedded in the nature of the conventional national product. As described in Part I, the GNP provides an unsatisfactory standard for the measurement of comprehensive welfare because, *inter alia*, it ignores many activities that meet important human requirements but cannot be given the necessary monetary tag. Planners are guilty of ignoring the human costs of producing the values that are chalked up in the GNP totals, and of paying relatively little attention to the achievement of goals which do not aid the conventional GNP to grow.

'The economic welfare of a community,' wrote Pigou (23), 'consists in the balance of satisfactions derived from the use of the national dividend over the dissatisfactions involved in the making of it.' This profound truth is shrugged off as irrelevant by the state interventionists, who measure happiness by the record output of nylon stockings and telephones. When a lazy nation works only seven hours daily, five days a week, planners dream of a dictator who would make these indolent creatures toil eighteen hours daily for six days a week. This would almost certainly lessen the overall national welfare, but it would make the conventional GNP bigger. Planners have little patience with the Pigou criterion of *net* welfare.*

* Although Pigou probably never reached the apex of intellectual enjoyment by becoming a television addict, he would (I hope) agree with the following prosaic elucidation of his thesis. On the assumption that there is no quality distinction between commercial television in the US and the BBC in the UK, is it correct to say that the cost of viewing the former is zero, whilst the viewing cost of the latter is measured by the £6 licence fee? In formal accountancy language the answer must of course be in the affirmative. But, if one measures the real welfare of viewers, one might conclude that the net satisfaction obtained by UK audiences (calculated by deducting from the pleasure of viewing the cost of the £6) is higher than that derived by US audiences (whose net satisfaction is computed by deducting from the pleasure of viewing the displeasure of having the viewing periodically interrupted by inane commercial breaks).

State interventionists usually seek out planning objectives that are materially tangible, measurable—and seen to be so. (As the neglect of mental health in Western countries proves, planners often want their objectives to be also politically attractive; relatively few votes are gained by improving the standards of mental hospitals.) Planners are prejudiced in favour of state aid for power stations, university buildings and fast aeroplanes as against the provision of social amenities. Yet in affluent societies growth in scenic improvements, aesthetics and noise abatement may generate more human happiness than augmented physical production. The state measures its health investments by the number of hospital beds and doctors. To cut down the waiting period before a patient can see his doctor or to provide greater privacy in hospitals are both costly objectives. When given the choice of augmenting either such indeterminate satisfactions or procuring additional apparatus, planners will tend to opt for the latter. That the country's X-ray equipment has been doubled appears as a greater triumph than that the average waiting period has been reduced from sixty to thirty minutes; the first achievement will also find its place in the annals of the GNP whilst the second cannot be recorded in the national accounts.

The imposing new state capital of Brazil, the Aswan Dam of Egypt, and the Durgapur steel plant in India all bear testimony to physical planning in under-developed countries, aided by the half-political, half-charitable contributions from the governments of the US, the USSR and the UK. All are objects of pride to the native and foreign planners who directly and indirectly aided in their construction. Plaques may properly be affixed to these GNP pillars, which undoubtedly will prop material growth in these poor countries. Yet cold historical analysis can leave no one in doubt that if these funds had been invested in less spectacular forms—particularly in population control—the net impact on welfare in these impoverished economies would have been far greater.

Brazil's planners have justified the investment of state funds in the building of a new capital by pointing to the augmented welfare which will flow from a streamlined and more efficient administrative centre. Undoubtedly this investment will lay golden eggs in a country with a relatively high GNP growth. Yet the degrading poverty of the majority of Brazilians is due to the slow growth rate of the *per capita* GNP which is determined by a population explosion that is only slightly held back by the high incidence of infant mortality and up to two million illegal abortions every year. Brazil has increased its population in the last twenty-five years from 50 to 90 million and expects to double the present number by 1990. Whilst all economists are agreed that there is no investment project in Brazil which would raise the average standard of living as fast as funds spent on birth control, the Brazilian authorities oppose population control; they neither allow foreign aid to be given in this field nor are prepared to allocate state funds for this purpose.

India, lacking the Brazilian religious and political scruples, has finally come round to the need for massive investments in birth control, and is even prepared to have some of the international aid funds – that might in the olden days have been destined for new steel mills and electronic machine tools – diverted to stem the unhealthy, and economically disastrous, growth of its population. This belated conversion still leaves the question unanswered why donors, like the U K, provided India (at her request) with funds to put up the Durgapur steel plant whilst – on Britain's own admission (18) – doing little to help with family planning.

Egypt's Aswan Dam was conceived to increase the area of her arable land by one third. Judged by this goal, the investment constituted a very worth-while objective. One may, however, arrive at a different answer when one considers the alternative of investing a fraction of the Aswan funds in sponsoring birth control. After a ten year construction period the Aswan Dam is now finished but in the meantime Egypt's population has increased by more than one third, so that today there are fewer acres under cultivation *per capita* than before the Russian and Egyptian planners had commenced to build the dam. Only in 1966 did Egypt's socialist government finally agree to begin a state campaign to halt the population growth.

Lipton of the Institute of Development Studies at the University of Sussex quotes estimates that investments in family planning in India yield fifteen times as much extra income per head as the next best investment (3). Enke arrives at an even more dramatic conclusion: if resources of a given value are devoted, in many less developed countries, to retarding population growth, rather than accelerating production growth, the resources are ' 100 or so times more effective in raising *per capita* incomes' (202). It does not matter greatly whether one accepts Enke's or Lipton's figures to conclude that investments in birth control were and are more prolific in creating welfare for the impoverished masses in the poorer parts of the world than any other form of investment. Indeed this has been true for twenty-five years. Why then has it taken so long to force a change in emphasis as between the procurement of steel mills and massive support for birth control? Why even today are birth control investments measured in thousands of dollars as against millions spent on acquiring sophisticated industrial machinery? The unpleasant truth, which alone can explain this nefarious misapplication of public funds which were supposed to raise efficiently and quickly the standard of living of the poorer countries, is embedded in the nature of state planning and closely linked with the mentality of planners in both the donor countries and the under-developed economies. Steel plants and airports are visible signs of wealth and recognizable forms of aid — birth control is an undramatic way of raising living standards. The output of factories increases the registered size of the GNP — augmented happiness induced by means of family planning is not recorded in the conventional national product. This issue sums up the inherent contradistinction between those who seek to enlarge the volume of true human welfare and those who aim at the largest possible GNP. Planners are mostly fond of the GNP.

Was Wilson a Bad Planner?

'Planning is what planners think and do.'

JOHN JEWKES

According to Myrdal the depth of the social and psychological causes of the destruction of liberal economic society is manifested in 'planned parenthood'. This is said to be a phenomenon 'intrinsically related to those very changes in people's attitudes which, on the political plane, have been causing the trend towards economic planning' (6). Such a weird proposition will strike many as far-fetched, arrant nonsense. Yet Myrdal, anticipating such criticism, is at pains to emphasize that his birth control analogy is not an intellectual pleasantry but to be taken seriously. Though unable to keep a straight face when told that planning parenthood is ideologically linked to state interventionism in the nylon stocking industry, I agree that Myrdal's thesis contains a chastening thought about what many political decision-makers believe to be the place of economic planning in modern society. They earnestly think that because man has evolved techniques to control nuclear fission and procreation, comprehensive centralized planning has become both possible and desirable. Above all, they regard it as an inevitable adjunct to our lives. It is a view which is held widely, and not only by those who openly profess adherence to socialist philosophy.

In my youth many anti-socialists proclaimed wildly that a centrally directed economy must ultimately break down or at best degenerate into a stagnant society. The achievements of the USSR and other communist countries in building Sputniks and generally raising the standards of living of their people—with television sets, better food and more education—prove decisively that centralized planning can deliver useful material benefits. Leaving out the vital consideration of human liberty in a highly controlled economy, the question to ask about the material successes of the communist countries is whether these economies would not have generated more output and welfare under conditions of less state planning. Most of the communist countries now implicitly admit this by slowly introducing the price mechanism, making allowance for the interest factor in production, and cutting down on centralized directives. A balanced judgement on the performance of communist countries does not therefore deny the advances made, but compares them with how much greater they could have been without the restraining shackles of omniscient state planners.

Mutatis mutandis, the improvements in Britain's economy during six years of Labour rule must be viewed in terms of what might have been achieved under different political conditions. It has now become fashionable to explain away the mistakes of Labour planning by saying that their published plans were only intended as 'indicative planning', targeting, guidelights, etc. This alibi does not stand up when one recalls the many instances of state interventionism in which the Labour government did not seek to persuade but acted through controls and prohibitions. Wilson's administration applied statutory force to further its planning objectives. The assertion that its intervention in economic life was passive is a travesty of truth. It is true that Labour's planning did not bring about the desired results, but this surely does not substantiate the pathetic plea that they did not plan resolutely.

Now that Labour has lost the general election, a stab-in-the-back theory may well be propounded to reveal the causes of the socialist government's failures. Conspiratorial allegations would have no basis in fact. Wilson began to rule with the docile assistance of the leaders of most trade unions and employers' organizations. As one would expect in Britain, the controls produced very few evasions, and illegal resistance to state interventions was at a minimum. The nationalized corporations of course had little choice but to obey sheepishly the 'wishes' of Whitehall. The vast majority of unions and corporations also went out of their way to comply with the requests of the state planners even when these were not backed by statutory powers. A few outcries here and there merely proved the rule that Wilson enjoyed the cooperation, or at least did not meet with the active opposition, of the leaders of the non-state sector.

There is no better example to confirm the charge that Labour planned, in the active sense of the word, than to cite the enforcement of the artificial $2.80 = £1 exchange rate for three years. Even a superficial analysis of the purchasing power of Sterling, or a quick examination of the forces determining the supply of and demand for Sterling, showed as early as 1963 that the $2.80 rate was an economic absurdity and could only be maintained by government force, and to the detriment of the welfare of the British people.* Notwithstanding tendentious stories to the contrary, few UK-resident individuals or corporations were technically able to sabotage the official exchange rate and only a small number did in fact contribute, by illegal means, to its ultimate downfall. Sterling did not have to be devalued, because some wealthy landlords unlawfully opened number accounts in Swiss banks. Whatever apologists for Labour may say in the future, the (November 1967) forced Sterling devaluation did not come about because the City of London disliked Wilson, but because foreign holders of Sterling could not be 'planned' by Whitehall. If blame must be apportioned, it ought to be placed on the Labour government for its vain efforts to plan something which is best left to the free interplay of commercial forces.

A serious thesis is propounded by the extreme left-wing to elucidate why the Wilson planners stumbled and fell. Wilson is not attacked for planning, but for not planning and controlling the *whole* of the economy. They point out that non-comprehensive state interventionism left private—individual and corporate—initiative enough room to manœuvre to frustrate many of the planning objectives. A sound observation! Harold Wilson could indeed have continued until today with his beloved $2.80 rate had he draconically prohibited the entry of half of Britain's conventional imports. He could have stopped inflation by compelling all savers to invest in 2·5 per cent. interest deposits at the Post Office Savings Bank. He could have averted labour shortages in industry by closing down two-thirds of all hairdressing establishments restaurants and bingo halls. He could have left the motorways free for nationalized coaches if half of all private cars had been taxed off the streets. He could have trebled British exports if industry had been forced to export half of its output even if this would have left much of home demand unsatisfied.

The communist experiments have demonstrated that even under

---

* A handful of economists advised Wilson to stick stubbornly to the old anachronistic $2.80 rate. The majority of UK economists pleaded for devaluation, but most of these did not thereby abandon their devotion to the planning of currency rates by governmental wisdom. They were in fact saying to Wilson: We do not object in principle to the rigidity of a fixed exchange rate... You are right to plan and control the price of sterling... We only request that you shift the numerals on your planning board.

fully centralized control, planners are helpless in implementing all their planning objectives. Nevertheless, it is obvious that a more ruthless and all-embracing planning strategy would have enabled Wilson to succeed in places where he failed – certainly, had he taken the necessary steps, he could have delayed the 1967 devaluation for many years. More energetic planning and nationalizations, as demanded by the left-wing critics of Wilson, would have affected adversely the material and non-material welfare of the British people. This, however, is not the main point to counter the criticism of lukewarm planning. When Wilson proclaimed his love for the National Plan, to the loud applause of members of all British political parties, he (and his admirers) did so in the conviction that it is both praiseworthy and feasible to practise centralized planning in a *mixed* economy. The Wilson philosophy does not embrace full control of every nook in the economy; this makes it difficult for the Labour Party to justify its dismal planning record on the grounds that it did not plan everything. The left-wing wants the Labour Party to resolve this ideological predicament by revising its political philosophy and accepting the ideas of totalitarian planning. Others will draw the conclusion that Wilson's planning dilemma calls for a reappraisal of the role of state interventionism in a mixed economy.

No doubts have been cast in this book on the personal abilities of Harold Wilson or the dedication of George Brown. I admire the intellectual zeal and altruism of the Whitehall planners whose labours have been castigated in the preceding pages. It is much more important to dissect the nature of planning than to inquire for what political party the protagonists of state interventionism vote.

In September 1964, Quintin Hogg stated at a public meeting in Birmingham: 'Consultation and willing cooperation are the conditions of any successful economic plan in a free country... It is not planning to which we are opposed but socialist planning' (174). This goes to the very heart of the Conservative Party. If one believes that Wilson, Brown and his administrators are incompetent planners, and that Conservative leaders are more intelligent and capable in planning the economy, then of course the main lesson to be drawn from Labour's failures is that Harold Wilson was a bad planner. If socialists are to be derided as bad planners, it follows that other people could be good planners. This negates the proposition that centralized state planning is not suitable for countries with a climate of free enterprise.

The senior minister of the DEA opened a House of Commons debate in November 1965, saying that 'the Leader of the Opposition is advising his right hon. and hon. Friends to accept a Motion to welcome the National Plan' (11). Reading Hansard today, one is astounded at the sentiments expressed on planning by most of the Conservative speakers.* When the debate was closed and the last speaker, the junior minister of the DEA, Austen Albu, rose he repeated almost word-for-word the opening statement of George Brown: 'The Motion is to welcome the Plan. I gather that hon. and right hon. gentlemen opposite will support us.' They did indeed, and the Motion was passed without a division. Even when the fabulous National Plan was officially buried, the Conservative Party (or parts of it) did not despair of state interventionism. Reginald Maudling put it as follows: 'Must we assume that the concept of planning has foundered with it? I do not, myself, believe that we should ...I think it would be a tragedy if these recent developments led to the idea of economic planning being abandoned altogether' (175).

When forecasters are proved wrong, they frequently tend to say that this does not invalidate the notion of forecasting and that their next efforts will be more successful. This is almost a standard answer to critics who suggest that there may be intrinsic reasons why the GNP cannot be predicted with a significant degree of accuracy. This, too, is the last line of defence manned by those planners who consider that extensive state interventionism in a mixed economy is not incongruous. The top civil servant of the DEA conceded to a parliamentary committee that the growth rates set by the government were not working 'perfectly'. Did they despair? '...it may well be that the third time round or the fourth time round we shall be a lot cleverer at this' (44). Michael Shanks, the ex-planner of the DEA, has remained buoyantly enthusiastic about government planning. He admits that the National Plan of 1965 has failed – but does this mean that planning is dishonoured? 'The next time we ought to do better' (176).

* Some Conservatives dissented. Enoch Powell, for example, described the National Plan in a speech delivered outside Parliament as 'a nonsense, a silly nonsense, a transparent nonsense, and, what is more and worse, a dangerous nonsense'. Today this will generally be regarded as a sound historical judgement, but at the time Powell was treated as an eccentric for saying it.

Conclusions

'As for growth, that is good, very good, provided you want growth and provided the growth is in the things you want.'

ENOCH POWELL

I trust that the preceding pages have helped to shake confidence in the accuracy of the GNP and economic forecasting, which serve as the sacramental instruments of the planning bishops. Some statistical tricksters have been exposed on the way, though this was not the main purpose of the exercise. Those who want the state to intervene decisively in the economy and control our lives 'for the public good' have a vested interest in demonstrating that economics is a science, and that the GNP and forecasting models are not merely academic concepts but accurate working tools usefully employed in centralized planning. The case that was implicitly argued throughout the book has a negative flavour. By exposing the hollow nature of the GNP and economic forecasting, one automatically challenges the competence of planners to achieve their sacrosanct aims.

Ought one therefore to denigrate all GNP calculations? No, provided the 'limits of error' of the indices are transferred from the footnotes to the body of the published national accounts.*

Are glimpses into the economic future never worth publishing? No, provided one spells out exactly what they purport to mean and emphasizes the conjectural basis of the predictions. It was improper to sell at home and abroad the National Plan as a document setting out what Britain would look like in 1970, but there is clearly room for speculating in public how the UK economy might perform if conditions A, B and C

---

* Ian Lloyd has pleaded that the prodigality of an enhanced governmental statistical machine, enormously reinforced by the power of the computer, should not be allowed to swamp the necessary fundamental caution and scepticism with which all statistical output, however respectable and virtuous its parentage, ought to be treated. He wants the 'limits of error' to be attached to statistics like the kitemark of the British Standards Institution or the stars attached by the Automobile Association to the names of their listed hotels (60).

are fulfilled. (Such conditional prognostications will clearly arouse much less interest than definitive forecasts; consequently the modest prognosticators will probably not be considered important enough to be interviewed on television.)

Is growth always a good thing? No, growth is neither good nor bad and it is fatuous to suggest that one can answer this with a simple 'yes' or 'no'. The main thing is to beware of what Mishan called 'growthmania' (54).

Is planning to be encouraged? This is a prevalent catch question. Of course planning is an inevitable function of every forward-looking family, company or government department. Yet, lurking behind this vague, general inquiry there usually hides the politically explosive question of whether one believes that the state should attempt to forcibly determine the production and distribution of a large part of the GNP. It is sociologically significant—or is it psephological fear?—that many non-socialist politicians dread to give an explicit answer to this challenge. Many believe that to oppose resolutely centralized state planning is to invite condemnation as a fossil of Adam Smith.

Hicks places the devotion to the sacred GNP cow in a revealing historical perspective. In a personal reminiscence, he recalls how forty years ago he had first learned about the concept of the national income from his socialist teacher, Hugh Dalton (59). Planners were in those days not as enthusiastic about GNP growth as they are today. Between the two world wars socialists were not primarily concerned with increasing the size of the national cake but, instead, concentrated on the advocacy of redistributing it in a more just manner. Why has the past ideal of redistribution become submerged by the present visionary drive to augment the GNP? Hicks thinks that this philosophical change occurred when it began to dawn on intelligent socialists 'that the gains that could be got by mere redistribution were disappointing'. Once social reformers realized that to take income away from the rich and spread it amongst the poor does not go far to raise the standard of living of the mass of the population, they shifted their position and commenced to shout loudly for the growth of the material output.

I believe that this latter phase is now coming to an end. The rich countries of the West will again have to change their social priorities and no longer place the same emphasis on a growing GNP (in their countries) as has been the custom in the last thirty years.* GNP growth in the past expressed itself in such concrete ways as providing an inside lavatory for every household, a seaside holiday for even the poorest, and medicines for ill persons who might previously have died prematurely without them. Most of the remaining pockets of poverty and housing shortages—the latter are in the UK largely the result of state interventionism—that still exist in the West will be almost entirely eradicated by the end of the next decade (irrespective of the political party in power).

What will happen to the extra output generated by advances in the volumes of the Western GNPs in the seventies? In theory it might be used in its entirety to erase the special features of unhappiness that are extant in our affluent societies: impoverished old age pensioners, permanent invalids, fatherless families, the mentally afflicted, drug addicts, etc. Something like 10–15 per cent. of Britain's population would gain greatly from larger social aid, and undoubtedly a portion of the augmented GNP will be devoted to help them. Living in an electoral democracy, however, one can be near-certain that the major part of the growing GNP will be consumed by the others who constitute 85–90 per cent. of the population. They will use the additional income, resulting from a higher national product, to replace their colour television set before it is obsolete, add a porch to the country cottage, travel to the moon instead of to the Costa Brava. Clearly all this expenditure will provide some additional happiness, but one may safely make the value judgement that the incremental welfare created by GNP growth in the seventies will be smaller than that which was begotten by a similar percentage increase in the national cake during Hicks's younger days. When more and more people are faced with the

---

* I am deliberately mentioning in a footnote a contingent development that might invalidate my conjectural thesis on GNP growth in the rich Western countries. The citizens of the developed countries may one day freely decide—or be forced by a dictator—to allocate a large portion of their national output to the poorer parts of the world. (I have my doubts as to whether such an international slumming operation would really further world peace and be of lasting economic value to the under-developed countries.) If this happened, the continued growth of the Western GNPs would then not necessarily lead to material superabundance in the West. I think that this is unlikely to happen on a large scale on a voluntary basis. The workers of Germany and Britain are not willing to work an extra hour daily to finance the erection of more steel mills in India. Their motivations may not be noble but I predict that this is how they will behave. If my ignoble conjectures are correct, one may proceed from the premise that the overwhelming part of the Western GNPs will continue to be consumed directly by their national producers.

alternative of either buying a second car or going for a winter holiday to Switzerland, the significance of GNP growth recedes in importance. An augmented national income forty years ago meant that electricity was installed in homes enabling its occupants to enjoy their evening leisure by reading or switching on the radio. GNP growth in the thirties enabled some lucky manual workers to buy for the first time in their lives oranges as a Christmas treat for the children. Surely, all these comparisons highlight the need to reappraise socially the changing function of the present GNP growth.

The conclusion that I draw from this new scale of material output is that Western society can afford today to pay much greater attention to non-material values even when their creation impedes the speed of continued material growth. On a dark July day in 1966, Harold Wilson proclaimed rigid price-wage-dividend controls in order to propel the UK GNP to grow at a faster rate. Even if these controls had achieved the aims formulated by their originators, was it worth while for a rich nation to suffer actual and contingent restrictions on its liberty to push the GNP up by another percentage point?

There is no evidence that centralized state planning can pull up a country to a higher material plateau than can the working of free enterprise. Having said this I am, however, ready to accept that there are people who genuinely believe that economic decision-making by a powerful state bureaucracy is needed to fight poverty efficiently in India today, just as there were sincere British politicians in the hungry thirties who advocated tough state interventionism in the UK—unencumbered by parliamentary trappings—to wipe out the misery and squalor of mass unemployment. One may concede the theoretical possibility that in India today material growth constitutes something which is worth buying at the price of having to live in a society regimented by benevolent state officials. I see, however, no reason why anyone should hesitate in making a different choice in the rich Britain of 1970, even if one believes that the alternatives are a fast GNP growth induced by more centralized planning or a slowing down of GNP growth but more freedom and less state controls.

The merits of a bigger GNP must be carefully scrutinized in the light of the demerits of attaining it. If the discussion is raised to this intellectual plane, many of the traditional arguments for and against the ability of the state to plan a fast growth rate lose their urgency. Jewkes believes that a historian of hallucinations ought to include in his domain the idea that governments possess the knowledge and power positively to determine the rate of economic growth through centralized planning (61). Drawing on her experience, Joan Mitchell, a member of the National Board for Prices and Incomes, has penned a heart-felt book (introduced by George Brown) which seeks to persuade that British state planning will raise production faster than a market economy (42). Whether Jewkes or Mitchell is right—does it really matter so much? We have the means today to be inefficient, we can afford to have less output rather than more, and—to cite the heading of the last Appendix—we can allow ourselves the luxurious right to waste.

Some prosaic numerate data illustrate the meaning of GNP growth. In the sort of business game they like playing at Harvard, it has been calculated that if the people of the US would continue to increase their productivity at the same pace as in the last thirty years, and work the same number of hours, the $550 billion national product of 1963 would become a (constant-price) GNP of $1,250 billion in 1993. The authors, however, warn that if Americans become indolent and cease to worship the sacred cow of the GNP with the same dedication as in the past, if they should degenerate and reduce their annual working time from the present 1,900 to 1,600 hours, and if they slow down their regular productivity spurts, then the 1993 US GNP will only be $800 billion (32).

If the 1968 UK GNP continuously grows at 4·5 per cent. per annum, then the (constant-price) national product in the year 2,000 will be about four times as big as today's. It is not suggested that this growth rate will in fact be achieved. Many people, however, think that it is an ideal to be aimed at and worth suffering for. Is it an ideal?

The concluding remarks are addressed to members of my discipline. I appreciate the temptations beckoning those who feel themselves condemned to a passive life of thinking, teaching, writing and counselling. State planning offers an opportunity to do, to perform and to mould the economy—not by persuasion but by statutory orders. It is the exhilarating emotion of putting theory into practice that has made so many economists, all over the world, rush away gleefully from their desks and podia to embrace the power to act which state interventionism offers. Whether in government service or not, it is pleasing to declaim before the lay public scientific truths, and to proclaim with certitude what the future holds.

It is part of the psychological make-up of mortals that they regard sins of commission as morally more depraved than sins of omission. An economist who can persuade his client to desist from continuing with an unprofitable venture is as useful as his colleague who is able to propose a profitable course of new action—yet, the latter will ordinarily reap more rewards because his advice is said to be constructive. I am well aware that my book is a debunking exercise which stresses why it is incongruous to forecast, and undesirable to plan, the national product. I have no recipes to sell and know of no panaceas. I have sought to destroy popular images and to demolish shibboleths; I am bound to fail the test of 'tell us how to do it better'.

Yet, I like to think, there is after all something constructive in the generation of healthy scepticism. It may influence the wider public to evaluate more critically pleas for growth-at-all-costs; it may lead voters to scorn a government which thinks that the maintenance of a bankrupt shipyard is a greater source of happiness than the building of a supermarket; it may even make people think twice about the barren assertion that exporting is always good and importing always bad.

Should the ideas put forward in this book become widely accepted, then this will undoubtedly lead to unemployment amongst economists who now earn their bread-and-butter by selling pompous forecasts and ready-made plans of the economic future. Regrettable though this may be for the individuals affected, I believe that it is wholesome to break the link between economic analysis and soothsaying, and to strip economists of their pretentious connotation as scientists. Shorn of its magic frills, economics can then be restored to the status of a discipline with sane and purposeful functions.

Appendix I

National Accounts Definitions[*]

The first national income estimate was made, more than three centuries ago, by William Petty. Until the Second World War, A. L. Bowley, L. Grünbaum, C. Clark, A. Flux, S. Kuznets and J. Stamp did pioneering work in laying the conceptual foundations of the modern national acounts; they were mostly, however, concerned with the national income, the net output of the economy which aggregates the factor shares of labour and property. Prodded and inspired by Keynes, James Meade and Richard Stone prepared for publication in April 1941, a British White Paper on war finance which included national product estimates at market prices. Their example was followed by American statisticians who published similarly constructed data on the US economy in 1942. These exercises, intended for the purpose of helping the government to harness the economy to war purposes, were the forerunners of the GNP data which are now prepared all over the non-communist world. When hostilities ceased, there was a temporary statistical hiatus in Britain, but in 1947 a complete set of national accounts, based on the double-entry principle, was introduced. National Blue Books, with GNP data going back to 1938, have been issued regularly since 1952. From 1957 onwards, backdated to 1955, the UK calculates also quarterly GNP figures.

[*] The British methods are admirably outlined in (105), whilst the varying national accounting practices in 60 countries are the subject of a special UN study (106). The statistical office of the United Nations brought out its first detailed report on the measurement of national income in 1947 (86), but this has been revised in a 1964 publication that serves as a model for comparative national studies (180). The OECD issued a revised edition of its standardized system of national accounts in 1958 (181). The US definitions of the GNP, and its tributaries, are succinctly summarized in the introduction to the Department of Commerce's national accounts tables for 1929–1965 (182).

National Income	= net domestic product at factor cost *plus* net factor income from the rest of the world.
Gross Domestic Product at Factor Prices	= net domestic product *plus* capital consumption.
Gross Domestic Product at Market Prices	= gross domestic product at factor prices *plus* indirect taxes *minus* subsidies.
Gross National Product	= gross domestic product *plus* net factor income from the rest of the world.

Those not concerned with the intricacies of national accounts may nevertheless be interested in three features that are found in all GNP presentations. (1) Exports are counted as part of the national product on the principle that the end-uses and destinations of output are statistically irrelevant; imports are not included and the value of the GNP is therefore calculated by deducting from expenditure figures the import content. (2) The basic difference between the GDP (gross domestic product) and the GNP (gross national product) is the inclusion in the latter of net property income from abroad, i.e. the income accruing from abroad less the domestic income accruing to foreigners. As the UK has larger investments abroad than foreigners have property assets in the UK, the British GNP is invariably larger than the GDP. This item, however, accounts for only a 1 percentage point difference. (3) The GNP includes production for both consumption and investment, the latter classified as gross domestic fixed capital formation. The data for the *gross* national product inflate the actual value of the annual production of wealth, because they make no allowance for the fact that some capital goods produced in the past have become partially or wholly obsolescent. Though statistically subject to larger errors, it is often more meaningful to measure the annual accretion of produced values by deducting from the gross totals the depreciation of capital goods, classified as capital consumption; if such deductions are made the *gross* national product becomes the *net* national product.

There is no great difficulty about reconciling national product totals at market and factor prices respectively, because the difference is the easily ascertainable volume of 'indirect taxes less subsidies', which is incorporated in the former but excluded from data at factor prices. British national accounts are usually presented at factor cost, whilst the UN and OECD prefer market cost figures.

THREE ROUTES

The first of the three ways in which the national product can be viewed is from the income angle. This route aggregates all forms of actual — and also some imputed — income, directly derived from the current production of goods and services. (Other types of income — such as gifts, family allowances, old age pensions — are not included because they are treated as transfer payments for which no current goods and services are created; they are registered in the national accounts as part of factor incomes or taxes.) In the UK accounts, the major income items are:

Income from Employment (wages, salaries, forces pay, some employer costs of fringe benefits);
Income from Self-Employment;
Profits (companies, nationalized corporations);
Rent.

The second route measures the GNP by the size of the total output of goods and services. It is an aggregate of value-added in different industries* and activities, i.e. the value of their gross output less the

---

* When patients visit doctors in Harley Street, they pay with their fees for medical and non-medical services, the latter include pleasant waiting rooms, receptionists to arrange appointments, privacy, etc.

Using hypothetical (constant price) figures, the average British housewife spends today £9, as against £6 ten years ago, on what the GNP connotes as food. Part of this increase represents a larger consumption of food measured in calories, proteins and carbo-hydrates, but a large part is accounted for by the acquisition of convenience elements such as pre-cooking, superior packing, hygiene, etc. A loaf of unwrapped bread is a different product from a hermetically-sealed plastic bag containing slices of fresh bread; in buying the latter the buyer acquires bread plus labour-saving plus freshness plus aesthetic enjoyment.

These examples are cited to cast doubts on the validity of subdividing the GNP into separate compartments. In suggesting that some of the values now attributed to industry A really belong to industry B, no criticism is implied of the total size of the GNP. It is, however, argued that *per capita* category comparisons, relating to expenditure on food, fuel, medicine, transport, etc., may at times be even more misleading than country and time confrontations of overall GNP totals.

inputs from other domestic industries and activities, and less the import content.

The third route, the GNP expenditure approach, adds up all expenditure on final goods and services less their import content. The main categories are current expenditure by consumers, corporations, and the government, and accretion to wealth by the physical increase in stocks and fixed capital investment.

These three GNP totals are calculated by more or less independent methods and from different sources. It is not surprising that the end-results vary though all three methods purport to measure one identical concept and each of the routes is supposed to lead to the same truth.

The movements of the three GNP approaches are erratic. They are slightly inconsistent and no correlation can be established which would indicate that a particular route tends to overstate or understate the actual GNP fluctuations. According to a recent Treasury statement (44), the biggest annual divergence noted between them has been 1·5 per cent. A study in *Econometrica* (20) concludes that the US gap between the calculated expenditure and income approaches has in some postwar years been more than 2 per cent.

Quarterly results obviously show a larger differential. In the example quoted below the discrepancy between one route and a second is as high as 4 percentage points! Whilst the expenditure data indicate a drop in the national product by 3 per cent., those based on the output approach report an increase by 1 per cent.

CONSTANT-PRICE GDP GROWTH
ACCORDING TO THREE CRITERIA

	Expenditure	Income	Output
1968 over 1967	+3·0%	+3·5%	+4·0%
2nd 1969, over 4th 1968, quarter	−3·0%	−0·5%	+1·0%

National accounts comparisons must, in order to have any semblance of meaningfulness, be expressed in constant prices. But which constant prices? Until the beginning of 1969, the UK GNPs were calculated with '1958 prices'. In 1969 the series of past GNPs was re-calculated with '1963 prices'. No one appreciating the methodology of working with different constant-price foundations will be surprised to learn that the past annual GNP growth rates have now had to be revised with discrepancies of up to half a percentage point. This is but another, perhaps pedantic, factor which introduces vagueness and indeterminateness in the recorded fluctuations of national accounts. It helps to show how silly are the people who suggest that a country with a constant-price GNP growth of 4 per cent. has necessarily had a faster time growth than a country with a constant-price growth of 3·5 per cent. which has been calculated on a different time basis. Until 1953 the British national accounts statisticians 'cheated' by so manipulating the least reliable estimates of the different routes as to reconcile the three GNP calculations. There were then no admitted discrepancies, as there are none today in many other countries' published GNPs (105). Since 1953, British national accounts appear in three slightly conflicting—but honestly presented—versions. The Central Statistical Office deserves to be congratulated for rejecting spurious accuracy in the different GNP approaches and, like their colleagues in the US Department of Commerce, they warn users to take these discrepancies into account when applying GNP data to an assessment of the economic situation. This intellectual honesty of governmental statisticians in the Anglo-Saxon countries (and in some others too) cannot be praised highly enough. Implicitly, however, it ridicules those politicians and economic commentators who attach great significance to 1 or 2 percentage points movements in the GNP, when the girth and weight of this sacred cow is not measurable except by statistical standards that themselves vary by 1 or 2 percentage points.

THE COMMUNIST MODELS*

National accounting in Marxist economies rests on one massive foundation: labour is only considered fruitful when expended on production proper or an immediate extension thereof, i.e. when it creates tangible material goods. The United Nations publish the Communist national accounts, headed *Expenditure on New Material Product*. An introductory note explains that this is an official estimate of the net material product, defined as the total net value of goods and 'productive' services, including

---

* I have drawn heavily, and gratefully, on the writings of A. Nove, particularly his Chapter X in (107), and have also benefited from Kaser (108).

turnover taxes. The ideological craze for material values induces the communist countries to omit the output of most services.*

The communist countries disdain the Western concept of the GNP and instead publish two main national accounts indicators. The first is the so-called gross social product which is an aggregate of the *gross* output of all branches of material production; this entails much double counting, because no deductions are made—as in the Western GNP—for inputs from other branches. The other is the more meaningful net national income, which is calculated on the basis of the final selling price of material goods (including turnover taxes, but net of double-counting and capital consumption).

Three conceptual difficulties arise in both types of calculation.

I

The official Soviet view (108) is that in a socialist society factor cost and market-price valuations are identical—yet the so-called market price is a misnomer in a centrally planned and directed economy, because it has little to do with costs or consumer demand but is arbitrarily determined. This market price valuation distorts the communist national accounts considerably, for—in the absence of much direct taxation—the state obtains most of its tax revenue from the turnover tax which constitutes about one quarter of the market price of material output. (The difference between the UK GNPs at factor, and market, prices is about 10 per cent.)

II

The definition of what is material and productive is subject to many interpretations, and indeed the communist priests in various countries argue amongst themselves as to what the prophets Marx and Engels would have ruled to be truly productive. The UN consequently warns

* The UN Committee on Contributions, theoretically at least, works on the basis of the national income estimates supplied by the member-countries. To bring the communist national output data on to a common denominator with those of other countries, UN officials scale up the former by adding to their official figures the guestimated value of services, etc., which constitute part of the published national accounts of the non-communist countries.

us that not only are comparisons between planned and non-planned economies full of pitfalls, but there are also statistical dangers in national income confrontations 'among the planned economies themselves' (109).

III

In the cited definition of the communist national accounts, at the beginning of this section, included services were described as productive in inverted commas. This is due to an absurd conceptual division of non-material service labour into 'productive' and 'non-productive'. Those services which are performed directly in conjunction with activities yielding material goods qualify for the Marxist crown of 'productive', whilst the other services are capped with 'non-productive' thorns.* Thus a railway signalman is productive when he lets a freight train past his box, but unproductive when he performs an identical action on the approach of a passenger train. A typist in the Russian Foreign Office is not productive, but her sister-typist in a machine tool factory is.†

The apparently irreconcilable communist and Western national accounts—one measuring material output at artificial market prices, whilst the other calculates material plus non-material output at factor

---

* The transportation item, for example, appears in the net material product of the USSR but is circumscribed as follows: 'goods transport and communications for "productive enterprises" only'. Kaser (108) has cited documentary evidence that this dogmatic approach is by no means applauded everywhere in the USSR. Without being sent to Siberia, some Russian statisticians have, in public, profaned the Marxist saints by demanding that passenger transport, education, and other services be incorporated in the net national income.

† In Britain, at least, we ought not to laugh ourselves hoarse at this funny dichotomy of the treatment of service output in the communist national products. The 1965 Selective Employment Tax, for which Wilson-Callaghan-Kaldor must take personal responsibility, was based on a similar ideological separation. It assumed, as the Marxists do, that the creation of material wealth is more deserving of public support than the generation of non-material wealth. The analogy with the communist national accounts continues. SET whitewashed (ordinarily parasitical) service activities as productive, and therefore worthy of being given a state subsidy, if they were carried on in conjunction with the production of material wealth. An English typist in a Sunderland shipyard earns her employer a payroll subsidy whilst the employers of a typist in a doctor's surgery or a City export house are punished for engaging in unproductive activities, and have to bear the full burden of the punitive SET.

prices—can in fact be made roughly to tally. The communist material output is notionally redistributed in the following manner: first the factors creating the material net output are rewarded and then the remaining values (consisting largely of profits and turnover taxes) are considered to be paid by the state to those factors in the economy which are engaged on unproductive tasks. Thus, whilst teachers are not treated as creators of output *per se*, the taxes levied on the output of iron and cabbages are deemed to be paid into a fund out of which teachers' emoluments are paid.

TOTAL AVAILABLE RESOURCES

The GNP is a statistical measurement of national output. The main purpose of collating GNP data, and employing them for comparisons over time and space, is to measure relative standards of living implicitly gauged by the numerate size of the GNP volumes. Leaving aside the criticism of national accounts comparisons, developed in Part I, I want to raise now the issue as to whether (on the premises employed by the statisticians of conventional national accounts) the national standard of living is always identical with welfare generated by the GNP.

The CSO, on p. 1 of its handbook (105), defines national income as a measure 'of the money value of goods and services becoming available to the nation from economic activity'. On p. 5 an important qualification is introduced and the definition is adjusted by the introduction of one word 'own'; the extended definition now says that it is appropriate to treat the 'national income as a measure of the goods and services becoming available to the nation through its own economic activity'. It implies that one ought to count those goods and services which 'become available' to the nation—not to the world as a whole. It also suggests that only those goods and services should be counted which are created through the nation's 'own' activities. Conceptually, there is a significant clash between these two notions.

GNP accounts include goods produced for exports. This certainly fits in with the idea underlying national accounts that all types of production, irrespective of their purpose and destination, must be included. For welfare comparisons, however, this is absurd because goods that are exported do not become available to the society producing them; they do not *per se* constitute an accretion to national welfare. Let it be assumed that two countries have the same GNP and both import nothing; one exports 1 per cent. and the other 10 per cent., of the GNP. Clearly — in terms of the standard of living — the latter is worse off. In practice, however, there is not much harm in incorporating exports within the GNP, because by the same rules imports are excluded (from 'total domestic expenditure plus export and property income from abroad') in calculating the GNP. In most countries of the world exports and imports of goods and services and net (negative or positive) property income are roughly equal. Even the temporary balance of payment deficits of the UK in the sixties did not exceed 2 per cent. of the GNP. Conceptually it may appear incongruous to include production-for-exports within a statistical vessel measuring national welfare, and to exclude from it imports which distinctly help to raise the standard of living. Yet, there is no urgency about abolishing these existing rules because of the mentioned self-cancellation of the two incongruities.

There are, however, countries where the traditional national accounts give a misleading picture of welfare. The national welfare, measured by 'total available resources', i.e. GNP plus the import surplus, may in extreme cases differ by up to 30 per cent. from the GNP. The military-political aid received by Vietnam, the charitable support given by Jewish sympathizers and friendly nations to Israel, and the remittances sent to their native countries by emigrants from Puerto Rico, Cyprus, Eire* and Greece, radically raise the standards of living in these economies above those that are notionally measured by their GNPs. The *per capita* GNP figures of countries in receipt of substantial — currently unrequited — grants, gifts, remittances, loans and investments do not provide data that are comparable with those adduced by countries in which 'total available resources' and the GNP are more or less identical. The *per capita* acquisition of refrigerators in Eire, the consumption of electricity in Vietnam, and the burden of military expenditure in Israel, ought to be seen within the framework of 'total available resources' — and not the GNP — because they are partly financed through the import surplus.

On p. 219, I discussed the contingent possibility that the rich Western countries might in future feel themselves so affluent as to devote a substantial portion of their GNP to aid for the under-developed economies.

* Eire has in fact adapted its national accounts presentation to the underlying principle of 'total available resources'. The net inflow of emigrants' remittances is treated as part of net factor income from abroad, and consequently included in Eire's national income. This is an explicit deviation from the standards set by the United Nations (106).

If this should ever come about and exceed, say, 10 per cent. of their total national cake, it would be necessary to employ for the donor countries too the principle of 'total available resources', i.e. to deduct from their GNP unrequited exports of goods and services. For comparative welfare purposes, they would be considered to have a smaller national cake than is calculated by the present national accounts.*

To summarize this section: if one wishes to collate output figures, then of course the GNP is the right statistical tool. If, however, one wishes to measure welfare—related to what the CSO calls 'goods and services becoming available to the nation'—one ought only to count those values which are in fact the determinants of the standard of living. I have suggested above that 'total available resources' can be calculated by adding to the GNP the import surplus. In the short run this is the right way. Yet, the import surplus ought to be split up between those transfers from abroad that represent investments from which foreigners will later draw a property income, and unrequited aid and remittances, i.e. pure gifts. In the sixties, the UK 'total available resources' were larger than its GNP, and to that extent the British standard of living was higher than was justified by the country's 'own economic activity'. The differential, however, will have to be repaid over the years to come in one form or another. On the other hand, in Eire, the remittances sent home by Irish emigrants have augmented that country's national welfare without this creating a drain on its future resources.

* Some sophisticated thinkers will no doubt argue that when a rich country sends unrequited exports to a poor country, it is augmenting its own welfare through spiritual pleasures derived from giving.

Appendix II

Ex Post GNP Revisions

The Attlee socialist administration was much more convinced that it could safely forecast detailed national accounts than the Wilson government. In the immediate post-war period, the Treasury stuck out its neck and published forward estimates of 'manpower budgets', imports and overall GNP figures. For obvious reasons the government of the day was made to look rather foolish and publication of specific forward estimates has been stopped since 1952. Of course governments have continued to act on non-published future estimates but it is now much more difficult to prove that the Treasury pundits are not really planning with accurate projections. To provide prima facie evidence of the Treasury's erroneous ex ante estimates, a rather indirect — but, I hope, no less convincing — route will be explored.

The first published ex post GNP data for year I are ordinarily published in the spring of year II as part of the budget package. Within a few months they are revised and corrected figures appear in the Blue Books published in the autumn of year II. This, however, is not the end of it. Every year, the Central Statistical Office (CSO) adjusts the GNP totals for all the previous years.

To some extent these revisions are due to conceptual changes in the GNP, which are announced periodically. The effect of this element upon the revision of *overall* GNP totals is minute, but it does play a not insignificant role in the historical adjustment of GNP *components*. Thus, for example, an early CSO definition of investment included 'repairs and maintenance', and when these were later excluded the re-written totals for the investment item showed a large discrepancy from the original published entries. The main reasons for the periodic revisions of the overall GNP totals are, however, not conceptual changes of this kind but — to cite the CSO — additional information and improved methods of estimation. In the following table, the GNPs of the first four years of the fifties and sixties have been noted, as originally issued, and are then contrasted with the 1967 estimates of the government statisticians.

UK GNP, AT CURRENT PRICES, EXPENDITURE BASIS, FACTOR COST

GNP Year	Original Estimate* £ Mn	Revised Estimate† £ Mn	Discrepancy £ Mn	%
1951	12,414	12,958	544	4·4
1952	13,648	14,009	361	2·6
1953	14,719	15,062	343	2·3
1954	15,543	15,924	381	2·5
1961	23,703	24,428	725	3·1
1962	24,824	25,555	731	2·9
1963	26,358	27,129	771	2·9
1964	28,691	29,231	540	1·9

Laymen will probably be astonished to learn that the (arithmetical) average of the annual GNP errors in the early fifties was £407 Mn, and in the early sixties £692 Mn; even allowing for the reduced value of the currency this hardly indicates an improvement in national accounts estimating. The (arithmetical) average percentage error in these eight years is 2·7 per cent. If this undermines faith in the Treasury statisticians it is comforting to know that the National Income division of the US Department of Commerce, also engaged on regular revisions, has recalculated past American GNPs to expose similar statistical fallacies. There are few more ludicrous spectacles than the annual homilies of Chancellors and economic commentators, discoursing on the need 'to

* 'Preliminary Estimates of National Income and Expenditure' published in March/April of the year following the completion of the calendar GNP year, in conjunction with the Chancellor's budget speech.
† These revised data are taken from the CSO's 'Blue' book on 'National Income and Expenditure', August 1967.

take out' or 'put into' the economy—through budget measures—£200 Mn or £400 Mn; the unwarranted assumption is made that the size of tomorrow's national cake is ascertainable today with numerate accuracy.

Actually, in outlining new measures bearing on the external exchange rate and on fiscal and monetary policy, the Chancellor of the Exchequer is more interested in projections of GNP components and the balance of payments than in general GNP prophecies. Yet the forecasting errors of these detailed, and much more relevant, categories are considerably greater than the overall GNP fallacies. Three striking examples will elucidate this. In April 1969, the Treasury reported that UK overseas private investments in 1968 had been £621 Mn. This was a vital piece of information because government policy in 1969 in relation to the balance of payments depended upon the size of this outflow which was largely under the control of the government. Yet by August 1969, the ex post 1968 estimate had already been revised to the startlingly higher figure of £736 Mn. In 1955 an estimate was given of the amount of personal savings in 1954, but in every subsequent year this was whittled down until the Treasury estimated in 1962 that this item was in fact only half of what had been originally published in 1955 (44). Only in 1968 did the preliminary results of the 1966 Census of Distribution reveal that the calculated output of service industries, estimated by the Board of Trade and incorporated between 1961 and 1966 in the respective GNPs, had been far out; thus former estimations of increased turnover of laundries, dry cleaners, etc., by 26 per cent. had now to be replaced with 62 per cent. This certainly was not a phenomenon that made the CSO lose much sleep, because it had previously intimated (105) how unreliable its consumer expenditure categories are.

A study of ex post revisions is revealing, because it bears on the accuracy of forward projections by the government. If the Treasury is unable to know with a high degree of accuracy, three months after the GNP of year II has ended, what the statistical performances have been —and up to ten years must elapse before a final estimation can be authoritatively published—how much more wrong must ex ante predictions of year II be when they are prepared, and acted upon, in year I? One can only applaud a system of government that permits state-employed statisticians to publish regularly revisions which implicitly prove that the state is not equipped to make accurate forecasts. There are cynics who say that the government is not harmed by these revisions, and that the Treasury and Board of Trade are not really held up to public ridicule, because the electorate obviously does not know of the implications contained in an exposure of wrong GNP estimates. How many Members of Parliament know, care and realize how fatuous are some of the budget speeches which outline new measures by quantifying their impact in relation to national accounts projections that will ultimately be proved to have been wrong?

The last people to blame for the errors of national incomes and expenditure items are the statisticians. They are fully aware of the true worth of GNP data. The official CSO handbook (105) spells it out: 'New sources of information, for example new kinds of statistical returns, may however make it apparent that the estimate of an item for some years was even further from the truth than the estimators thought likely.' The CSO goes on to say that it is the duty of the estimators to warn the users of the statistics about these weaknesses. Undoubtedly this is done in inter-office memoranda but clearly government statisticians cannot give a press conference to denounce their political masters for having used, without reservations, figures for which the evidence is relatively weak. The ideology of economic planning entails knowledge of the economic future. To tear the forecasting carpet from under the feet of the planners is wholesome political labour; by disseminating ex post national accounts errors (in addition to all the other criticisms of the GNP), healthy public scepticism is created in face of ex ante declamations.

Appendix III
The Investment Conundrum* .

The output data of an economy do not differentiate between production of consumer and capital goods. The expenditure uniform of the GNP, however, makes a distinction between current consumption and gross domestic fixed capital formation. There are certain exceptions to this rule. By convention, all expenditure on military equipment is treated as consumption. Consumer durables (except houses) are statistically presumed to be consumed in the year of production. In practice a substantial amount of business expenditure is listed improperly as current expenditure (e.g. acquisition of small tools), and the same applies to Research-and-Development costs. (Most investments in human capital—this is further discussed at the end of this chapter—also do not qualify as capital formation.) The result is that the true proportion of the GNP, furnished by capital formation, is almost certainly higher than that registered in the official national accounts. This, by itself, does not change in the *year of production* the overall size of the GNP, but merely affects its composition. Why is it then worth raising? In some political arguments, the investment segment of the national cake is considered a decisive criterion for the economic performance of countries. On that score developed countries, compared with under-developed ones, have a higher investment segment than is officially admitted.

The National Bureau of Economic Research is now engaged on a project, under the leadership of J. W. Kendrick (100), in which the 1965 US national accounts are being recalculated by shifting certain consumption expenditure to gross investments. For the purpose of his analysis, Kendrick has also augmented the US GNP by about 50 per cent.; he has imputed value-creation to housewives' services, privately-

---

* Capital formation in stocks is not discussed in this chapter, which deals only with investments in fixed assets and human capital.

owned capital goods, student compensation, etc. Whilst the official capital formation is 16·3 per cent. of the conventional US GNP, the Bureau's total gross (tangible and intangible) investment is 53·4 per cent. of the enlarged national product model. Even when the GNP is not swelled by these notional increments, the real investment proportion is still seen to be considerably higher than the 16·3 per cent, arrived at by the present conventional methods.

Country A produces in 1970, 100 tons of bread and pineapples, 200 houses, 10,000 washing machines, one giant computer, and completes 10 per cent. of a dam project which will become operative only after another nine years of construction. Each of these items is registered with an identical £1 Mn output-value in A's £5 Mn GNP. This arithmetical sameness hides a variety of current welfare meanings that can be given to these products. The bread and pineapples are immediately consumed. The houses, washing machines and the computer are put to immediate economic use, but their use-values—in the year of production —are not equal to their registered output-values. The users-buyers expect to amortize their acquisitions only after 40, 5 and 10 years respectively; the partial completion of the dam produces no current use-value. The welfare utilities enjoyed by the citizens of country A in 1970 depend upon their consumption of goods valued at £1,325,000. Not everyone will accept this figure as a sound basis for calculating the standard of living of country A. But there will probably be no dissent from the thesis that the current welfare benefits of country A are considerably fewer than those generated in country B, which has an identical £5 Mn GNP but one consisting exclusively of output of immediately consumed bread and pineapples. Depending on one's preference for immediate or delayed consumption, the size of the investment portion within the GNP may be of greater welfare significance than the size of the GNP itself.

According to Jostock (56), the national product comprises goods, services, and the yields *(Nutzungen)* of capital assets. The first group is relatively easy to establish statistically, whilse the second group already presents more methodological and computational problems. It is the third group which, in Jostock's view, is the most sadly neglected, with half of its values left out of the GNPs of the developed countries. I agree that the yield on the aggregate of capital assets is not fully registered in the national accounts, but—for purposes of comparison—it is even more significant that a given amount of investment-dollars do not lay the same number of golden eggs in all countries and at all times. $100 of investments may produce in Ceylon an annual yield in the fifties of $40, whilst $100 of investments in Canada in the sixties may only produce an annual $20 yield. When the national capital-output ratios diverge considerably—in our hypothetical example they are 2·5 and 5—a confrontation of the respective GNPs is, on that score alone, misleading.

Many have sought to draw far-reaching conclusions from the fact that since the last war Germany has devoted a larger proportion of its national cake to investment than has Britain. Correct but largely irrelevant! What is really decisive is the choice of the German investments. The UK has lagged behind Germany and other competitors because of massive misinvestments, by pouring capital into the wrong branches — much of it into declining industries (textiles, shipyards, coal, railways). If we leave statistical considerations aside, then it is not the proportion of the GNP, taken up by capital formation, which matters but the purpose to which it is put. As T. P. Hill (185) has demonstrated in his international comparison of growth-induced-by-investments, the welfare generated by capital formation is very much influenced by the type of assets produced, e.g. in the short run the construction of residential dwellings is much less 'productive' than machinery.

Many investments in backward economies yield more income than the average investment in the developed countries, but they do not always, on balance, help to speed economic growth. In a Full Employment economy the manufacture of pea-picking machines is beneficial, because through their use more peas can be sown and harvested with the same labour force. (Alternatively, even when the tonnage of peas remains unchanged, the farming community may enjoy higher welfare through increased leisure.) However, in a country with an under-utilized labour force, the portion of the GNP derived from manufacturing pea-pickers (which are not exported) does not enhance welfare, if as a result the tonnage of peas does not increase but labourers, hitherto gathering this crop manually, are displaced by the machines and transferred to the pool of unemployed.

Country A manufactures 100 buses in 1970 for domestic use. For the purpose of incorporating their output-value within the 1970 GNP, it is sufficient to know the market prices, but this is not enough in order to estimate the total *volume* of welfare which the buses will ultimately generate. If they are sent to Manchester to ferry daily thousands of commuters, they will have a higher 'investment yield' than if used by dukes to bring a few visitors to their estates one day a week. The intensity of exploiting a capital asset supplies a pertinent piece of economic information that is unavailable from a reading of the official national accounts. Pictures hung in a private castle and the National Gallery respectively beget varying yields of enjoyment. If the UK and the US both note in their GNPs that the annual *per capita* output of books is $5, but in the former ten – and in the latter only two – people, on average, read each copy, there is then surely a different connotation to this output. To measure the benefits of capital formation one must have recourse to the example of the teacher, whose costs of preparing a lecture are unchanged whether he imparts his knowledge to a class of 10 or 50 pupils.

In one respect the GNP, as a gauge for the generation of economic values, distinctly exaggerates the size of the national product. As its name implies, the GNP measures the *gross* output of investment goods without simultaneously deducting capital consumption. The arbitrary employment of this gross concept disguises the fact that one is told of accretions to the nation's productive wealth but not about its diminutions. If one seeks to measure output, then the gross measure is useful, but output *per se* conveys little that is worth knowing. An inquiry into the relationship between national output and welfare leads to a consideration of net national investments, calculated by deducting the yearly obsolescence and depreciation of past assets from the output-values of newly created assets. Imagine that an earthquake destroyed half the physical assets of a country. To make up for the losses, people work extra hard and by doubling the conventional GNP in the subsequent year they succeed in producing enough investment goods to replace one quarter of the destroyed capital assets. The conventional GNP relates clearly that the productive effort has been vastly improved, but of course it does not say that despite the doubled GNP the standard of living is lower than that prevailing before the earthquake. The architects of conventional national accounts defend the gross approach on the grounds that estimates of depreciation – which would have to be ascertained to arrive at the more meaningful net national product – can be made only on the basis of arbitrary calculations. No one will dispute that net national product figures are even more inaccurate than gross national product data, but—for welfare comparisons—the former are more suitable because they are more significant. Denison agrees that it is easier to measure the gross, than the net, product but he adds that this provides 'no reason for analysing an irrelevant series' (124).

The gross criterion is particularly inappropriate for comparisons of investment volumes as between countries at different stages of development. Let us assume that Brazil buys a $100 Mn nuclear power station. The unsatisfied fuel demand nevertheless remains so great that its existing coal-fired generating stations continue to supply electricity. The new investment, in this case, does not displace old investments and is to be valued at $100 Mn. The US brings into operation a $100 Mn nuclear station, which makes commercially obsolescent several coal-fired stations that physically could have continued to supply energy. The welfare value of the new investment, in this case, ought to be arrived at by deducting the value of the displaced plants from the $100 Mn.*

From the section above it is obvious that the national product is overstated by the gross convention. In another important sense, however, the national product—whether measured gross or net—is decisively underestimated. The outstanding feature of a capital asset is its contingent ability to lay annual golden eggs. These pickings, in the period subsequent to the year in which the output-value of the capital asset was enshrined in the GNP, ordinarily appear indirectly in the national accounts. With fixed capital assets in the ownership of (privately or publicly controlled) businesses, selling their output at market prices, the GNP registration of this annual yield factor presents no problem, because it is incorporated in the prices of the goods currently produced. The matter, however, becomes sticky when the state or non-profit organizations employ capital assets. In general no income is imputed by the state in respect of non-trading assets, other than buildings.†
Thus roads, bridges, some medical facilities, etc., are treated as if they

* If I own a black-and-white television set in perfect working order but throw it away because I have bought a colour set, I have been enriched only by the differential value of the two, whilst my neighbour acquiring a colour set—his first ever television set—will derive a greater benefit.
† Sometimes buildings too are considered to have a zero annual rental value in the UK national accounts, e.g. hospitals operated under the National Health Service, and establishments used by the Atomic Energy Authority for R & D.

provided no annual yield enhancing welfare. The larger the state owner-ship of infrastructure, the larger does this omission under-estimate the GNP.

At the beginning of this chapter, it was suggested that expenditure on consumer durables (cars, washing machines, etc.) ought to be shifted to the investment category, because these are capital goods (even though they are not employed as factors in the creation of material output). They clearly generate annual welfare, which in most cases is larger than their annual depreciation. People buy these durables, rather than rent or lease them, because they expect to have derived from them by the end of their useful lives an accumulated benefit which is larger than their acquisition price. Theoretically this is fully admitted by all concerned with national accounts, and many economists—cf for example (110)—have urged that imputed value-creation should be recorded for consumer durables. The principle is accepted so far as owner-occupied houses are concerned; the GNP records rental income as a regular income factor calculated on a notional basis. For technical reasons this policy is not pursued with the ownership of pianos and washing machines. This means that the GNPs of economies in which consumers own rela-tively many durables understate, in this respect, the true size of the national product that should, but does not, include these golden eggs.

I have discussed elsewhere (cf pp. 72–76) under what circumstances investment in human capital* can today augment the conventional GNP, and concluded that in the developed economies large amounts of additional educational expenditure are needed to produce a minute increase in the tangible values of the GNP. This conclusion— which is hotly disputed by many economists— does not detract from the import-ance of restructuring the contributions of present educational and health expenditure to the national product. This job entails three separate assignments:

---

* Investment in health is methodologically akin to education. It is, however, even more difficult to draw an accepted line between the consumption and capital aspects of health expenditure; most of its golden eggs are already re-corded in the conventional GNP by output that would otherwise have been lost through sickness, absenteeism or the premature death of members of the labour force. As to the intangible benefits, such as absence of pain, these of course are indeterminate and can only find a theoretical place in the genuine GNP.

I

Capital, as distinct from consumer, goods have been defined above as having the characteristic of yielding benefits in the period subsequent to the year of their creation. On that ground expenditure on the formation of human capital ought to be transferred (like consumer durables, R & D, etc.) from the consumption to the capital component category of the GNP. This would not by itself change the overall size of the national product.

II

In the case of education, however, much of society's expenditure is not registered at all in the GNP; I particularly refer to the 'foregone costs', i.e. the national income notionally lost as a result of keeping people at school when they are already physically capable of manufacturing machine tools and stockings. At an international conference (21), economists clashed amongst themselves on the merits of incorporating these notional output-values within the GNP; Vaizey and Balogh were amongst those who vociferously raised their voices in opposition. There are estimates showing that these notional, foregone, educational costs represent expenditure which is as large as all the conventional educational costs already registered in the GNP. Kendrick (100) has calculated these unregistered 'student compensation' costs in the US — by imputing to students fourteen years of age and over the average earnings in the same grouping of those who are at work — at $54 billion in 1965 compared with $6 billion in 1929. These represent expenditure items which are 9·6 per cent and 5·5 per cent of the size of the respective official GNPs.

Machlup (21) has rightly argued that 'one should not use statistical inability to calculate income foregone with any exactitude as an excuse for ignoring the concept altogether'. Merrett (115) and others have elaborated upon the methodological difficulties in arriving at a shadow wage, which would be appropriate for the lost wages of youngsters in education after fourteen. To be fully aware of the practical obstacles, awaiting a reasonably accurate calculation of these notional costs, does not alter the fact that theoretically it is right to register *all* educational costs. (I have developed my views on this in the chapter on A New GNP Dimension; the genuine GNP certainly has room for these notional costs.) Today the conventional GNP merely records actual expenditure, in the form of blackboards, teachers' salaries, and class rooms. I submit that the measure of the opportunity cost is a more comprehensive gauge. When a doctor takes a sabbatical year to specialize in dermatology, the costs to society do not consist only of his tuition fees but are determined by these *and* the necessary expenditure to pay for his locum. When a company sends an executive to the Harvard Business School, it does not measure the costs solely by the tuition and maintenance fees but considers as even more important the disturbance costs incurred by this step.

III

Having decided that educational expenditure belongs to the capital category, it now becomes necessary to register its indeterminate annual yield within the GNPs. Part of it presents no difficulty because many of the golden educational eggs show up in the relatively higher salaries and the higher output already noted in the GNPs. What conventional GNPs omit to show are the non-material yields generated by educational capital. John, at the age of 50, is capable of deriving pleasure from Beethoven because of the tuition he received at school when he was 16 and did not manufacture machine tools. These intangible — and at present unregistered — welfare benefits make our Western society richer than is evident from the conventional GNPs.

Appendix IV

Forecasting Coal Demand

Translated into 1970 prices, investments in the coal industry since nationalization have totalled about £3 billion, some of it interest-free and the rest at subsidized interest rates. Most of these were meant to be amortized over 20–30 years. A number of the modernized pits – such as the Mosley Common colliery which has absorbed £11 Mn investment capital since nationalization – have been closed altogether, many are under-utilized and others are only kept working by state support.* Tens of millions of pounds were expended on first attracting workers to the mines and then paying redundancy emoluments to re-settle them. The economy, in addition to providing investment capital, has had to pay higher fuel costs because electricity, gas and oil prices were artificially heightened in order to bolster the coal industry. Before quantifying the coal industry's output it must be recalled that the National Coal Board has exported at a loss, and also accumulated large stocks of unsold coal, 'some of which has been lying on the same tips for many years – unsold, deteriorating, poor in quality and not worth the value in the books' – as was charged by a Member of Parliament in 1967 (65). This issue was raised when the government requested that the National Coal Board's borrowing power be raised to £950 Mn, largely to cover the financing costs of 30 Mn tons of stocks (over and above the seasonally conditioned summer stocks). How did Britain get into this mess?

In 1949 coal output was 203 Mn tons. In that year 'Plan for Coal'

---

* In this tragi-comedy E. Shinwell has played a leading role since the days when he was the minister responsible for the creation of the Coal Board. At the end of his long parliamentary career, he had to admit: 'The most modern machinery, the most modern equipment and the most modern methods have been deployed at great expense, and many of the pits upon which vast sums of money have been expended for this purpose have been closed' (65).

was prepared, and was published in the subsequent year by the National Coal Board (NCB), predicting a demand of 230–250 Mn tons in 1961–65. The demand schedules were drawn up as if coal had no competitors and the country's anticipated additional fuel demand would accrue almost automatically to coal. In April 1956, the NCB published a revised projection ('Investing in Coal') providing for an output of 228 Mn tons in 1960 and 240 Mn tons in 1965. 'The Board has come to the conclusion that an output of 250 Mn tons a year cannot be attained before 1970 instead of 1965 as they had hoped...' In October 1958, the NCB issued a 'Revised Plan for Coal', estimating the 1965 demand at 200–215 tons.

In real life things worked out differently. Despite continued subsidies for the NCB, the government recognized, in a 1967 White Paper, that it could not force the economy to absorb more than 155 Mn tons in 1970 and even this would have to be scaled down to 120 Mn tons in 1975 and perhaps 80 Mn tons in 1980. As the Ministry of Power (184) put it, even this 155 Mn target could only be achieved if the electricity industry was reimbursed from the public purse for being compelled to use coal instead of oil, and the gas industry prohibited from making substantial bulk sales to power stations.

On the 28th November 1967 a devoted apostle of nationalization, the socialist Member of Parliament for the West Fife constituency, attacked Labour's handling of the coal situation:

'If our post-war experience of the fuel industries and the coal industry has taught us one thing, it is never trust the experts, particularly, never trust fuel ministers, however glib and smooth they may be. They have produced more wrong forecasts than the most hapless football pools punter, and they have been a lot more expensive.'

In several respects this is an unjust attack on the predictors of the NCB. No one could have demanded that they be clairvoyants. There was nothing wrong in NCB economists' dreaming, in 1949, of the future and conjecturing possible future demand.* The culprits of the coal débâcle are the governments, which treated predictions as forecasts, and acted upon them as if they were gospel truth.

In an address to a learned society, the director of statistics at the

---

* The coal industry has a place of honour amongst those British economic branches which recorded a steep increase in production per man-hour during the sixties. Managerial and labour efficiency, however, cannot keep a dying industry alive.

Ministry of Power, C. I. K. Forster, debunked forecasting in a manner, which implicitly constituted a sharp attack on the planning ideology of post-war British governments (184). He ridiculed the political and economic commentators who imagine that with sufficient technical care 'forecasts will come out right...this is a complete fallacy'. In this senior statistician's view, however good the method and however skilled the operators, there are never any guarantees that predictions will turn out to be good forecasts. He suggested two specific reasons for this in the energy industries. First, the forecaster has to work on specific assumptions, such as that there will be no future changes in government policy, which may be wide of the mark for reasons that have nothing to do with the particular product. Secondly, he made the obvious point — though not obvious to planners — that unforeseen technological changes may occur. He asserted that even the most sophisticated methods in the late fifties could not have forecast the demand for gas in 1967, or predicted a relatively low increase in electricity sales between 1963 and 1967.

His civil service status prevented Forster from continuing the analysis to ask why the conjectural thoughts of the NCB were allowed to assume the tragic *dimensions* they did, when they were translated into economic facts. The inimical effects flowing from the fallacious NCB predictions can be directly traced to the nationalized status of the coal corporation. (1) Even when it had become obvious that coal was a dear fuel, which was being displaced technologically and economically by its competitors, the government did not radically reverse its bigoted support for coal. Once having committed itself, it preferred to continue — albeit at a slower pace — to prop coal production at the expense of other sectors of the economy. Governments do not like to cut their losses demonstratively and quickly — for all to see. (2) The Whitehall planners realized that in a free market coal production would slump fast. Possessing statutory powers to coerce fuel users, they deliberately intervened in the economy to work against the market trend. They succeeded, by force, in holding back the increased use of new fuel products, to keep alive something outdated. (3) When the executives of the NCB were conjecturing about a large future demand for their products, they thought aloud in order to recruit investment capital. Industrialists in the non-state sector also conjecture about the growing demand for their products, but they do not find it so easy to attract risk capital. In a free enterprise economy predictions are always treated with some scepticism by the private suppliers of capital. On the basis of the knowledge available in the fifties, a privately-owned NCB would undoubtedly have been able to make out a case of sufficient potency to attract private investments. It would, however, not have been successful in obtaining the same volume of (cheap) funds that benevolent governments transferred to it from the pockets of the taxpayers. Predictions by nationalized corporations are considerably more dangerous than those by privately owned companies; governments lack the healthy scepticism which armours the private owners of risk capital.

Appendix V

The National Plans

It is very unfair to put all the blame on George Brown, and call his masterly document THE national plan—after all it was all started by the Tories. In 1970, when planning documents issued by Her Majesty's Stationery Office have a low credibility rating, it may be difficult to recall the mood of the country in 1960 when the authorities were engulfed by a sea of banners—the biggest one was prepared by the Federation of British Industries—proclaiming the need to emulate the brilliant French in their imaginative, yet authoritarian, planning. The pressure was strong and bore fruit. In July 1961, Selwyn Lloyd appointed the National Economic Development Council. Bickerings prevented it from meeting till March 1962 but Neddy soon settled down to work and when Christmas had come, the first British five-year plan (76), covering growth between 1961 and 1966, was ready and was published in early 1963. A revised version had to be prepared quickly and this too came off the government printing presses in record time to allow the public to buy the green-covered copy for their Easter holidays (186). Selwyn Lloyd had certainly smacked the Labour Party hard. Only a few years previously the socialists had been able to assert with impunity that the Tories refused to plan (189). The Labour Party had been proved wrong!

Neddy's five-year projections (or whatever one seeks to call them) suggested that the gross domestic product would rise in that period by 4 per cent. annually. The actual increase was 3 per cent. When one looks at the data, in the Green Books, concerning manufacturing investments, exports, etc., and compares them with the historical performance of the UK economy, one readily grasps how wrong or irrelevant these arithmetical games had really been.

The two Neddy plans were undoubtedly the genesis of the National

Plan (75) that the Department of Economic Affairs was later to prepare, and all three have two features in common:

I

However erudite the reader, and however many hours he cares to spend on perusing them, he will be unable to discover exactly what they purport to be—targets? forecasts? strategy? psychological warfare? hopes? Many commentators have since elucidated what *they* think these plans were meant to convey, but as yet no one has shown where in the documents the purport of the Tory or Socialist plans is spelt out explicitly and lucidly.

II

The planning documents of George Brown and his predecessors are largely based on data obtained from approaches to industry to elicit their expectations of the future. At best this gives non-committal answers, and at worst replies that have been deliberately contrived to please the framers of the questions. A parliamentary investigation in 1966 discovered that it was farcical to send questionnaires to individual firms,* because most of them did not in fact have plans of the kind

---

* Most of the people who filled in the questionnaires regarded it as a bureaucratic 'duty' to be completed in the shortest space of time and without wasting much effort on it. A few paid attention to the 25 per cent magic figure and actually made returns which amended their tentative corporate plans in the light of this 'target' or 'forecast'. None of the companies which I have interviewed was prepared to be quoted on the meticulousness and conscientiousness with which they filled in the questionnaires. Thanks to the published evidence of the managing director of the Royal Dutch Shell group, history has on record at least one authoritative witness. McFadzean (197) begins his evidence by recalling that the National Plan questionnaires reached his company on the 10th of February with the replies demanded by latest the 17th of March. Shell indeed had plans of its own but refused to adjust them to the higher demand schedule implied in the 'figure of 3·8 per cent plucked out of the air'. McFadzean ridicules the thought that Shell 'would actually implement the level of investment we submitted in reply to the questionnaire. We did not, in practice, disturb our engineers with the counter-productive exercise of revising design and cost estimates; they were engaged in more essential work. We submitted the best guesses we could and carried on precisely with what we were doing before the planners intervened.' I can personally testify to the intelligence of some of the senior staff of the DEA. Surely they must have known what the quality of the replies to

demanded for the purposes of the National Plan. As a DEA spokesman later put it: '...it is quite useless going to individual firms and asking them what they will be doing in five years' time or even in many cases in three years' time.' Consequently the inquiries centred on trade associations but these did not prove particularly helpful either, because they also had little experience of forward planning, not much knowledge of the relevant industrial statistics, and member-firms did not provide them with direct indications of individual future plans and expectations. There are many other criticisms in the report of the Estimates Committee (44), which imply that the returns obtained from the questionnaires are not very trustworthy. Although the National Plan abounds with hundreds of projections about the future state of the economy in 1970, said to have been derived from these questionnaires, most industries were in fact only asked to provide estimates on output and exports up to 1967. Did Neddy and the DEA publicize these, belatedly revealed, facts, which cast additional doubts on the 1970 projections of output of valves, administrative staff in the heavy electrical industry, export of chocolates, and imports of hosiery?

George Woodcock has been quoted as saying this of Neddy: 'Recently it has been a mere talking shop. It is getting quite frustrating' (188). This is intolerant, cruel—and foolish. From its inception in 1962, Woodcock was a member of Neddy. What has changed in its planning and deliberations to provoke this assertion in the autumn of 1968? There is not the slightest foundation for the implication that Neddy was a meaningful policy-making organ under the Tories and has become a talking shop under Woodcock's socialist friends. It has always been the same—with one exception. In November 1962 it had a full-time staff of 61 persons. In February 1969 it employed 178, aided by many part-timers and volunteers.

Labour came to power in October 1964, and immediately organized the DEA which assumed the mantle of Britain's planning. By hard work, long weekends and late nights, its staff succeeded in knocking into shape the National Plan within ten months; it saw the light in September 1965. The GNP was expected to grow annually, in the years

---

their hallowed questionnaires would turn out to be! I am sure they knew, but the innocent buyer of a copy of the National Plan (said to be based to a considerable extent on the answers to these questionnaires) did not necessarily know.

between 1964 and 1970, by 3·8 per cent, so that at the end of this six-year period Britain's (constant price) national output would be 25 per cent bigger than at the beginning — 25 per cent. is a nice round figure! In the foreword to a succinct summary prepared in simple language for the common people who cannot, or do not want to, wade through the full masterly document, George Brown wrote:

'It isn't a Plan to tell us all what to do and when and how. That wouldn't be acceptable to a nation like ours. But it does show us what is necessary and possible. What is available to do it with' (187).

It serves little purpose to point out the contradictions in this popular exposition. One untruth, however, deserves to be exposed. On p. 1 of (75) it says that 'The Plan is designed to achieve a 25 per cent. increase ...' This definition is shown to be a blatant dishonesty when one looks up Appendix C, in which the receipients of the questionnaire are informed that they are to formulate their answers 'on the assumption of a 25 per cent. increase...' The readers of the National Plan are led to think that the government has concluded that a 25 per cent growth is to be expected, or is feasible, or possible, because the returns obtained from industry indicate an anticipated 1970 performance which *in toto* is 25 per cent. above that of 1964. The data on chocolate, perfumery, steel and fur production in 1970, however, tell a different story. They are figures which are based on the arbitrary assumption of a 25 per cent. growth that had been fixed a *priori*.

Did the National Plan fail because it was prepared in such a haste? This alibi is now being built up. When the senior officials of the DEA gave evidence to the Estimates Committee, the point was put to them that extra time would have been most welcome in the preparation of the Plan. Honourable men that they are, they gave an honest answer: '...it would not have made much difference...I doubt even with more relative time, another three or four months, you would have got a very much different result...I am not sure that even if we had had all the time in the world we would have decided differently' (44).

There is something intellectually cowardly about the presentation of the National Plan projections in the form of six-year overall figures. A glance at the questionnaire shows that the industries were requested to give year-by-year estimates of their future output, employment, etc. Why were yearly targets or projections not published? One need not be a cynic to answer that had the government done this it would quickly have destroyed the myth of their plan. Only by waiting till 1971 can a final judgement be made on the validity of the various DEA projections. This may save some political skins but of course condemns the National Plan to a high degree of uselessness for practical business decisions. In 1966 it seemed as if the 25 per cent. target would remain more than half unfulfilled. Because of the 1968–70 recovery induced by the 1967 devaluation, the 25 per cent. target may not turn out not to have been quite so wrong. The DEA's reputation may be partly saved by a decision that was forced upon the economy against the wish of the government. In 1966 and 1967, when Harold Wilson still had his way and kept up the old exchange rate, the GNP grew annually by 1·5 per cent. When in those years critics quoted these low growth rates to compare them disparagingly with the stated 3·8 per cent. rates in the National Plan, government spokesmen told them that two years prove nothing, because 3·8 per cent. was only intended to indicate the average overall six-year performance.

Whilst many facts have already come to light to demonstrate the loose foundations on which the National Plan was built, it will suffice to give one outstanding illustration, which was first uncovered by G. Polanyi in his brilliant introduction to (136). Enough statistical experience was available in 1965 to show that UK employment figures are liable to an error of more than one million, i.e. 5 per cent. of the labour force. To make the DEA plan look scientific and accurate all these past statistical errors were put aside to make room for a dogmatic statement that a 'manpower gap' of 400,000 would appear by 1970, i.e. the labour force would then be short by that number to make the 25 per cent. GNP growth feasible. The government undertook so to shape regional policies as to reduce this forecast gap to 200,000. The DEA economists nevertheless continued to scratch their heads in order to remove this projected labour shortage.

Alas, the world does not pay much attention to the sleepless nights of people who know what the future has in store—a shortage of up to 0·8 per cent. of the required labour force! The National Plan was based on a mid-64 labour force of 25,430,000. In 1966 the Central Statistical Office spoiled the calculations by revising that figure to 25,890,000. Polanyi comments unkindly: 'The manpower "gap" has been closed by the simple expedient of revision and without the need for intervention by the planners.'

In a highly emotional speech, interspersed with offending remarks addressed to Members of Parliament who said that they did not understand his defence of planning, George Brown announced simultaneously the collapse of the National Plan and his continued faith in national plans:

'For almost two years now we have tried to manage the economy in a way that no economy has been managed before... How does this affect the National Plan? I will be absolutely frank with the House. It means that the rate of growth we intended to get, and were set to get, and on the basis of which we predicted all other things for 1970, is no longer available. Therefore I must sit down again with my advisers...and have a new look at the rate at which we now think we can go, and the changes we now think we can make. But it does not destroy the idea of a plan to which the government are committed' (77).

Writing shortly after this speech, Brittan (157) came to the—to him—despairing conclusion that the ideas underlying the Neddy Green Books and the National Plan had 'suffered a resounding defeat. One particular approach to economic policy had lost its credibility in this country for the rest of this decade and probably beyond'. I wished that he were right, but all the signs point to new planning documents.

Indeed George Brown returned from his parliamentary clarion call to rally the DEA staff and encourage them to engage on National Plan, Mark II. Work commenced and various versions were ready in 1967. Then came devaluation which disastrously upset the planners' new blueprints. It appears that at some stage in 1968 the new minister of the DEA, Peter Shore, finally decided not to tempt the economic gods; he cancelled the proposed publication of a revised National Plan. Instead, in collaboration with Neddy, the DEA prepared a harmless paper, modestly headed, *Economic Assessment to 1972*.

How should a gentleman act in the moment of his glory? He must not rub salt into the open wounds of his political opponent. He must not behave like a bully, who hits a man when he is down. He must not smile gleefully. It seems so ungentlemanly to relate the misfortunes that have befallen George Brown and his Plan. If Brittan's prognosis were sound, one could let all this rest in peace and leave it to historians to deal with. I suspect, however, that human memory is short. Michael Shanks is probably right when he says: 'It is remarkable that, after the débâcle of the 1965 Plan, both sides of industry should be so ready to try again' (103). As preventive medicine, to avert this danger, I recommend reading the euphoric comments which greeted, at the time, the publication of the Neddy and DEA plans.

Appendix VI

Long Live Waste!

The following article appeared in the *Railway Review,* the organ of the National Union of Railwaymen, March 1963. It is reproduced with the courteous permission of its editor, Frank Moxley, on condition that I state explicitly that these are his personal, editorial, opinions. The feature has been reproduced *in toto,* so that there can be no question of tearing any pieces out of context. The contents may seem so startling that it is worth recalling that this was not published during the hungry thirties but in the year before Harold Wilson became Prime Minister. Its author is not a crank but a good socialist; it appeared as an unsigned editorial in a journal sponsored by a powerful trade union. Admittedly, it is very frank and therein differs from the publicly spoken or written words of many who plan, or aspire to plan, our lives for the general good of the country. I know of no more powerful document with which to conclude this book — it illustrates superbly my thesis.

PRIVATE OWNERSHIP OF MOTOR CARS?

It was not expected that the study group on the transport needs of Great Britain in the next twenty years should come out with a blue-print. Indeed, all they have done is to carry the logic of present trends onwards to 1980.

True, the report of Sir Robert Hall and his colleagues have something to say about policy. But generally they ask questions rather than answer them. It is obvious, anyway, from what they say that the transport picture is vague and much more research is needed.

They do say, however, that 'a better and wider understanding of the value to the economy of investment in transport is essential, because it is through investment that the Government exercises the greatest measure of control over transport development'.

We do not think that this Government can control, or better still shape, transport development properly without economic planning not just of transport but of the main structure of our economy.

This, they are not prepared to do. Control of investment is a clumsy device. And we have seen through the years that it has failed miserably.

It is strange that the authorities in this country are so afraid of making real decisions which are biased towards the common good. Minority, especially rich minority, groups have far too much influence. And pressure organizations play a great role in preventing logical development of plans for the general good of the country.

Take the vast expansion of private motor cars. The group merely records the possible growth and suggests an extension of certain checks. We do not expect, of course, any revolutionary ideas from such a group.

But it seems clear to us that the growth of private ownership of cars is in itself a trend which in the national interest should be reversed.

We say this not because we are against private motoring; not because we want to force people to travel by public transport.

But consider what the private ownership of road vehicles entails. We must stress the 'private ownership' aspect of this problem.

*

In many respects the big difficulties of the motor car age arise out of the fact that the vast majority of licensed vehicles are most of their time underused.

In no field of investment is there such waste as in the private ownership of motor cars. The majority of cars are driven for only a fraction of the time they are licensed.

This means that hundreds of millions of valuable investment, productive effort and actual physical space are wasted every day.

Hundreds of thousands of man-hours have been expended on vehicles that are standing idle much of the time.

From this it is evident that there are in fact too many vehicles for the needs of the community. If the utilization of private cars was worked out we are pretty certain that we could actually do with only a fraction of the cars now in circulation, provided each car was fully used.

The inference from all this is that if we were concerned with the use of cars instead of the ownership of cars we could organize ourselves a lot better.

And the conclusion must also be that the private ownership of cars is uneconomic, a waste of national resources and quite unnecessary.

*

We suggest that status consideration, and the false notions about the value of personal property in this field should be superseded by a movement towards concern with motor cars for practical use.

There seems no reason why stocks of cars could not be held—a vast extension of hiring organization—for use by those who at any time and for any fruitful period need them.

Investment could be controlled. Garaging and maintenance of road vehicles would be more efficient and safer. Insurance and licensing would be simplified. It should be as easy and convenient to borrow a car as it is to borrow a television set.

If a person wished to own a car he would have to convince the authorities that it was absolutely necessary, a very difficult plea if cars were available freely for hire.

*

The result of this organization would, of course, be that there would be a vast reduction in the number of cars. And this would have its effect on the motor manufacturing industry and all the industries which supply it. That, probably, would be the main obstacle to such a sensible arrangement. Which is what we meant earlier.

Minority interests do prevent logical development. They should be resisted where the common good is at stake, as in this case.

In the ultimate we would like to see cars as common property administered by the authorities just as living accommodation should be, and is by local government.

Why not, we would like to know?'

Those who reject as distasteful the proposals in the above article—to create a vast state car hiring organization and to make the ownership of a car dependent upon convincing the authorities that it is absolutely necessary—may do well to remember that the author's analysis is basically correct: 'The private ownership of cars is uneconomic, a waste of national resources...Valuable investment, productive effort and actual physical space are wasted every day.' Frank Moxley repeatedly uses the word 'waste' because he thinks that his readers, the railwaymen and others, think that 'waste' is something bad. But is it?

In a beleaguered city it is proper to husband economically and equitably resources needed to withstand the siege. Britain, and the affluent countries of the West, however, benefit now from such material abundance that the optimum physical exploitation of resources need no longer determine all our economic and social strategies. To use privately acquired goods in a manner considered wasteful by planners is part of our raised standard of living. So-called physical waste is not always the antithesis of human welfare but may actually enhance it. If one values leisure highly, and can afford to use it, one does not darn stockings or repair broken kitchen chairs, but buys replacements. In the olden days small soap remnants were saved in order to mould out of them a large cake of soap; Moxley's railwaymen are too affluent today to spend their time on this. Of course national resources are squandered—and valuable dollars wasted on increased pulp imports—when each family today buys one or two daily newspapers. Before the war, two or three penurious households sometimes clubbed together to buy jointly one copy of a newspaper. Shall we now return to this system? Or, perhaps better still, send everyone to read his papers in a public library?

Conspiracy theories always make fascinating reading. Moxley did not introduce a reference to the pernicious influence of motor manufacturing companies (and their suppliers) in order merely to embellish, journalistically, his demand to limit the private ownership of vehicles. He really believed that it is these commercial interests which largely prevented the then Conservative government from checking the wasteful private ownership of cars 'driven for only a fraction of the time they are licensed'. How fatuous! The people of Britain derive pleasure from underutilized television sets, cars and newspapers. The happiness, derived from their wasteful use, may not be recorded in the conventional GNP but it is no less profound for that.

Cited Sources

1 J. Brunner, 'The Dash For Planning', *The Listener*, London, 10 May 1962.

2 P. Studenski, *The Income of Nations*, New York University Press, New York, 1958.

3 M. Lipton, 'Supply Problems Matter', *Financial Times*, London, 20 January 1969.

4 P. A. Samuelson, *Problems of the American Economy*, Athlone Press, London, 1962.

5 J. Jewkes, *The New Ordeal by Planning*, Macmillan, London, 1968.

6 G. Myrdal, *Beyond the Welfare State*, Duckworth, London, 1960.

7 C. Onslow (edited), *Asian Economic Development*, Weidenfeld & Nicolson, London, 1965.

8 P. T. Bauer, *Economic Analysis and Policy in Underdeveloped Countries*, Cambridge University Press, London, 1957.

9 W. Beckerman and Associates, *The British Economy in 1975*, NIESR, Cambridge University Press, London, 1965.

10 K. Schiller, *Der Oekonom und die Gesellschaft*, Gustav Fischer, Stuttgart, 1964.

11 *Hansard*, House of Commons, London, 3 November 1965.

12 C. R. Rao (edited), *Essays on Econometrics and Planning*, Pergamon Press, Oxford, 1965.

13 I. M. D. Little and J. M. Clifford, *International Aid*, Allen & Unwin, London, 1965.

14 O. Morgenstern, *The Limits of Economics*, William Hodge, London, 1937.

15 M. C. Kemp, 'Economic Forecasting when the Subject of the Forecast is influenced by the Forecast', *American Economic Review*, Evanston (Ill.), June 1962.

16 O. Morgenstern, *On the Accuracy of Economic Observations*, Princeton University Press, Princeton, 1963.

17 J. R. Hicks, 'The Valuation of the Social Income', *Economica*, London, May 1940.

18 *Seventh Report from the Estimates Committee*, HMSO, London, 1968.

19 D. Usher, 'The Transport Bias in Comparisons of National Income', *Economica*, London, May 1963.

20 A. G. Gartaganis and A. S. Goldberger, ' A Note on the Statistical Discrepancy in the National Accounts', *Econometrica*, New Haven (Conn.), April 1955.

21 E. A. G. Robinson and J. E. Vaizey (edited), *The Economics of Education*, Macmillan, London, 1966.

22 H. Apel, 'Scope and Significance of Economic Misrepresentation', *The American Journal of Economics and Sociology*, New York, January 1962.

23 A. C. Pigou, *The Economics of Welfare*, Macmillan, London, 1960.

24 *Economics and Public Policy,* The Brookings Institution, Washington, 1955.

25 R. Frisch, 'Opening Address', *Econometrica,* New Haven (Conn.), July 1956.

26 F. Lutz, *Das Problem der Wirtschaftsprognose,* Mohr, Tuebingen, 1955.

27 T. Wilson, 'Liberty as a Problem of Applied Economics', *The American Behavioral Scientist,* New York, June 1965.

28 B. M. Gross, 'Findings and Fallacies', *Public Administration Review,* Washington, December 1965.

29 B. G. Hickman (edited), *Quantitative Planning of Economic Policy,* The Brookings Institution, Washington, 1965.

30 O. Morgenstern, 'Qui numerare incipit errare incipit', *Fortune,* Chicago, October 1963.

31 *The Quality and Economic Significance of Anticipations Data,* National Bureau of Economic Research, Princeton University Press, Princeton, 1960.

32 R. C. Garretson and F. F. Mauser, 'The Future Challenges Marketing', *Harvard Business Review,* Boston (Mass.), November 1963.

33 D. Usher, 'The Thai National Income at United Kingdom Prices', *Bulletin of the Oxford University Institute of Economics and Statistics,* Blackwell, Oxford, August 1963.

34 J. Mosak, 'National Budgets and National Policy', *American Economic Review,* Ithaca (New York), March 1946.

35 G. Bombach, 'Ueber die Moeglichkeit Wirtschaftlicher Voraussagen', *Kyklos,* Basel, 1962.

36 A. Hahn, 'Don't Predict Post-War Deflation—Prevent it', *Commercial and Financial Chronicle*, New York, 25 January 1945.

37 I. M. D. Little, *A Critique of Welfare Economics*, Oxford University Press, London, 1965.

38 F. D. Newbury, *Business Forecasting*, McGraw-Hill, New York, 1952.

39 M. H. Spencer, C. G. Clark and P. W. Hoguet, *Business and Economic Forecasting*, Richard Irwin, Homewood (Ill.), 1961.

40 T. Wilson, *Planning and Growth*, Macmillan, London, 1964.

41 D. H. Robertson, 'Utility and All That', *The Manchester School*, Manchester, May 1951.

42 J. Mitchell, *Groundwork to Economic Planning*, Secker & Warburg, London, 1966.

43 C. Clark, *The Conditions of Economic Progress*, Macmillan, London, 1951.

44 *Fourth Report from the Estimates Committee*, HMSO, London, 1966.

45 E. S. Phelps (edited), *The Goal of Economic Growth*, Norton, New York, 1962.

46 *Problems in the International Comparison of Economic Accounts*, National Bureau of Economic Research, Princeton University Press, Princeton, 1957.

47 J. Gould (edited), *Penguin Survey of the Social Sciences*, Penguin Books, Harmondsworth, 1965.

48 I. M. D. Little, 'The Strategy of Indian Development', *Economic Review*, NIESR, London, May 1960.

49 R. R. Neild and E. A. Shirley, 'An Assessment of Forecasts', *Economic Review*, NIESR, London, May 1961.

50 M. Chand and N. Sreeraman, 'A Note on Certain Forecasts in USA and India', *The Indian Journal of Economics*, Allahabad, July 1966.

51 *Studies in Income and Wealth*, Volume X, National Bureau of Economic Research, New York, 1947.

52 *Studies in Income and Wealth*, Volume I, National Bureau of Economic Research, New York, 1937.

53 W. L. Butler and R. A. Kavesh (edited), *How Business Economists Forecast*, Prentice-Hall, London, 1966.

54 E. J. Mishan, *The Costs of Economic Growth*, Staples Press, London, 1967.

55 S. Kuznets (edited), *Income and Wealth in the United States, II*, Bowes & Bowes, Cambridge, 1952.

56 P. Jostock, *Die Berechnung des Volkseinkommen und ihr Erkenntniswert*, Kohlhammer, Stuttgart, 1941.

57 N. Georgescu-Roegen, 'Economic Theory and Agrarian Economics', *Oxford Economic Papers*, Oxford, February 1960.

58 'Some Factors in India's Fourth Plan', *The National and Grindlays Review*, London, October 1966.

59 J. R. Hicks, 'Growth and Anti-Growth', *Oxford Economic Papers*, Oxford, November 1966.

60 *Hansard*, House of Commons, London, 4 May 1967.

61 J. Jewkes, 'The Perils of Planning', *The Three Banks Review*, Edinburgh, June 1965.

62 G. Denton, *The National Plan*, PEP, London, 1965.

63 J. Jewkes, P. Chambers and L. Robbins, *Economics, Business and Government*, The Institute of Economic Affairs, London, 1966.

64 S. E. Harris (edited), *Economic Reconstruction*, McGraw-Hill, New York, 1945.

65 *Hansard*, House of Commons, London, 5 December 1967.

66 M. Friedman, 'Foreign Economic Aid', *Yale Review*, New Haven (Conn.), Summer 1958.

67 G. C. Smith, 'The Law of Forecast Feedback', *The American Statistician*, Washington, December 1964.

68 J. A. Livingston, 'How Wrong can Economists be?', *The Reporter*, New York, 26 May 1953.

69 *Report from the Select Committee on National Industries*, HMSO, London, July 1961.

70 D. Burn, J. R. Seale and A. R. N. Ratcliff, *Lessons from Central Forecasting*, The Institute of Economic Affairs, London, 1965.

71 E. Devons, 'Statistics as a Basis for Policy', *Lloyds Bank Review*, London, July 1954.

72 E. B. Weiss, 'E. B. Puts his Annual Pox on Prognosticators', *Advertising Age*, Chicago, 17 December 1962.

73 S. Brittan, *The Treasury under the Tories*, Penguin Books, Harmondsworth, 1964.

74 R. Edwards, *Economic Planning and Electricity Forecasting*, The Electricity Council, London, 1966.

75 *The National Plan*, HMSO, London, 1965.

76 *Growth of the United Kingdom Economy to 1966*, NEDC, HMSO, London, February 1963.

77 *Hansard*, House of Commons, London, 27 July 1966.

78 'Effects of Weather Forecasts on Trade', *The NCT Journal*, National Chamber of Trade, London, November 1966.

79 V. Zarnowitz, *An Appraisal of Short-Term Economic Forecasts*, Columbia University Press, New York, 1967.

80 *Hansard*, House of Commons, London, 9 April 1957.

81 H. Koontz and C. O'Donnell, *Management*, McGraw-Hill, New York, 1964.

82 B. de Jouvenel, *The Art of Conjecture*, Weidenfeld & Nicolson, London, 1967.

83 L. Robbins, *An Essay on the Nature and Significance of Economic Science*, Macmillan, London, 1932.

84 D. N. Chester (edited), *Lessons of the British War Economy*, Cambridge University Press, London, 1951.

85 T. Balogh, *The Economics of Poverty*, Weidenfeld & Nicolson, London, 1966.

86 *Measurement of National Income and the Construction of Social Accounts*, United Nations, Geneva, 1947.

87 W. A. Lewis, *The Principles of Economic Planning*, Dobson, London, 1939.

88 'How to Plan for Declining Growth', *Sunday Times*, London, 2 July 1967.

89 R. J. Ball and T. Burns, 'The Need for Reflation', *Sunday Times*, London, 2 April 1967.

90 *Economic Review*, NIESR, London, February 1967.

91 J. K. Galbraith, *The Affluent Society,* Houghton Mifflin, Boston (Mass.), 1958.

92 *The Economist,* London, 28 December 1963.

93 *The Economist,* London, 31 December 1966.

94 G. D. Woods, *Address to the Board of Governors,* World Bank, Washington, 1967.

95 *Financial Times,* London, 21 October 1966.

96 J. L. Nicholson, 'The Measurement of Quality Changes', *The Economic Journal,* London, September 1967.

97 D. Usher, *Rich and Poor Countries,* The Institute of Economic Affairs, London, 1966.

98 J. Brunner, 'The Flight from Reality', *The Listener,* London, 17 May 1962.

99 W. Beckerman, *International Comparisons of Real Incomes,* OECD, Paris, 1966.

100 *Forty-Seventh Annual Report,* National Bureau of Economic Research, New York, 1967.

101 *Growth Through Industry,* The Institute of Economic Affairs, London, 1967.

102 E. R. Rolph, *The Theory of Fiscal Economies,* University of California Press, Berkeley, 1954.

103 M. Shanks, 'Off with the Old, on with the New?' *The Times,* London, 11 September 1967.

104 *International Definition and Measurement of Standards and Levels of Living,* United Nations, New York, 1954.

105 *National Accounts Statistics,* CSO, HMSO, London, 1968.

106 *National Accounting Practices in Sixty Countries,* United Nations, New York, 1964.

107 A. Nove, *The Soviet Economy,* Allen & Unwin, London, 1965.

108 M. C. Kaser, 'Estimating the Soviet National Income', *The Economic Journal,* London, March 1957.

109 'A Note on some Aspects of National Accounting Methodology in Eastern Europe and the USSR', *UN Economic Bulletin for Europe,* Geneva, November 1959.

110 A. L. Bowley, *Studies in the National Income,* Cambridge University Press, London, 1942.

111 T. W. Schultz, 'Reflections on Investment in Man', *Journal of Political Economy,* Chicago, October 1962.

112 T. W. Schultz, 'Investment in Human Capital', *American Economic Review,* Evanston (Ill.), March 1961.

113 J. E. Vaizey, *The Control of Education,* Faber, London, 1963.

114 *The Times,* London, 10 February 1968.

115 S. Merrett, 'The Rate of Return to Education', *Oxford Economic Papers,* Oxford, November 1966.

116 S. J. Mushkin, 'Health as an Investment', *Journal of Political Economy,* Chicago, October 1962.

117 *Report of the Committee on Contributions,* United Nations, New York, 1967.

118 G. S. Becker, 'Underinvestment in College Education', *American Economic Review,* Evanston (Ill.), May 1960.

119 *Sunday Times,* London, 5 November 1967.

120 J. K. Galbraith, *The New Industrial State,* Hamish Hamilton, London, 1967.

121 *Israel Investors' Manual,* Government of Israel, Jerusalem, 1968.

122 J. M. Keynes, 'The Concept of National Income', *The Economic Journal,* London, March 1940.

123 *A Report of the Cost of Living Advisory Committee,* HMSO, London, 1968.

124 E. F. Denison, *Why Growth Rates Differ,* The Brookings Institution, Washington, 1967.

125 H. Kahn and A. J. Wiener, *The Year 2000,* Macmillan, New York, 1967.

126 *The Times,* London, 29 July 1968.

127 S. Kuznets, *Letter to the Author,* Cambridge (Mass.), 29 May 1967.

128 J. R. Hicks, *Letter to the Author,* Oxford, 28 September 1966.

129 A. Rubner, *Fringe Benefits,* Putnam, London, 1962.

130 M. Crawford, 'Investment Grants', *Sunday Times,* London, 21 January 1968.

131 *Daily Telegraph,* London, 13 October 1959.

132 *The Economist,* London, 23 May 1964.

133 D. Vital, *The Inequality of States,* Clarendon Press, Oxford, 1967.

134 K. Richardson, 'Plan to Reshape Big Steel Groups', *Sunday Times,* London, 20 October 1968.

135 A. Marshall, *Principles of Economics,* Macmillan, London, 1898.

136 B. Marlow, *Charting the British Economy,* Longmans, London, 1968.

137 R. L. Merritt and S. Rokkan, *Comparing Nations,* Yale University Press, New Haven (Conn.), 1966.

138 *Readings in the Theory of Income Distribution,* Blakiston, Philadelphia, 1946.

139 *Economic Review,* NIESR, London, November 1967.

140 *Sunday Telegraph,* London, 5 November 1967.

141 A. Rubner, *The Economics of Gambling,* Macmillan, London, 1966.

142 'You can also use Tea Leaves', *Business Week,* New York, 17 November, 1962.

143 *News Release,* Labour Party, Transport House, London, 25 May 1968.

144 *Growth in the British Economy,* PEP, London, 1960.

145 *National Income and Expenditure,* HMSO, London, 1968.

146 *Monthly Economic Letter,* First National City Bank, New York, August 1968.

147 'Post Mortem', *British Industry,* CBI, London, 2 September 1966.

148 *The Times,* London, 7 November 1967.

149 *The Times,* London, 18 October 1968.

150 S. Klein, 'Recent Economic Experience in India and Communist China', *American Economic Review,* Evanston (Ill.), May 1965.

151 K. Fleet, 'De Gaulle's Financial Waterloo', *Daily Telegraph,* London, 22 November 1968.

152 S. H. Frankel, '"Psychic" and "Accounting" Concepts of Income and Welfare', *Oxford Economic Papers,* Oxford, February 1952.

153 K. Fleet, 'ICI comes out wrong on the right Side', *Daily Telegraph,* London, 29 November 1968.

154 'Short-Term Economic Forecasts in the United Kingdom', *Economic Trends,* HMSO, London, August 1964.

155 *Economic Review,* NIESR, London, May 1967.

156 A. Thorncroft, 'Taking a Long View in Biscuits', *Financial Times,* London, 7 July 1967.

157 S. Brittan, *Inquest on Planning in Britain,* PEP, London, 1967.

158 A. C. Chiang, 'Economic Forecasting when the Subject of the Forecast is influenced by the Forecast', *American Economic Review,* Evanston (Ill.), September 1963.

159 'The Sterling Hat Trick', *The Economist,* London, 6 August 1966.

160 'The Jugopipeline', *The Economist,* London, 9 November 1968.

161 *The Economist,* London, 30 March 1963.

162 L. R. Klein, 'A Port-Mortem on Transition Predictions of National Product', *Journal of Political Economy,* Chicago, August 1946.

163 W. S. Woytinsky, 'What was Wrong in Forecasts of Postwar Depression?', *Journal of Political Economy,* Chicago, April 1947.

164 'The Day the Experts Tore up their Forecasts', *Evening Standard,* London, 5 December 1967.

165 W. B. Stewart, 'Mr Computer Looks at his Crystal Ball', Paper read to New York chapter of *American Statistical Association*. (Undated.)

166 E. Boyle, *Conservatives and Economic Planning,* Conservative Political Centre, London, 1966.

167 'Back to the Drawing Board', *The Economist,* London, 30 July 1966.

168 A. Rubner, *The Ensnared Shareholder,* Macmillan, London, 1965.

169 *Fortune,* New York, April 1959.

170 'Intermediate Technology', *Far East Trade & Development,* London, July 1967.

171 E. F. Schumacher, 'Economic Development and Poverty', *Bulletin of Intermediate Development Group,* London, September 1966.

172 D. Allen, *Planning — A Development Science in Industry and Government,* British Institute of Management, London, March 1968.

173 M. Shanks, 'The Quiet Revolution', *Sunday Times,* London, 27 September 1964.

174 *The Times,* London, 17 September 1964.

175 R. Maudling, 'The Tories and Planning Now', *Daily Telegraph,* London, 10 August 1966.

176 *Financial Times,* London, 13 March 1968.

177 R. Jallow, 'Forecasting Season is upon us', *California Business,* 16 October 1968.

178 M. Gilbert, 'Quality Changes and Index Numbers', *Economic Development and Cultural Change,* Chicago, April 1961.

179 R. Edwards, 'Financing Electricity Supply', *Lloyds Bank Review*, London, July 1967.

180 *A System of National Accounts and Supporting Tables*, United Nations, New York, 1964.

181 *A Standardised System of National Accounts*, OEEC, Paris, 1958.

182 *The National Income and Product Accounts of the United States 1929–1965*, US Department of Commerce, Washington, 1966.

183 *Economic Trends*, HMSO, London, October 1969.

184 C. I. K. Forster, *The Statistical Basis to National Fuel Policy*, Institute of Actuaries, London, January 1969.

185 T. P. Hill, 'Growth and Investment according to International Comparisons', *Economic Journal*, London, July 1964.

186 *The Growth of the Economy*, NEDC, HMSO, London, March 1964.

187 *Working for Prosperity*, HMSO, London, 1965.

188 'TUC Urged to Cut its Links with NEDC', *The Times*, London, 19 August 1968.

189 *Plan for Progress*, Labour Party, Transport House, London, 1958.

190 *Hansard*, House of Commons, London, 27 February 1969.

191 C. A. Blyth, 'Problems in Appraising the Forecasting Record of the NIESR', (unpublished) Paper presented to *CIRET Conference*, Madrid, 1969.

192 M. Ellman, 'Aggregation as a Cause of Inconsistent Plans', *Economica*, London, February 1969.

193 *Hansard*, House of Lords, London, 4 November 1969.

194 *The Times,* London 27 June 1969.

195 'Business Outlook', *Business Week,* New York, 27 September 1969.

196 P. Hutber, 'Economic Opinion', *Sunday Telegraph,* London, 9 March 1969.

197 F. S. McFadzean, *Galbraith and the Planners,* University of Strathclyde, Strathclyde, 1969.

198 M. Young (edited), *Forecasting and the Social Sciences,* Social Science Research Council. Heinemann, London, 1968.

199 G. Myrdal, *Economic Theory and Under-Developed Regions,* Duckworth, London, 1957.

200 W. and P. Paddock, *Famine 1975!,* Weidenfeld & Nicolson, London, 1968.

201 G. W. Ball, *The Discipline of Power,* Bodley Head, London, 1968.

202 S. Enke, 'The Economic Aspects of Slowing Population Growth', *The Economic Journal,* London, March 1966.

203 'Cuba Postpones Christmas', *The Times,* London, 29 October 1969.

204 C. E. V. Leser, *Can Economists Foretell the Future?,* Leeds University Press, Leeds, 1969.